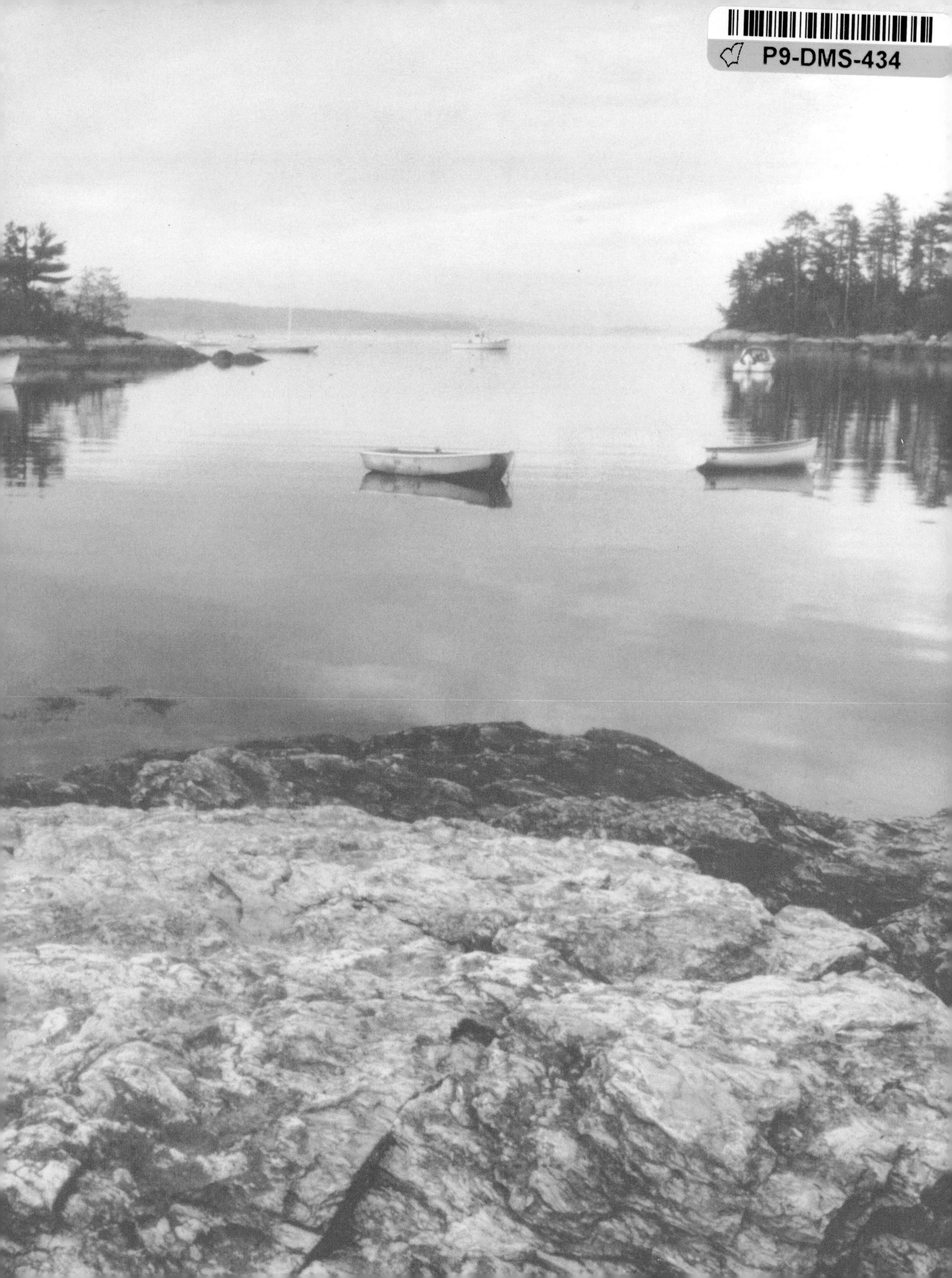

Saltwater Seasonings

Also by Sarah Leah Chase

The Nantucket Open House Cookbook

Cold Weather Cooking

The Silver Palate Good Times Cookbook
(co-author)

Saltwater Seasonings

Good Food from Coastal Maine

SARAH LEAH CHASE AND JONATHAN CHASE

Photographs by Cary Hazlegrove

Little, Brown and Company

Boston   Toronto   London

FIRST EDITION

LIBRARY OF CONGRESS CATALOGING-IN-PUBLICATION DATA

Chase, Sarah Leah.

Saltwater seasonings : good food from coastal Maine / by Sarah Leah Chase and Jonathan Chase ; photography by Cary Hazlegrove. — 1st ed.

p.   cm.

Includes bibliographical references and index.

ISBN 0-316-13812-6

1. Cookery, American — New England style.   2. Cookery — Maine.

I. Chase, Jonathan, 1954-   . II. Title.

TX715.2.N48C43   1992

641.5974 — dc20

91-40565

10   9   8   7   6   5   4   3   2   1

RRD-OH

Designed by Barbara Werden

Published simultaneously in Canada by Little, Brown & Company (Canada) Limited

PRINTED IN THE UNITED STATES OF AMERICA

We dedicate this book to:

The memory of our grandparents who so bountifully shared the good life in Maine with us when we were young

and

Our parents who continue to enrich in infinite ways our experiences Down East.

We miss you immensely, "Ma" and "Ish," and we love and cherish you, Mom and Dad.

Acknowledgments

EQUAL to the overwhelming magnitude of Maine's four thousand miles of sprawling coastline is the task of thanking each and every person along that craggy coastline who added to the fabric of this book in ways both meek and magnificent. While space unfortunately does not allow for Jonathan and me to acknowledge here all *Saltwater Seasonings* contributors by name, there are a handful of extra special and impassioned supporters of this project to whom we are most grateful. They are Bob and Kathe Bartlett, Paul and Mollie Birdsall, Sam Hayward, Dana

Holbrook, and Phyllis Schartner. We would also like to thank the staffs at Jonathan's Restaurant and Maine Shellfish for their enthusiastic cooperation. Behind-the-scenes acknowledgment is due Downeast Properties and Leigh and Drew Deeley for making the 350 miles that separate Nantucket from Blue Hill no more than a fax number away. And, a final allotment of appreciation goes to all those at Little, Brown and Company whose talents transformed our raw manuscript into this beautiful book.

Contents

Saltwater Seasonings

Introduction

What happens to me when I cross the Piscataqua and plunge rapidly into Maine at a cost of seventy-five cents in toll? I cannot describe it. I do not ordinarily spy a partridge in a pear tree, or three French hens, but I do have the sensation of having received a gift from a true love.

E. B. WHITE
"Home-Coming," 1979

AS ONE inexplicably compelled to seeking self-expressive fulfillment through the culinary arts, I am always intrigued by the often unstated interrelationship between cooking and other sensory arts. In the process of trying to capture for print and palate the essence of Maine food and flavors, I fell in love by chance, not predictably with a faded file of no-nonsense Yankee recipes, but rather with a collection of choice paintings gathered together in a little book succinctly titled *Paintings of Maine*. Author Carl Little's introduction, addressed to profiling the wide range of artists drawn to this most northerly New England state, begins by citing painter William Kienbusch's explanation of attraction: "When I arrive in Maine," Kienbusch reflected, "I start seeing again."

The reading of this simple statement at once made lucid to me the hitherto inarticulable basis of my own enchantment, thereby illuminating how I could have become so readily able and willing to twirl my whisk away from more complex and fashionable ingredient combinations — so much a trademark of my three previously published cookbooks — in order to champion the straightforward purity of Down East fare. Indeed, I have delightfully come to realize that each and every time I arrive in Maine, I start tasting again.

But a cookbook is not built merely on a bounty of delicious indigenous food resources and odd flashes of *trans*creative insight. Gastronomically inclined maternal grandparents who some forty years ago adventurously purchased a Maine island laden with wild blueberries and raspberries, as well as secret birch-shaded clusters of startlingly orange chanterelle mushrooms and infinite shoreline nooks and crannies embedded with troves of purpled mussels and long-necked steamer clams (not to mention the luxurious offshore supplies of lobsters and other fishy kin), unknowingly laid the foundation for this book. Blend in parents seeking cool summer solace Down East with a station wagon full of energetic children, and the seeds of Maine mania become more firmly established. Thousands of tides, shore dinners, and double-crusted desserts later, cumulative generational influences and/or fate came to bear by conspiring to propel my brother Jonathan from an early passion and career as the golf pro at the scenic Blue Hill Country Club into a job as a prep cook at the local Seagull Restaurant in tiny downtown Blue Hill and then onto eventual proprietorship in 1982 of the same restaurant, renamed Jonathan's.

While Jonathan enthusiastically began charting his life course away from putting greens toward home-grown salad greens, I remained obliviously immersed in my Que Sera Sarah specialty food business many nautical miles away on Nantucket Island. As Jonathan's Restaurant developed into a highly acclaimed, uniquely Down East coastal bistro — garnering from 1985 onward the coveted *Wine Spectator* "Award for Excellence" — I found myself increasingly lured by the promise of sanity seemingly inherent in trading grueling and hot hours of stoveside toil for equally challenging but more flexible hours devoted to writing and researching personally inspired cookbooks. At long last unburdened from the endlessly cyclical diurnal/nocturnal constraints of shopkeeping on Nantucket by the beginning of 1989, I began to broaden my New England coastal horizons with occasional forays to Blue Hill to seek that particularly nurturing blend of R&R that only a spell back home with parents, replete with restaurateur brother proffering ready goblets of exciting Maine wines and recipes for the latest of menu raves, can provide.

As such escapes became understandably habit-forming, I soon registered that no Down East jaunt ever passed without my father persistently planting the idea for a new cookbook on Maine in my forever restless culinary consciousness. Along the way, Jonathan took the bold initiative of inviting me into his restaurant kitchen to test recipes for my then current cookbook projects on his customers. When equally suspicious brother and sister discovered with a huge sigh of relief that such a potentially volatile joint venture bred instant cooking camaraderie rather than sibling rivalry, the concept for the *Saltwater Seasonings* cookbook emerged as crystal-clear as islands in Penobscot Bay struck by strong, blue-sky sunlight after long stretches of indecipherableness in thick fog.

Fueled in unison by delectably vivid memories of foraging for food with our grandparents during childhood summer vacations in Maine, on land and sea as well as in any good grocery establishment falling between Camden and Bar Harbor, Jonathan and I knew that the thrust of our collaborative efforts would be directed toward documenting these simple yet immensely rewarding pleasures of taste as they continue to exist today.

Maine's rugged terrain and remote location have allowed for a more untainted flourishing of practical and austere Yankee spirit than in other New England states. To be sure (and sorry), irrepressible progress has seen to the building of strips of discount outlet stores in places that were, no more than twenty years ago, still quaint rural outposts and outports, but Maine is an amazingly large and durable frontier and there is still much that is both palpably and palatably pristine. One of the first Mainers we interviewed for this book was a mussel diver from Jonesboro, who replied when queried on his favorite way of cooking his catch: "The less you do to 'em, the better they are." We have been guided by this advice time and time again during the process of determining the recipes to be included in this book. Thus the pages that follow are filled with the likes of Baked Beans, Bakewell Cream Biscuits, Sardine Dips, and Camp-fire Smelts rather than affected listings for Chateaubriands and Lobster Thermidors.

Bringing readers these time-honored Maine foods and flavors has not always been the easiest of tasks for two chefs who achieved their culinary savvy and sophistication during the megatrend eighties. Frequent were the moments that both Jonathan and I found ourselves slapping each other's hands as they instinctively reached for that normally staple bottle of balsamic vinegar or sun-dried tomatoes! At the same time, the dawn of the health-analytical nineties has made us all too aware that recipes for meals that begin by trying out salt pork and end by calling for scoops of ice cream churned from *real* cream atop sugar- and shortening-rich pies don't exactly command high esteem with today's nutrition-fixated media. Yet, because occasional indulgence in hearty Down East fare has never been known to induce immediate cardiac arrest, we feel a guiltless and over-riding obligation to document these foodways, which until recently were long lauded for their thrifty wholesomeness. Indeed, we have managed to become both haunted and driven by the belief of Octavio Paz that "Every view of the world that becomes extinct, every culture that disappears, diminishes a possibility of life." Paz, of course, was speaking in far broader anthropological terms, but food has been, is, and always will be a piece that can guarantee cultural longevity. It is our wish to see both salt pork and edible seaweed (a recent harvesting trend along the Maine coast) find ways to coexist in the diets of this decade as well as those in the twenty-first century.

Once firmly and philosophically tied together at the apron strings, Jonathan and I directed our energies to the more nitty-gritty task of dividing and delegating cookbook work loads. Years of running his restaurant in Maine had furnished Jonathan with a wealth of contacts with native food people and resources, so it was natural for him to take charge of setting up the majority of our interview appointments. While complicated personal schedules and geographic logistics dictated conducting these interviews apart as much as together, almost all of the recipes were cooked together either in Jonathan's Restaurant or our parents' South Blue Hill kitchen. As the more experienced author, I took on the lion's share of the actual writing of the text, though Jonathan eagerly put his pen to the three chapters of his greatest familiarity and expertise — Fin Fish, Saltwater Farms, and Maine Meat. For the sake of clarity

and consistency, however, the book has been written as if it were my voice throughout. Photographer Cary Hazlegrove added a final irreplaceable component with her miraculous ability to capture on film exactly the mood we wished to convey with our hearts. I simply could not have imagined a greater compatibility existing between emotionally rooted visions and photographic reality.

While composing this introduction, I coincidentally began reading Norman Mailer's recently published *Harlot's Ghost*, which begins with a stunningly crafted depiction of the Mount Desert area of coastal Maine. Mailer himself, while writing, became struck by his uncontrollable tendency toward prosaic hyperbole in describing a place where there is almost "no sand beach" and "the shore is pebble and clamshell strand" and "twelve-foot tides inundate the rock." I, on the other hand, could relate at once, for *Saltwater Seasonings* is precisely about the unexpected hyperbole in a scarcely adorned meal of steamed lobster or simple supper bowlful of parsnip stew.

Lobsters reign as the king of crustaceans Down East.

Chapter One

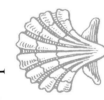

Right-Tasting Lobsters and Their Crustacean Cousins: Crab and Shrimp

Let me straighten all readers out on one point. Lobsters are known in other parts of the world besides the New England coast. But they are a sad mistake and poor imitation of the New England kind. They are not built right in their claws. They grow all to tail. They do not have so much brain. And, worst of all, they taste about as much like a Yankee lobster as a piece of corn-pone. . . . . Now I come down to facts, the fact is that the only right-tasting lobster, and right-looking lobster — and looks are mighty vital in a lobster, let me tell you — is my Casco Bay kind.

ROBERT P. TRISTRAM COFFIN
Mainstays of Maine

IT IS the lobster first and foremost that marks Maine as a major player in the global culinary hall of fame. Fifty percent of all lobsters fished in New England emerge from cold Maine waters, and any lobsterphile will swear that the best-tasting lobsters in the world are Maine ones. This, however, is in no part due to any superior culinary expertise lurking in Down East kitchens, for most Mainers insist that recipes for cooking this mighty king of crustaceans should require no more than two pots — one to trap the critters in, and one to steam them in! We too are convinced, as was the great poet of Maine foods Robert P. Tristram Coffin, decades ago, that simply, arrogantly, and irrefutably the only right-tasting lobsters come from the state that is the subject of this book.

Given this truth, it is most logical that much of the man-made aesthetic appeal of the already exquisite natural coastal landscape of Maine should stem from enterprises involving the catching, cooking, and consuming of lobsters. Fishing villages such as South Bristol and Port Clyde, so isolated on fingery peninsulas of craggy coastline, appear at times too quintessentially postcard-picturesque to be truly real and functioning. The basic charm of a well-tended flower patch, ramshackle general store, and waterfront dock piled high with bright buoys and interlacing lobster traps can't be beat when the view is paired with the experience of eating an alfresco shore dinner replete with steaming scarlet lobsters, briny clams, buttery yellow corn on the cob, and boiled new potatoes. Even with numerous years of Maine living and lobsters under our straining belts, we have yet to resolve the question of whether the scenery improves the flavor of a lobster dinner in the rough, or whether the sweet and inimitable savor of Maine lobster meat

7

adds that much more splendor to the coastal panorama.

For most of the years in which Jonathan and I have come to know Maine, it has been fashionable for urbanites to romanticize the life-style of a Maine lobsterman — the independence of a daily life on the open sea and in fresh, unpolluted air being thought enviable. As of late, however, a different story of hardship and woe in the lobstering industry has been reported in publications both local and national. Headlines in the *New York Times* proclaim that "Lobstering Life Is Losing Allure," while those of the *Bangor Daily News* read: "Catching Maine Lobster Takes a Lot of Hard Work." Jonathan and I recognize and sympathize with problems such as oversupply in a time when new technology takes the human smarts out of catching a lobster, making it almost too easy. The results are ridiculously low wholesale prices paid in an overabundant market and an uproar over the state law that since 1988 has restricted the size of keeping lobsters to those measuring no less than three and a quarter inches and no more than five inches from eye socket to the edge of the carapace, or part where main body meets tail. While we recognize that Maine's $180-million-per-year lobster industry is suffering environmentally, economically, and technologically induced pain, we also celebrate the fact that the innate character of the Maine lobsterman remains intact.

The first lobsterman we knew as children was named Seth, and he conducted business on Sand Point in Blue Hill Bay, a short row in a dinghy or low-tide beach stroll away from our family summer cottage. Like many other Maine lobstermen, Seth did not know how to swim. Quirkily, he would always row backward when traveling to and from his fishing vessel. This amused us, but not nearly as much as the fact that Seth always carried a wad of dollar bills in one pocket of his well-weathered trousers and a loaded pistol in the other.

At the time we had a huge rock in front of our house aptly called "the big rock," and my sisters and I would often pass lazy summer days in our bathing suits sunning, sprawled on the big rock. Seth, we soon found out, liked to look at us through his binoculars. One afternoon my mother decided to row down to Sand Point to fetch some lobsters from Seth

for our dinner. The date might best be placed by noting that Mother carried only a five-dollar bill in her pocket for the purchase of three or four lobsters. As she pulled the dinghy onto Seth's shore, she observed a transaction taking place between Seth and some customers with New York state license plates. The tourists' lobsters had just been weighed up, indicating a price of $19.50, which Seth kept insisting was "about twenty dollars." When at last the exasperated New Yorkers realized that many dinner hours could pass before change would ever be forthcoming from their twenty-dollar bill, they retreated to their car with their lobsters.

My mother took the next place in line, at which point Seth immediately noted that "there's a lot of pretty girls down your way." My mother's lobsters were then weighed up, and they came to six dollars. Apologetically, my mother explained that she had only five dollars but would be happy to row right back with the additional dollar. Seth refused, stating simply, "It all evens out somehow in the end."

Another time, my mother paid a visit to Seth for lobsters on the day of an annual craft fair in town and mentioned by way of conversation that ticket sales had already indicated one more person in attendance over the previous year. Seth scratched his wispy head of salty hair and replied in earnest, "Wonder who he was?"

As we have collected and related our Seth stories over the years, we imagined him to be legend only to our family and relatives. Recently, however, I purchased a book put out by the Women of the Lobster Industry called *A Lobster in Every Pot* and was touched to read the following in the Cook's Introduction:

My father loves to eat. He is motivated by food. He always made it his business to know where the fiddleheads grew, where the trout were biting, and where to pick the wild strawberries. He cultivated friendships with farmers who allowed him to pick his own sweet corn and fresh peas. And, best of all, he knew lobstermen. He would make the hour's drive to Blue Hill just to see his friend Seth and come home with a dozen lobsters for supper.

Since Seth passed away many tides ago and can only be a rich memory and not an interview for this

Lobsterman Dana Holbrook and his canine first mate, Lady.

book, Jonathan put me on the trail of another lobsterman in Buck's Harbor, the father of one of the waitresses in his restaurant. On an unusually hot August afternoon for coastal Maine, I headed out from Blue Hill on the faded gray pavement of Route 175, forewarned that lobsterman Dana Holbrook had a Maine accent thicker than fog and was a real character.

I was not disappointed, as Dana manifested none of the reticence toward a taped interview that I had encountered with many another Mainer. At one point, amid an impassioned discussion of lobster recipes, he even stopped to remind me that it was time to flip the tape over! I met Dana on the rocks of the cove where he anchors his lobster boat, *Shady Lady,* as he was coming in at about 4 P.M. after a long day of fishing that had begun close to sunrise. He was in a gregarious mood and looking forward to unwinding in his shanty (defined by him as "the place where

I put my boots on in the morning — my place of business") with an "attitude adjuster" — a crude but satisfying blend of Diet Pepsi and vodka poured from a half-gallon jug into oversize plastic cups. I accepted the offer of an attitude adjuster of my own, and we began to talk, tape rolling.

Dana, too, harbored a host of gripes against the current state of lobstering caused, according to him, in large part by the legislature in Augusta making laws to adjust lobster size restrictions by sixteenths of inches and devising trap regulations enough to entangle more well-intentioned lobstermen than lobsters. Yet a genuine and glowing love for lobstering kept this twenty-two-year veteran of the industry from sounding the least bit deterred or defeated. As a grammar-school teacher for part of the year, where life runs on a schedule kept by "the ringing of bells," it is the self-determination in his life as a lobsterman from April to December that Dana revels in. He

Right-Tasting Lobsters and Their Crustacean Cousins: Crab and Shrimp

even rejoices at the smell, repulsive to most, of the herring oil in the lobster bait and the fact that it can be removed, only for his wife's sake, with a rigorous scrubbing using Lemon Fresh Joy. "What comes from the sea returns to the sea," justifies Dana. "If I want to pull a hundred and sixty or a hundred and seventy traps, I do; and if I want to pull only fifty, I do. It's a chance to measure your success every day — you against the elements and nature." As a person who has spent almost all his life on the ocean, Dana still manages to see the mystery and excitement in the daily rigor and routine of pulling traps. "Every day is just like Christmas out there." He beamed, swilling another gulp of his attitude adjuster.

Rumor frequently has it that lobstermen never eat their catch. I personally can't understand how this false impression gained currency, as Robert P.

Lobstering paraphernalia enhances Maine's coastal splendor.

Tristram Coffin had explained back in the forties: "Of course the lobsterer eats lobster at least once a day, even though it is a kind of drinking of his pearls." And Dana Holbrook certainly proves the notion wrong as well. Dana's very favorite lobster dish is called Lobster Fried Over Cold, a recipe far easier to make than to decipher through a heavy Maine accent. The story behind the recipe begins with Dana liking, on occasion, to boil up three or four lobsters from a daily catch for overnight refrigeration in the shell. The following day, he picks out the meat in fairly sizable chunks, and then, Dana explains, "I heat up a black spider [cast-iron skillet], whomp it with butter, and fry the cold lobster in the hot butter" until heated, about ten minutes. Lobster Fried Over Cold is best enjoyed, according to its inventor, with "a mess of biscuits." "Gawd, Sarah deah, it's some good" serves as an apt final footnote to the recipe.

Come fall, Dana likes to make a rich and old-fashioned Maine lobster stew with "no taters and no onions," for it is mustering up the patience to let the simple ingredients — lobster, butter, and cream — age and mellow over hours, even days, that makes the dish a rare and extraordinary treat.

One controversial area of lobster cooking about which Jonathan and I don't share a firm opinion is whether to cook the lobster, in the first place, by boiling or steaming. A visit to the Trenton Bridge Lobster Pound on the road to Bar Harbor, where lobster after lobster is boiled in the same caldron of seawater heated by the flames of a birch fire, can easily make one into a true believer in boiling. On the other hand, one is just as easily persuaded by the merits of steaming when reading Robert P. Tristram Coffin lobster odes:

And this law you must observe above all: Only a half cupful of water to a whole kettle of lobsters. For these are viands that must steep in their own juice, to come out in full gorgeousness of flavor. Fresh water is poison to them. The little you sprinkle in the kettle is merely a magnet of steam to call out the blood of the crustaceans to do all the cooking. Some people, Christian people, drown lobsters. They go in for total immersion. There ought to be a law against such cruelty to nature. Good lobsters are steamed,

Fixin's for a traditional Maine lobster bake simmer at sunset on the rocks of panoramic Flye Point in Brooklin.

not boiled. And steamed for only about ten minutes, on a fast fire. They are over seventy percent liquid anyway. They have enough juice to do themselves justice.

No matter which method you choose, use seawater, if at all possible, for either boiling or steaming, and if not seawater, then salted water. Bear in mind that 1- to 1¼-pound lobsters take only ten to twelve minutes to cook, and not the fifteen or more minutes recommended in many other cookbooks.

Lobsters are not the only crustaceans to meet their fate in traps, as inadvertently ensnared crabs make for a thriving by-product of lobstering. Most of the crabs caught in Maine are rock crabs conveniently lured by the same bait used in lobstering — smelly scraps of sardine herrings or alewives. Some fishermen set traps strictly for crabs, because the laws are more relaxed, with the escape vents required in all

lobster traps not a regulation in crab traps. Crabs may also be fished in harbors by baiting a hook and line.

Summer and fall are the best times for crabbing, and signs for picked crabmeat crop up in front of residences up and down the coast of Maine. But it is wise to be particular about where you buy crabmeat, since it is difficult to patrol sanitation standards in home kitchens. We vividly recall that one of the worst insults our normally sweet grandmother could cast upon a person was "I wouldn't buy crabmeat there!" Our grandmother bought her crabmeat from Mr. and Mrs. Sherman, who lived in a neat little house just across from the IGA market on the fringes of Blue Hill proper. Our mother still gets her crabmeat today from the Shermans, and even Dana Holbrook sings the praises of the Shermans' crabmeat from miles away in Buck's Harbor. Indeed, those in the know always say that the Shermans'

Right-Tasting Lobsters and Their Crustacean Cousins: Crab and Shrimp

A secret to the simple Lobster Fried Over Cold crabmeat recipe is to heat the cold meat in a buttered "spider," or cast-iron skillet.

crabmeat is "the cleanest, best-looked-over crabmeat" that they have ever purchased.

We went to visit the Shermans and found that their renown lay in keeping an immaculate kitchen and in packing only leg meat, and no body meat, into their half-pint and pint containers. Leg meat is the most flavorful part of the crab, and it also keeps the longest. Picking crabmeat as impeccably as the Shermans do is arduous work, and they say that on the average they pick three pounds of crabmeat per hour. The crabs are boiled the night before, allowed to cool in a refrigerator, and then pounded with a special mallet on a stainless-steel surface to expose the sweet meat within. During the busy summer season the Shermans will pick five to eight pounds of crabmeat a day, though if they are really lucky they may score some special crabs from down Stonington

way that can yield close to five pounds of picked meat per hour.

A favorite Maine use for crabmeat is in a simple sandwich known as a crab roll. Numerous roadside stands sell crab rolls along with lobster rolls and fried clams to hordes of tourists all summer long. As would be expected, there are good crab rolls and bad crab rolls. Good crab rolls start on a base of a *buttered and toasted* hamburger or hot-dog bun, which is then filled with an ample quarter-pound of fresh crabmeat bound lightly with good-quality mayonnaise and absolutely no additional celery or minced onion as fillers — an incredibly simple and pure affair. Bad crab rolls consist of inferior crabmeat further bastardized by celery and onions slopped lazily onto an unbuttered and untoasted bun. We are especially fond of the good crab rolls sold at the scenically splendid Bagaduce Lunch stand in Brooksville and have based our recipe on those.

In the winter, when most lobstering and crabbing pursuits take a vacation, rugged Maine fishermen with indefatigable energy return to the iciest of waters to go dragging for shrimp. The season lasts for a brief and brutal three months, during which the catches are sold both raw and cooked in fish markets and from mobile fish trucks parked along coastal Route 1. Maine shrimp are quite petite, measuring a mere three inches from head to tail, and Jonathan used to think they weren't worth the bother until we

Small but sweet and savory Maine shrimp are harvested during winter months.

began experimenting with recipes for this book. Maine shrimp can easily turn to mush if the Down East axiom of cooking seafood "short," or briefly, isn't followed religiously. When making recipes such as our Maine Shrimp Toss, we have found that we achieve the best results using raw shrimp that are purchased in the shell and then shelled as close as possible to cooking time. Maine shrimp are toilsome yet addictive little morsels, and those in the shell yield half the weight of what you begin with. In other words, two pounds of shrimp-in-the-shell render the labor-of-love reward of one pound of fresh pink meat.

Lobster Fried Over Cold

Lobsterman Dana Holbrook's favorite lobster recipe contains only two ingredients — lobster and butter — blended with some good common-sense technique. Every rich and irresistible mouthful of this dish rings true to that Maine philosophy of life's best pleasures being simple and native. Accompany with "a mess of warm biscuits" and relish one of the greatest Down East feasts we know.

4 live 1- to 1¼-pound lobsters
8 tablespoons (1 stick) unsalted butter

1. The day before you plan to make the recipe, boil or steam the lobsters until done, about 10 minutes. Drain, cool, and refrigerate the lobsters in their shells overnight.

2. The following day, pick all the meat from the lobsters, leaving it in fairly large chunks. Discard the shells but save the tomalley, if desired, and add it to the lobster meat.

3. Melt the butter over medium heat in a large cast-iron skillet. Add the lobster meat and tomalley

These containers are chock-full of the Shermans' impeccably picked and packed crabmeat.

(if using) and sauté until the mixture is piping hot, about 10 minutes. Serve at once with the inventor's suggestion of warm biscuits.

Makes 3 to 4 memorable servings

Right-Tasting Lobsters and Their Crustacean Cousins: Crab and Shrimp

Lobster Stew

In essence this stew is incredibly easy to make and even more incredibly wonderful to consume. The secret to success is twofold: First, there must be an extravagant ratio of half lobster meat to soup liquid, and then the stew must age in order to intensify in flavor for at least 24 hours. Dana Holbrook lets his Lobster Stew mellow on the back of his woodstove for two to three days, but following modern guidelines for food safety, we suggest aging in the refrigerator.

4 live 1- to 1¼-pound lobsters
8 tablespoons (1 stick) unsalted butter
2 teaspoons paprika
4 cups scalded whole milk
1 cup scalded heavy cream

1. Boil or steam the lobsters until slightly under-cooked, 7 to 8 minutes. Let cool until easy to handle. Remove all the meat and tomalley from the lobsters and reserve all juices. Leave the lobster meat in fairly sizable chunks.

2. Melt the butter over medium-high heat in a heavy soup pot. Add the lobster, tomalley, and reserved juices. Stir in the paprika and sauté all together, stirring frequently, for 10 minutes. Very slowly, a drizzle at a time, pour in the milk and cream, stirring constantly, until all has been added. Simmer the stew uncovered for 10 minutes more over low heat.

3. Remove the stew from the heat, let cool, and then cover and refrigerate for at least 24 hours. When ready to serve, gently reheat the stew over low heat until heated through. Serve, ladled into deep bowls, with warm biscuits.

Makes 4 rich servings

Lobster Butter

This recipe is the product of childhood memories, good old New England thrift, and the continuous quest to utilize every last morsel of the abundant seafoods that are available on the coast of Maine. When we vacationed in Blue Hill as children, our parents would always set aside at least one night for a lobster dinner — the type that never strayed too far from the norm: steamers, lobsters, corn on the cob, and blueberry pie. Such a feast would always leave us loosening our belt buckles, falling asleep on the couch listening to a Red Sox game on the transistor radio, or venturing outdoors to a waning campfire to roast a marshmallow or two. One ritual that was out of the norm was our father's religious dumping of the lobster and clam shells into the ocean. After completion of this task, much to the delight of our mother, who would be wiping up the

Baskets of lobsters, mussels, steamers, and corn await their kettles for steaming in a traditional Maine lobster bake.

last scraps of tomalley and spilled butter from the vinyl tablecloth, our father, without fail, would search his closet for a flashlight and then summon the troops to view the eels that always came to feast on the shells that had been deposited in the water. Jonathan, thinking that the eels might know something that we didn't, came up with this recipe (much to the dismay of Blue Hill Bay eels) as a way to utilize the tasty scraps from a picked-over lobster. The lobster butter can be used as a substitute for regular unsalted butter in seafood sautés or as a flavor accent in other seafood preparations that call for butter. Lobster butter keeps for several months in the freezer and for three weeks in the refrigerator.

4 carcasses of 1- to 1½-pound lobsters
2 pounds unsalted butter
¾ cup dry sherry
2 teaspoons paprika
Pinch of cayenne pepper (optional)

1. Place all the ingredients in a heavy stockpot over low heat. Lightly crush the lobster shells with a potato masher. Allow the ingredients to simmer for 1 hour.

2. Strain the liquid into a large container, pressing down on the solids to extract as much flavor as possible. Refrigerate for at least 6 hours.

3. With a table knife, cut around the perimeter of the container to loosen the solidified butter. Carefully pour out the liquid that has accumulated at the bottom of the container. Discard the liquid.

4. Place the now bright-orange-colored butter in a saucepan to melt. Pour into smaller containers and refrigerate or freeze.

Makes about 4 cups

Lobster and clam rolls tempt many at the beautiful picnic area of the Bagaduce Lunch in Brooksville, but our favorite remains the crab roll.

Maine Crab Roll — Bagaduce Lunch Style

The roadside Bagaduce Lunch stand beckons as a midday destination for three reasons. The crab rolls are the best around, the view from the outdoor picnic tables over the tidal river is gorgeous and refreshing, and the word *Bagaduce* is fun to say. No one is quite sure what the Indian word for the river means, but our favorite speculative meaning is "Where your daughter floats out with the tide!"

1 pound fresh-picked Maine crabmeat
⅓ to ½ cup mayonnaise, preferably Hellmann's
4 store-bought, split hamburger buns
2 tablespoons butter or margarine

15

1. In a bowl, combine the crabmeat with just enough mayonnaise to bind. Refrigerate until ready to use.

2. Spread the butter or margarine lightly over each half of the hamburger buns. Toast the buns, butter side down, on a griddle or in a large frying pan until golden. Divide the crabmeat mixture evenly among the 4 buns, sandwich together, and serve at once.

Makes 4 sandwiches

Crabmeat Casserole

When natives want to do something extra special with crabmeat for company, they'll make a casserole, or supper pie. Some casseroles are topped with basic buttered bread crumbs, while others are made even fancier with crunchy sliced almonds. Most have the addition of either Cheddar or American cheese. We think that Cheddar, in this instance, is too strong and overpowers the delicate flavor of the crab, yet our culinary consciences won't let us use processed American cheese. Monterey Jack seems to offer the perfect mild solution. We have also added a touch of grated lemon zest to the standard Maine recipe as we feel lemon always further enhances pure flavors. The casserole may be baked in one large dish or divided among individual au gratin dishes or ovenproof scallop shells.

4 tablespoons unsalted butter
4 tablespoons unbleached all-purpose flour
1½ cups milk
1 tablespoon fresh lemon juice
2 tablespoons cream sherry
1 teaspoon Worcestershire sauce
3 tablespoons finely minced onion
2 teaspoons grated lemon zest
1 pound fresh crabmeat
½ pound Monterey Jack cheese, shredded
Salt and freshly ground pepper, to taste

½ cup sliced almonds
1 tablespoon unsalted butter, melted
Paprika

1. Preheat oven to 350°F.

2. Melt butter in a saucepan over medium heat. Whisk in the flour and continue to cook, stirring constantly, for 3 minutes. Slowly whisk in the milk, stirring to make a smooth sauce. Continue cooking and stirring until the sauce is quite thick, 4 to 5 minutes longer. Blend in the lemon juice, sherry, and Worcestershire. Remove from heat.

3. Fold the onion, lemon zest, crabmeat, and cheese into the sauce. Season to taste with salt and pepper. Turn the crabmeat mixture into a buttered 1½-quart baking dish or 6 individual gratin dishes. Toss the almonds with the melted butter and sprinkle evenly over the top of the crab. Sprinkle paprika evenly over the top as well.

4. Bake the casserole until lightly browned and bubbling, about 35 minutes for the single large one or 20 minutes for the individual ones. Let sit for 5 minutes before serving.

Makes 6 servings

Maine Shrimp Toss

The Italian way of preparing shrimp, or "scampi," with olive oil, garlic, and lemon has universal appeal. When the technique is applied to tender Maine shrimp, the resulting dish is more delicate than the foreign counterpart but no less satisfying. Serve on a bed of plain rice or pasta to absorb the delectable juices and sauce.

4 tablespoons olive oil
2 cloves garlic, minced
Grated zest of 1 lemon

1 pound freshly shelled Maine shrimp
2 tablespoons fresh lemon juice
2 tablespoons dry white wine
2 tablespoons minced fresh parsley
2 tablespoons minced fresh dill (optional, but a nice touch if available)
Salt and freshly ground black pepper, to taste

1. Heat the olive oil in a large skillet over medium-high heat. Add the garlic and lemon zest and sauté for 30 seconds. Stir in the shrimp and toss in the skillet until just cooked through, 2 to 3 minutes total.

2. Stir in the lemon juice, wine, parsley, and dill. Cook just 1 minute more. Season shrimp to taste with salt and pepper and serve at once.

Makes 4 servings

Maine Shrimp Boil

A peel-'n'-eat shrimp feast is always messy and a great deal of fun. We love sweet Maine shrimp boiled in lager beer with mustard and fennel seeds and then dipped in melted butter jazzed with hot sauce to taste. Place a heaped communal platter of the hot boiled shrimp in the center of a table spread with newspaper — we can never decide whether the *Bangor Daily News* or the *Ellsworth American* makes the best place setting. Have lots of napkins, little bowls of melted butter, and iced Geary's Ale within easy reach. The shells can be discarded right onto the newspaper, and all can be rolled up for easy cleanup in the end.

If any shrimp are left over, we like to make a rarebit the next day using some of the yeasty boiling liquid to thin the cheese in the rarebit base.

5 pounds fresh Maine shrimp, in the shell
3 tablespoons olive oil
1 tablespoon mustard seeds
1 tablespoon fennel seeds
4 bottles (12 ounces each) lager beer
½ teaspoon hot red-pepper flakes
4 whole bay leaves
2 cloves garlic, peeled and cut in half lengthwise
1 whole lemon, quartered

Melted sweet butter
Hot sauce or Tabasco, to taste

1. Remove and discard the heads from the shrimp by breaking them off with your fingers. Rinse the shrimp under cold running water.

2. Heat olive oil over medium heat in a 4-quart pot. Stir in the mustard and fennel seeds. Cook until aromatic but not popping, 1 to 2 minutes. Pour in the beer and add the red-pepper flakes, bay leaves, and garlic. Squeeze the juice from the lemon quarters into the pot and add them, rind and all, to the pot. Bring mixture to a boil and then simmer, uncovered, for 5 minutes.

3. Bring mixture back to a full boil and add the shrimp. Cook a scant 2 minutes, keeping in mind that Maine shrimp cook very quickly. Drain, reserving the cooking liquid if desired for Shrimp Rarebit. Mound hot shrimp onto a platter and have melted butter seasoned with hot sauce ready for dipping. Serve at once.

Serves 4 to 6

Right-Tasting Lobsters and Their Crustacean Cousins: Crab and Shrimp

The owner of the Trenton Bridge Lobster Pound boils lobsters in seawater heated by a roaring birch fire.

Shrimp Rarebit

This comforting, rosy rarebit is a wonderful luncheon dividend if you are lucky enough to have any leftover shrimp and their liquid from a boil.

3 tablespoons unsalted butter
3 tablespoons unbleached all-purpose flour
1½ cups shrimp boil liquid, strained
1 can (10 ounces) stewed tomatoes
1 teaspoon Worcestershire sauce
1 teaspoon dried mustard
1 teaspoon paprika
Pinch of cayenne pepper
½ pound sharp white Cheddar cheese, shredded
2 cups cooked Maine shrimp, shelled
Salt, to taste
Toast for serving

1. Melt butter in the top of a double boiler over simmering water. Whisk in the flour and cook, stirring constantly, for 3 minutes. Gradually pour in the shrimp boil liquid, stirring to make a smooth sauce. Continue cooking and stirring until thickened, about 5 minutes.

2. Add the stewed tomatoes to the rarebit, breaking up any large pieces of tomato with the back of a spoon. Season with the Worcestershire, mustard, paprika, and cayenne. Add the shredded cheddar by handfuls, stirring until smooth after each addition. Continue to cook the rarebit over barely simmering water, stirring occasionally, for another 10 minutes to allow the flavors to mellow.

3. Just before serving, add the shrimp and warm through. Season with salt if needed. Serve the rarebit spooned generously over your favorite toast.

Makes 6 servings

Chapter Two

The Myriad of Maine Mollusks

When the tide is out, the table is set.

Old Indian saying

WE have no argument with letting the bold and bright lobster steal most of the limelight in Maine's seafood spectrum. But, at the same time, we are not about to clam up over our passion for the state's comparably abundant mussels and steamers. Indeed, if shellfish Academy Awards existed, these two bivalves would certainly garner best-supporting-role honors for dependable appearances in the ritualistic production of all Down East lobster bakes and shore dinners.

As avid mussel gatherers since childhood, it seems incomprehensible to us that a food so readily available, so visually attractive, and so delectable could have been ignored for so many years by Americans while simultaneously being relished by Europeans. Even Robert P. Tristram Coffin, a man normally given to rapture when confronted with living off the natural bounty of the land in Maine, harbored an unenlightened bias against *Mytilus edulis*, or the edible blue mussel. In a 1946 essay, "Brains from the Sea," he wrote:

Mussels we have, whole dark continents of the small triangular azure ones, built up through hundreds of years of generations on generations of mussels. Our tidal thatch is crinkled with the tapered, fluted ones. And the giant mauve ones are

the anchors to our forty-foot kelp ribbons out in bold water. These last we use for bait to tempt a reluctant pollack. But we have not yet learned to eat any of our mussels ourselves. We have so many other more tasty bivalves which need no sauce but their own juice that we have not got around to eating mussels. We are beginning to ship them out to others, though.

The first cookbook directed exclusively to mussels that we know of was written by Sarah Hurlburt and published in 1977 by Harvard University Press. The book opens with this line: "This book is devoted to a virtually new seafood for Americans." A cookbook published in celebration of Maine's Sesquicentennial Year in 1969 contained but one mussel recipe, although a previous book by Willan C. Roux, *What's Cooking Down East*, published in 1964, contained eight recipes and the following enthusiastic introduction to the mussel section:

Mussels are possibly the most neglected and unappreciated seafood in America. But in Italy, France, and Maine they are neither neglected nor unappreciated: they are thoroughly enjoyed.

At their best in the early spring, Maine mussels are plump and tender. And the supply is unlimited. They are to be found along the entire length of the coast, clinging to the rocks and ledges in great clusters, blue-black beauties waiting to be picked when the tide is out. It's a pity that more don't seem to reach other parts of the country. We'd like to share their goodness with you.

Evidence of just how recently mussels have come to shed their pejorative reputation can be seen by looking at the harvest figures from the Maine

Fresh and briny Spinney Creek oysters.

Department of Marine Resources. They show a dramatic consumption increase from two thousand pounds of mussel meat per year in the early sixties to approximately 4.8 million pounds by the end of the eighties. The broadening appeal of mussels and recent emphasis on eating foods that are low in fat and cholesterol have led to the development of commercial mussel farms, based on European models, in selected places along the Maine coast. In fact, roughly twenty percent of all Maine mussels are now farm raised.

Currently, the largest commercial mussel producer in the country is The Great Eastern Mussel Farms in Tenants Harbor. Owner Chip Davison started the business a little over a decade ago and practices the Dutch technique of dragging for mussels offshore in deep waters, a method that is not technically aquaculture. Great Eastern's fishing boat, the *St. George*, leaves Tenants Harbor with storage bays on board filled with ice. When the mussels are dredged from deeper sea waters, using a process that allows smaller seed mussels to return to the ocean's bottom, they are immediately stored on the ice until they are brought back to the production base at the dock in Tenants Harbor. Once on dry land, the thirty employees of The Great Eastern Mussel Farms attend to getting the catch ready for market. The mussels are first put into a tumultuously loud scrubbing machine and then sent down a conveyor belt for sorting, bagging, and sealing. Ready now for nationwide distribution, the mussels maintain a shelf life of nearly a week so long as they are kept cool and moist by continual ice insulation. The Great Eastern Mussel Farms has recently expanded product line and distribution to include cultured Mahogany clams and oysters. The oysters are the only ones available from the midcoast of Maine, since these elegant bivalves are normally fonder of bedding in warmer waters. These oysters are named for the two places they are independently farmed — Spinney Creek and Pemaquid — and Maine chefs such as Sam Hayward become euphoric at the mere mention of their name.

There are also small and independent mussel farmers like Ed Myers of Abandoned Farms on the Damariscotta River in picturesque South Bristol. Myers, seventy-three, a one-time philosophy major at Princeton and a self-described "elderly eccentric," started the first commercially licensed mussel farm in the country back in the mid-seventies. Chip Davison, in fact, apprenticed with him before starting The Great Eastern Mussel Farms. Myers employs a truer form of aquaculture than Davison, based on a modification of the Spanish system of growing mussels on rope lines in a semiprotected sea environment. Once the spat, or fertilized mussel eggs, attach themselves to dangling ropes, it takes eighteen months for them to grow to market size, in contrast to the eight-year average for wild mussels. We are sorry that we did not have the pleasure of meeting Ed Myers to interview him for this book, but an extensive profile of him in a 1991 issue of *Eating Well* magazine made clear that Ed Myers shares in an admirable philosophy common among people dedicated to championing Maine's native foods — that of trying to make a living on an increasingly complex planet while "doing as little to insult it as possible."

Jonathan and I cannot help but applaud the marketing advantages of mussels that are commercially raised. Mussels, like all bivalves, are filter-feeders, which obtain nourishment by swishing water in and out of their shell-enclosed systems. The current of water that gets swept through mussels is stronger than that of any other mollusk, making the purity of the water in which the mussels thrive of tantamount importance to the consumer. Aquaculturalists, as opposed to amateur foragers, tend to be religious in making certain that their products are drawn from waters free of toxins such as red tide. Cultured mussels also score points for being of uniform size and shell color (an inky dark purple) and yielding plumper meats that are pearl-free, due to the short time it takes for farm-raised mussels to reach maturity. Nevertheless, we must confess that we still find our greatest satisfaction comes from gathering our own wild mussels amid the natural serenity of a coastal cove.

This predilection, along with many another in this cookbook, is most readily attributable to Maine childhood experiences with our grandparents. One of our favorite summer memories is of crossing Blue Hill Bay to anchor on Long Island to jointly harvest mussels, clams, and blueberries. Despite the raw unpleasantness of frequently getting soaked by the chilly and choppy waves of the bay as we made the mile trip in our grandfather Ish's fourteen-foot skiff, we loved these outings for the family competition they engendered. Since mussels could be gathered almost as effortlessly as picking up rocks along the shore, most of the rivalry centered on digging soft-shell clams, or "steamers," which tend to be far more prevalent in Maine than hard-shell quahogs. While our father directed his energies to locating the "mother lode," Jonathan applied deductive reasoning to his efforts by figuring that the faster he filled the clam basket the sooner he could return to the mainland to watch the ballgame on television. Our grandmother always managed to scrounge some steamer, obscenely larger than anyone else's, from the common digging grounds. Manifesting my earliest signs of quiet but fierce competitiveness, I would con my younger sister into manning an inflatable boat while

A hearty and warming bowl of Maine Clam Chowder made with whole steamer clams.

I dove off it into six or seven feet of frigid water to glean the prize of the deep — huge hen clams, or "ashtray" clams, as they are nicknamed. Smug, yet disgusted by the size of these clams, I wanted them out of my sight as quickly as possible and gladly handed them over to my grandmother, who would grind them up as chowder base.

We would enjoy those grand halls of mussels and steamers back at our grandparents' Brooklin camp by letting them all nestle together like blood brothers in the same pot for steaming open over the outdoor bonfire that Ish built every night, whether or not he was intending to cook over it. Melted butter and moonlight over Mount Desert were the sole accompaniments save for the adult cocktails of sixteen-ounce bottles of Haffenreffer Malt Ale. Dessert, more often than not, was blueberry pie. If we were very lucky, the pie would be topped with our Uncle Kiki's homemade vanilla ice cream churned from local Tamworth Farm heavy cream.

These are the edible memories that guide and follow us into the kitchen today. Last year, our childhood predispositions were reinforced by a trip to Jonesboro to visit Dave Thompson, who along with his son dives for the mussels that supply Ducktrap River Fish Farm's smoking operation. When asked about his favorite way to prepare mussels, Dave replied succinctly: "The less you do to 'em, the better they are." We couldn't agree more, and in the restaurant Jonathan adds no more than some slivers of onion to his steamers and a splash of wine and a scattering of dried herbs to the mussels.

When it comes to the topic of chowder, Maine clam chowder is concocted quite differently from its Cape Cod counterpart, with sweet and succulent *whole* steamers preferred to the Cape base of chopped quahogs. Pale green and crunchy celery, coarsely chopped, is also often included as an ingredient. Our recipe is quite similar to the award-winning chowder ladled forth at Cappy's, a popular Camden meeting and eating place. Preliminary instructions for preparing clams for all recipes include ridding the steamers first of possible mud and grit either by simply rinsing them well under cold running water or by letting them soak for half an hour in a pot of cold water sprinkled with a little cornmeal to encourage disgorging. Mussels should, at the very least, be

Maine Clam Chowder

This hearty chowder utilizes the tasty briny broth that results from steaming the clams, which accounts for the absence of salt in the recipe.

5 dozen medium-size steamer clams, rinsed several times
    to remove sand
3 cups cold water
8 tablespoons (1 stick) unsalted butter
1 large onion, diced
3 stalks celery, diced
3 tablespoons unbleached all-purpose flour
3 large Maine potatoes, roughly cut into ½-inch chunks
2 cans (12 ounces each) evaporated milk
2 cups half-and-half
Freshly ground black pepper, to taste

Steamers steamin' to accompany a bountiful shore dinner.

scrubbed before steaming. Jonathan doesn't bother with removing the tough bundle of threads (known as debearding) remaining on the mussel from its salt-water anchorage before cooking, finding it just as easy to let the eater do the debearding afterward. When cooked mussels are to be used as an ingredient in soups and salads, I tend to debeard before steaming them open. Food safety dictates that mussels be debearded as close to cooking time as possible to lessen the danger of the mollusks dying.

Last but not least in our Maine bevy of bivalves is a mussel homonym, the scallop *muscle*, the splendid flesh with which the clever creature opens and closes its shell. Maine scallops are sea scallops and, in the words of Robert P. Tristram Coffin, "almost the size of bread-and-butter plates." The current rage in the harvesting of Maine scallops is diving rather than dredging. Diving allows the wet-suited scalloper to handpick the choicest specimens from hard-to-dredge underwater ledges and crevices. We like to think of this method as analogous to being let loose in Cartier or Tiffany on a spree where price is no barrier to selection.

The downside to diving for scallops is that the season runs from November 15 to April 15, the cruelest and coldest time even to contemplate immersing oneself in Maine waters. Many divers work in three-somes off another person's lobster boat, giving the boat owner a third of the catch, the currency being scallops rather than money. The scallops are shucked almost immediately on board the boat and an average take per day is 35 pounds per person.

Since commercial draggers in New Bedford, Massachusetts, determine the wholesale prices of all New England scallops, diver-harvested scallops cannot currently be sold for more than those that are dredged. This is not to say, however, that they don't bring added cachet to menus in renowned restaurants across the country. It is not unusual to see "Maine Divers' Scallops" on Le Bernardin's menu in Manhattan or that of The Seasons in Boston. Jonathan won't buy anything but diver-harvested scallops and has taken to freezing enough of them to sustain his restaurant through the off-scallop-season. The scallops freeze well, and there is nothing like a bowlful of Northeast Harbor Scallop Soup to warm the raw edge of a foggy summer day.

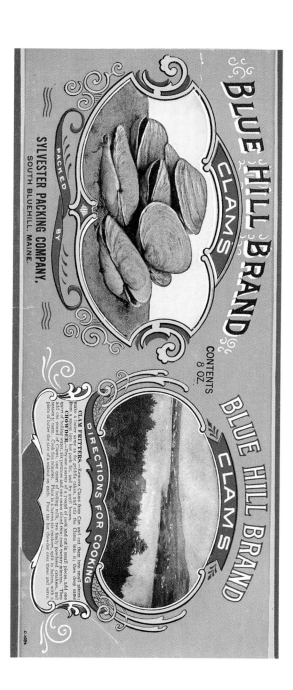

2 tablespoons chopped fresh parsley
4 slices bacon, cooked until crisp and then crumbled
Paprika (optional)

1. Place the steamers and cold water in a heavy stockpot. Turn heat to high, cover, and steam until all the clams are open, about 8 to 10 minutes. Remove the clams from the pot and set aside to cool. Strain the broth through several layers of cheesecloth and reserve.

2. In another pot, melt the butter over medium heat. Add the celery and onions and sauté until the vegetables just begin to soften, about 5 minutes. Do not let the vegetables brown. Add the flour and stir constantly for 3 minutes. Slowly add the reserved clam broth and stir. The liquid should thicken immediately. Add the potatoes, reduce heat to low, and cook until the potatoes are just tender, 15 to 20 minutes.

3. While the soup is cooking, remove the clams from their shells (making sure also to remove and discard the coarse sleeve over the neck) and reserve. When the potatoes are cooked, add the clams, evaporated milk, and half-and-half. Increase the heat to medium and cook until the soup returns to serving temperature. Season with black pepper.

4. Ladle the chowder into large bowls. Sprinkle the chopped parsley and bacon bits over each bowl.

A dash of paprika on the top adds a colorful final touch. Serve at once with oyster crackers or hot biscuits.

Makes 8 generous servings

Steamed Clams

6 dozen steamer clams, rinsed several times to remove sand
4 cups cold water
1 medium onion, halved and thinly sliced
1 teaspoon freshly ground black pepper
1 stick unsalted butter, melted
Lemon wedges for garnish

1. Place the clams in a large stockpot. The clams should not fill the pot by more than two-thirds. Add

the water, onion, and black pepper. Cover the pot and place over high heat. Cook until all the clams have opened, 8 to 10 minutes.

2. Ladle the clams into large bowls and garnish with lemon wedges. Serve at once with small bowls of broth from the pot and ramekins of melted butter for dipping.

Makes 4 servings

Clam Cakes

I tasted my first clam cakes several years ago on a dark and cold winter's evening in a little waterfront restaurant in Thomaston, which at the time seemed like the coziest and warmest place on earth. Such fond memories make these clam cakes, known often in Maine as sea burgers or Down East hamburgers, a welcome treat any time of the year. Tartar sauce is the traditional accompaniment.

1 pint freshly shucked clams, chopped
2 tablespoons fresh lemon juice
⅓ cup minced scallions or onion
1 cup common cracker crumbs (unsalted)
½ cup Ritz cracker crumbs
2 tablespoons unbleached all-purpose flour
2 eggs lightly beaten
Freshly ground black pepper, to taste
Melted butter or vegetable oil for frying
Tartar sauce (recipe follows)

1. Drain the clams and reserve the juice. Toss clams with the lemon juice, scallions, cracker crumbs, and flour. Add the eggs to bind the mixture. Moisten the batter with enough of the reserved clam juice to make a moist, yet still fairly firm mixture. Season with freshly ground black pepper.

2. Melt a few tablespoons of butter or oil in a

One of many funky and good places to stop for "finest-kind" fried clams along the coast of Maine.

large frying pan over medium heat. Drop large spoonfuls of batter into the pan to make patties about 3 inches in diameter and about ¾ inch thick. Fry until golden brown on the underside, 3 to 4 minutes; turn and brown the other side. Repeat process, adding more butter or oil to the skillet as needed, until all the cakes are cooked. Serve the clam cakes hot with a dollop of tartar sauce on top.

Makes 8 to 10 small clam cakes

Tartar Sauce

This is how we make our tartar sauce.

1 cup mayonnaise, preferably Hellmann's
1 heaping teaspoon Dijon-style mustard
2 scallions, trimmed and finely minced
2 tablespoons chopped dill or sweet pickles
1 tablespoon capers, drained
1 tablespoon fresh lemon juice
1 teaspoon Worcestershire sauce
1/4 cup chopped fresh dill or parsley
Freshly ground pepper, to taste

Makes about 1¼ cups

Place the mayonnaise in a mixing bowl and whisk in the mustard until smooth. Mix in the scallions, pickles, capers, lemon juice, Worcestershire, and dill. Season the tartar sauce to taste with pepper and store in the refrigerator until ready to use.

Jonathan's Quick Fish Stock

Jonathan devised this recipe for a cooking class he was teaching on basic soups and stocks. Realizing that many people were intimidated by making fish stock in the classic manner by simmering scraps, frames, and heads cajoled from a gruff fishmonger, he invented this flavorful, easy-to-make stock using the plentiful mussels nestled into the rocks of a nearby beachfront. For those who don't have a favorite mussel-gathering spot along the Maine coast, mussels are often available at very affordable prices at seafood markets.

2 tablespoons extra virgin olive oil
1 tablespoon fennel seeds
1 large onion, coarsely chopped
6 cloves garlic, peeled and coarsely sliced
1/2 cup celery leaves
6 sprigs parsley
6 whole black peppercorns
1 tablespoon dried rosemary
1 teaspoon dried thyme
1 teaspoon saffron threads (optional)
2 cups dry white wine
10 cups cold water
48 mussels (2 pounds) scrubbed but not debearded

1. Heat the olive oil in a large stockpot over medium-high heat. Add the fennel seeds and sauté until they are quite aromatic, about 2 minutes. Reduce heat to medium and stir in the onion, garlic, and saffron (if using); sauté until the vegetables are softened, about 5 minutes.

2. Add all the remaining ingredients, cover the pot, and bring to a full boil. Reduce heat to a simmer and continue to simmer, uncovered, for 45 minutes.

3. Strain the stock through a sieve, pressing hard to extract the juices from the solids. Discard the mussels and vegetables. Store the resulting fish stock in the refrigerator for up to 4 days or freeze in plastic containers. Use as called for in the recipes.

Makes about 2½ quarts of stock

Steamed Mussels

6 dozen fresh mussels, scrubbed
1½ cups dry red or white wine
6 cloves garlic, minced
2 tablespoons minced shallots
1 teaspoon whole fennel seeds
1 tablespoon dried rosemary
1 teaspoon dried thyme
Freshly ground pepper, to taste
1 stick unsalted butter, melted (optional)

Steamed mussels

1. Place the mussels in a large stockpot. The mussels should not fill the pot by more than two-thirds. Add all the other ingredients except the butter.

2. Cover the pot and place over high heat. Cook until all the mussels are open, 8 to 10 minutes. You may want to stir the pot once or twice while cooking. Transfer the mussels to large platters or bowls, discarding any that have not opened. Serve at once with melted butter if desired.

Makes 8 servings

Marinated Mussels

While we never seem to tire of polishing off bowl after bowl of simply steamed mussels, we also often enjoy this cool salad of picked mussel meats for toting along on summertime picnics. The colorful sautéed vegetables make the bright apricot mussels taste all the sweeter. Marinated Mussels are also always welcome speared onto toothpicks come cocktail hour.

½ cup olive oil
3 carrots, peeled and diced
3 stalks celery, minced
2 cloves garlic, minced
2 large leeks, washed, trimmed, and minced
2 cups dry white wine
4 dozen mussels, scrubbed and debearded just before cooking

The Myriad of Maine Mollusks

2 tablespoons fresh lemon juice
¼ cup minced fresh dill
Salt and freshly ground pepper, to taste

Serves 4 to 6

1. Heat ¼ cup of the olive oil over medium heat in a pot large enough to cook the mussels. Add the carrots, celery, garlic, and leeks and sauté for 5 minutes. Reduce heat to medium and continue to cook the vegetables, stirring occasionally, until quite soft, 15 to 20 minutes.

2. Stir the wine into the vegetables. Add the mussels to the pot, raise heat to high, cover, and cook until all the mussels have opened, 8 to 10 minutes. (Discard any mussels that do not open.) Remove the mussels from the pot and let cool until easy enough to handle.

3. In the meantime, boil the liquid in the pot with the vegetables until reduced to 1 cup, 15 to 20 minutes. Remove from heat. Remove the mussel meat from the shells and add to the vegetable reduction. Stir in the lemon juice and remaining ¼ cup olive oil. Season with the dill and salt and pepper. Transfer to a serving bowl and chill in the refrigerator for a few hours before serving.

Northeast Harbor Scallop Soup

One foggy day I accompanied my parents on their boat for a sea rendezvous with a yacht from Northeast Harbor. We were invited on board the yacht for lunch, and our hosts served a wonderfully rich and warming Scallop Soup. I learned that the soup had been thickened in the old-fashioned way with crushed cracker crumbs, and that, along with a healthy splash of sherry, gave the soup its unforgettable, rib-sticking goodness on that raw day. The recipe here is a reasonable facsimile re-created from memory and hunger.

8 tablespoons unsalted butter
2 tablespoons bacon fat or 2 more tablespoons butter
1 medium onion, finely minced
½ cup cream sherry
1 cup Jonathan's Quick Fish Stock (see page 26) or bottled clam juice
1½ cups crushed Ritz crackers
3 cups milk
2 cups half-and-half
1½ pounds fresh sea scallops, coarsely chopped
Salt and freshly ground pepper, to taste
Pinch of cayenne pepper

Makes 6 to 8 servings

1. Melt the butter and bacon fat (if using) together in a large pot over medium heat. Add the onion and sauté until quite soft, 10 to 15 minutes. Stir in the sherry and fish stock. Slowly stir in the cracker crumbs, stirring until smooth and thick.

2. Pour both the milk and half-and-half into the soup, stirring to blend. Add the scallops and simmer the soup uncovered over medium heat until all is hot and the scallops are cooked through, about 15 minutes. Season the soup to taste with salt, pepper, and cayenne. Serve hot.

Scalloped Scallops

Mainers are fond of scalloping all manner of shellfish with melted butter and bread or cracker crumbs. We find that Ritz crackers produce the most sinful crumbs and that luscious sea scallops from Maine's icy winter waters make the best candidate for scalloping. This recipe epitomizes rich yet straightforward New England cooking. These plump and golden-crumbed scallops look as fabulous as they taste and are truly worth the guilt of every indulgent and buttery calorie.

Crusty, rich, and irresistible Scalloped Scallops.

¾ cup unsalted butter
2 cups Ritz cracker crumbs
1 cup fresh bread crumbs
1½ pounds fresh sea scallops
1½ cups light cream or half-and-half
Salt and freshly ground pepper, to taste
2 teaspoons paprika

1. Preheat oven to 350°F. Butter a 1½- to 2-quart baking dish.

2. Melt ¾ cup butter over low heat and combine with cracker and bread crumbs to moisten evenly and thoroughly.

3. Sprinkle one-third of the crumbs over the bottom of the baking dish. Top with half of the sea scallops. Pour half of the cream over the scallops and sprinkle with salt and pepper. Layer on another third of the crumbs, followed by the rest of the scallops and cream. Season again with salt and pepper. Top with the remaining third of the bread crumbs. Sprinkle the paprika evenly over the top.

4. Bake the scallops until just cooked through and bubbling, 30 to 40 minutes. Serve sizzling hot from the oven with a lemon wedge or two if desired.

Makes 4 to 6 rich servings

The Myriad of Maine Mollusks

A colorful fish market array of Maine's saltwater bounty.

Chapter Three

Fin Fish

There are smelts and swordfish, mackerel and tuna, herring and haddock, flounders and pollack, cod, stripers, hake, ocean perch, alewives — you name them and the odds are they're somewhere around the Gulf of Maine. There are no pompano or red snapper, mighty few blues, and the shad that once came up our river are long gone. However, there's enough variety to satisfy the most enthusiastic fish eaters and enough recipes extant to keep them eating a different fish dish twice a day for half a normal lifetime!

WILLAN C. ROUX
What's Cooking Down East

WHEN we began this book, it was inconceivable that a chapter on fin fish could be anything but an integral part of the whole story of coastal Maine cooking. Cookbooks that are now decades old bulge with recipes for fin fish that range from chowders to cakes, stews, smothers, outdoor bakes, fries, and simple Sunday suppers. We envisioned a typical coastal fishing community made up of fishermen, fish merchants, and boat crew members, with supporting industries such as canning or processing factories, boat builders, and sailmakers. The normal town necessities, such as pharmacies, general stores, banks, schools, and service stations, would be present, but the community itself would draw its lifeblood from the sea. Recipes for our book would come from fishermen's wives, who would combine Yankee thrift, their husbands' catch, and perhaps a bit of mischievous creativity (a touch of sherry?). As we researched the topic and delved into the commercial aspects of the fishing industry, once the backbone to the econ-

omy of many a Maine seaside town, we discovered that the fishing industry in Maine, New England, and the rest of the world, for that matter, does not live up to the one-dimensional bucolic picture we had prepainted for ourselves.

Today people on the coast of Maine have access to a greater selection of quality fresh seafood than ever before, whether from adjacent waters or those of another hemisphere. Credit or blame the internal-combustion engine, if you will, but modern technology has given us refrigeration, transportation, and fishing methodology that can actually ensure that a mature salmon raised in a fish pen in Norway can come to a Maine table in a pristine condition that cannot be matched in price or quality by a catch of any species brought in by the trawlers that leave Portland harbor on a ten-day stint. Modern technology has also created a global market for fish caught anywhere, Maine waters not excepted. The ton of groundfish (i.e., bottom fish) brought into Stonington harbor by a fishing vessel may wind up on the plates of businessmen in Tokyo, and it is not uncommon for this fish to find its way to Boston before it comes back to Jonathan's Restaurant in Blue Hill, just twenty miles away from its landing point. Such are the channels of distribution in today's world.

On the downside, this global demand for Down East products has put them into a price category that is beyond the reach of many a Mainer. The evolution of the fishing industry has seriously threatened a way of life and made it virtually impossible for small fishermen to make a living in the current environment. Years ago the enactment of the 200-mile limit prohibited foreign vessels from fishing the waters inside this range. This was critical in molding the structure of

A fishing village and shorefront scene such as this could soon become a memory as new and global technology threatens to change the independent ways of old-time Down East fishermen.

the fishing industry into what it is today. A decade ago venture capitalists and investment bankers were more than willing to finance seaworthy craft and state-of-the-art equipment to fish waters that were protected from foreign intrusion. The feeling was "It's ours, nobody else can take it, so let's go get it." But today the barriers to entry into this industry are virtually insurmountable. To be competitive, start-up costs are $250,000 or more; this goes for a boat and rigging, nets, radar equipment, underwater cameras to track schools of fish, insurance, routine maintenance, and so on. Once all this is assembled, good fortune comes into play — weather, equipment that functions as it is meant to, and an ability to play in a market that is driven by global, not local, forces. A nasty Nor'easter can keep a boat in harbor for days at a time; payments on that boat do not abate correspondingly. And let us not forget that hauling nets,

cranking pulleys, and bouncing around in ten-foot seas while fighting off frozen sea spray is hardly safe or pleasurable work.

Other nonindustry economic facts come into play also. The skyrocketing real estate prices for shore frontage in coastal Maine during the eighties have put access to the water beyond the means of most small fishermen; the demand for the recreational use of prime waterfront land put many fishermen into the unemployment lines. The climate is such that only the big guys can play the game. This all spells good-bye to our idealized notion; it is a sad but true fact that the small, local fisherman is a dying breed. Nothing is better testament to this than the picture of a crusty, retired fisherman that hangs on the office wall of seafood distributor Jimmy Markos, Jr., of Maine Shellfish Company in Ellsworth: David Hyde of Seal Harbor, a bearded man in his late fifties with

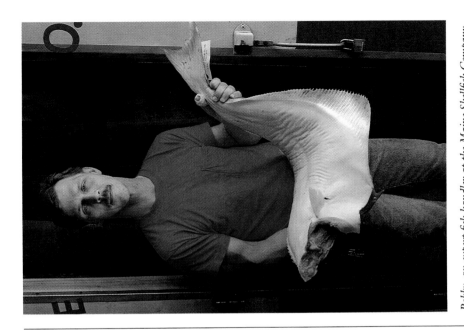

Bobby, an expert fish handler at the Maine Shellfish Company, proudly exhibits a halibut.

wrinkled tan skin, poses for a photographer on the back of his fishing boat *Sunrise*. Today, ironically, Hyde makes a better living taking summer tourists out on *Sunrise* to see how fishermen of another era made their living than he did when he was doing it himself.

Recently, several Maine entrepreneurs have taken their cue from the Norwegians and many new salmon farms have sprung up along the coast. Experiments with halibut, haddock, and other species have begun, and we perceive this all to be part of the evolutionary process. Purists will argue that aquaculture threatens a traditional way of life, but many regard it as a means of halting the continuing decline of the fishing industry. Proponents of aquaculture see it as the only viable way to take advantage of a rich resource (the sea) in a time when long-honored methods have become archaic in a competitive market. Species that have been traditionally dear (the Atlantic salmon, for example) are beginning to make their way into the marketplace at reasonable prices. Dissidents will argue that environmental impact studies are incomplete and that the high-tech equipment visually scars Maine's pristine coastline in ways that quaint yet unkempt boatyards and lobster shacks do not. The controversy continues as does the evolutionary process of the fishing industry as a whole.

Part of this evolutionary process unique to Maine is the revolutionary Portland Fish Auction. The only one of its kind in the country, it takes place in a state-of-the-art temperature-controlled warehouse (32 degrees) where buyers and brokers can actually see the fish they are buying in contrast to other fish auctions, where bids are placed on an unseen product not yet unloaded from boats that have been out for seven, ten, or more days at a time. Boat captains at the Portland Fish Auction have the power to refuse bids in efforts to coax up the price of their catch. The techniques applied at this auction go a long way toward ensuring that consumers receive Maine seafood of the highest quality. The Portland Fish Auction is a model that will undoubtedly be followed elsewhere in years to come.

Our own first childhood memories of Maine fin fish revolve around the mackerel run that usually starts in early July. As a boy, Jonathan would often go fresh-

water fishing with our father, spending hours watching a cork bob, slapping mosquitoes, and coming home empty-handed. Jonathan noticed early on that saltwater mackerel fishing was much easier, more comfortable, and eminently more rewarding. Twenty minutes on Blue Hill Bay early in the morning with nothing more than a dinghy, a pair of oars, and a dragline rigged with five white-feathered lures followed by a shiny "mackerel jig" would often yield breakfast for the family long before anyone had awakened to the smell of fresh coffee. Mackerel travel in schools; the way to catch them is to troll along the coastline with one of the aforementioned rigs until you run through a school. If you're lucky, you'll get a fish on all six hooks; if you're unlucky, you'll get only two or three, but you can throw your line in again. The fish are at a particular disadvantage if you happen to have a companion in the boat on the end of a second dragline. Mackerel do not have scales and are very easy to gut and clean; we often did it right over the side of the boat. They are oily fish and best cooked over a hot fire when very fresh. With bacon and home fries they make a very special and hearty Down East breakfast.

The pugnacious bluefish is of the same family as the mackerel and in recent years has been a frequent summer visitor to the waters of Maine. The father of a friend of Jonathan once hooked a bluefish while innocently playing in a kayak with a mackerel jig in a protected cove. The story, although not completely substantiated, is that the "blue" took him to Long Island (two nautical miles away) before he gave up his Hemingwayesque quest and cut his line. We're not sure how he knew it was a "blue," nor are we sure how he mustered the energy to paddle home. Nevertheless, very fresh bluefish, cooked in a dome cooker or baked in foil with onions and fresh herbs, is very good eating.

In July and August, Maine's tourist season, fishing tournaments are held up and down the coast. Every once in a while someone lands a multi-hundred-pound bluefin tuna or a blacktip shark, but most of this sport is relegated to bluefish and mackerel. An occasional swordfish will find its way into the southern part of Maine's coastal waters, but the remainder of Maine's fin-fish harvest lies in white-fleshed groundfish, namely, cod, pollack, haddock, sole, flounder, hake, whiting, cusk, halibut, and a few other obscure varieties. All but a very small portion is harvested commercially.

Haddock is indeed the quintessential Maine fish. Mainers consider it to be *their* fish. It does seem a bit unjust, however, that its price often makes it unavailable to the typical Mainer, but roadside seafood shacks and local restaurants such as the Fisherman's Friend in Stonington often serve up a fresh-fried haddock sandwich with the obligatory tartar sauce and French fries at a price that will not set the eater back much more than the unworthy counterpart at a typical fast-food chain restaurant. Home cooks can substitute less expensive pollack, hake, cusk, or cod in chowder and other recipes that call for haddock with almost always pleasing results. Halibut is often considered the king of Maine fin fish, perhaps because of its *size* (the smallest coming in around ten

A super-fresh fried haddock sandwich is a Down East treat hard to resist at the annual Common Ground Fair in Windsor.

pounds, the larger ones ranging up to three hundred pounds or more), but more likely because of its superb eating quality. The snow-white flesh is firm, and whether filleted or steaked, halibut needs little more than to be brushed with melted butter before spending ten minutes or so under a hot broiler; served with lemon wedges and parsley-boiled potatoes, this is the purest and most delicious of feasts. Fin-fish recipes that follow range from variations on tried-and-true old-time methods to a few of our own new and worthy creations.

Fish Chowder

If salt pork and bacon are the backbone of Maine cooking, seafood stews and soups certainly account for much of the flesh. In fact, it is more likely that the first chapter of a Maine cookbook will be comprised of chowders rather than the usual appetizer fare. When it comes to fish chowder, we personally think of it as more traditionally Down East than clam chowder. Any combination of white fish may be used — pollack, haddock, cod, hake, or cusk — and the most authentic chowder is made by adding the fillets whole to the soup pot. Once cooked, the fish will flake naturally as the chowder is stirred and ladled into soup bowls. For a change of pace, it is nice to pass the crisped salt pork pieces and common crackers in separate condiment bowls to allow each person to put the finishing touches on his or her chowder.

½ pound salt pork, cut into a fine dice
2 medium onions, minced
5 cups peeled and diced Maine potatoes
3 cups water
2½ pounds fresh, firm, white fish fillets, bones removed
1 can (12 ounces) evaporated milk
3 cups whole milk
Salt and freshly ground pepper, to taste
½ cup minced fresh parsley
Paprika
Common crackers

1. Sauté the salt pork over low heat in a large soup pot until browned and crisp, 6 to 8 minutes. Remove from pot with a slotted spoon and set aside to drain on paper towels.

2. Add the onions to the fat in the pot; sauté until soft and translucent, 5 to 7 minutes. Add the potatoes and water. Bring to a boil and then simmer the soup uncovered until the potatoes are almost tender, 8 to 10 minutes.

3. Place the whole fish fillets on top of the potatoes, cover the pot, and let the fish poach until just cooked through, 12 to 15 minutes. Add the evaporated and the whole milk. Season the soup to taste with salt and pepper. Let simmer for an additional 5 minutes.

4. To serve the chowder, ladle chunks of fish and soup into large bowls. Sprinkle the top of each serving with parsley and a little paprika. Pass the

reserved salt pork and common crackers in small bowls.

Serves 8 to 10

Codfish Pudding

Fish pudding, an almost forgotten old-time dish, is the ethereal seafood equivalent of meatloaf. Maine cookbooks sport pudding recipes calling for haddock, halibut, or cod. We prefer cod, although you may substitute haddock or halibut. Codfish Pudding becomes elegant when served with a drizzle of Lobster Butter (see pages 14–15). For a more down-home repast, accompany the pudding with Tartar Sauce (see page 26).

2 cups evaporated milk or light cream
2½ cups fresh, soft bread crumbs
2 tablespoons unsalted butter
1 pound codfish, boned and filleted
1 small onion, grated
1 tablespoon fresh lemon juice
1 teaspoon celery seeds
Pinch of cayenne pepper
Pinch of nutmeg
Salt and freshly ground pepper, to taste
4 egg whites

1. Preheat the oven to 350°F. Lightly oil a 9 × 4-inch loaf pan and set aside.

2. Scald the milk or cream in a medium-size saucepan, add the bread crumbs, and stir to make a smooth paste. Add the butter, stir until melted, and then remove the pan from the heat.

3. Cut the codfish into small pieces and place in a food processor fitted with the steel blade. Process until the fish is finely ground but not puréed. Add the fish to the saucepan, stirring until smooth. Mix

in the onion, lemon juice, celery seeds, cayenne, and nutmeg. Season the mixture to taste with salt and pepper.

4. Beat the egg whites until they form stiff but not dry peaks. Gently fold the whites into the fish mixture until thoroughly incorporated. Transfer the fish pudding to the prepared loaf pan.

5. Place the loaf pan in a larger pan filled with 1½ inches of water. Bake the fish pudding until set, 45 minutes to 1 hour. Unmold and serve with the sauce of choice. (Note: Any leftover pudding is excellent sliced cold for lunch the following day.)

Serves 8

Baked Stuffed Haddock

The origin of this version of baked stuffed haddock is a bit murky, but it has been handed down to various proprietors of the building that is now Jonathan's Restaurant. As a college student Jonathan worked at what was then the Sea Gull Restaurant, and this recipe was brought in by a local cook named Randy, who got it from his mother, who got it from her mother. We assume that we have here a real fisherman's wife's recipe of the sort we fantasized finding for our book. Who she was or where she lived is unknown, but her recipe is simple, satisfying, and delicious.

2 pounds haddock fillets
6 tablespoons unsalted butter
1 small onion, diced
1 cup diced celery
½ teaspoon dried thyme
4 tablespoons dry sherry
2 cups bread crumbs
Salt and pepper, to taste
1 can (14 ounces) stewed tomatoes

1. Preheat the oven to 375°F. Lightly grease a 9 × 9-inch baking dish.

2. Melt 4 tablespoons of the butter and sauté the onion and celery with the thyme until soft, about 8 minutes. Add the bread crumbs, remove from heat, and mix well. Season with salt and pepper, to taste.

3. Place half of the fillets in the baking dish. Cover with half of the stuffing. Repeat with the rest of the fish and the stuffing. Top with the tomatoes, making sure that they are broken into small chunks. Pour the juice from the can around the sides of the baking dish. Drizzle the remaining butter over the top.

4. Bake the haddock for 35 to 40 minutes or until the fish easily flakes when tested with a fork. Serve at once.

Makes 4 to 6 servings

Oven-Broiled Halibut

Halibut is the sort of fish that Mainers rate as "finestkind," and they say that it is a shame to spoil it with too much "fixing up." The following recipe is just about as basic and wonderful as they come.

4 fresh halibut fillets (6 to 8 ounces each)
2 tablespoons unsalted butter
2 tablespoons fresh lemon juice
½ cup dry white wine
Salt and freshly ground pepper, to taste
Chopped fresh parsley and lemon wedges to garnish

1. Preheat the oven to 450°F.

2. Arrange the halibut fillets in a shallow baking dish large enough to accommodate them comfortably. Cut the butter into small pieces and dot over

Atlantic salmon and garden-fresh peas are readied for a great Fourth of July feast.

each fillet. Drizzle the lemon juice and wine over and around the fillets. Season them with salt and pepper.

3. Bake the fillets in the oven until they are just cooked through, no more than 10 to 12 minutes. Serve at once with any pan juices drizzled over the top of the fillets. Sprinkle with parsley and accompany with lemon wedges.

Serves 4

Poached Atlantic Salmon with Dill Sauce

The lucky winner of the Annual First Hancock County Pea Contest will dine on this simple yet delicious dinner compliments of Jonathan's Restaurant. Steamed new potatoes, snap or shell peas, and a chilled glass of Bartlett's Coastal White wine complete this simple and traditional American summer feast.

Sauce:

2 tablespoons unsalted butter
1 tablespoon minced shallots
2 tablespoons chopped fresh dill
1 tablespoon fresh lemon juice
½ cup mayonnaise, preferably Hellmann's
½ cup sour cream

Poaching Liquid:
6 cups cold water
2 cups dry white wine
2 cloves garlic, peeled and halved
1/2 small onion, sliced
6 sprigs of parsley
2 thin slices lemon
2 bay leaves
6 whole black peppercorns

Salmon:
4 boneless Atlantic salmon fillets, 6 ounces each

1. To make the dill sauce, melt the butter with the shallots in a small saucepan over medium-high heat. Cook until the butter just begins to brown. Remove from heat and add the dill and lemon juice. Let the dill steep in the hot butter for 1 minute. Thoroughly mix the mayonnaise and sour cream in a small bowl. Fold the dill mixture into the mayonnaise and sour cream and chill for 1 hour.

2. To make the poaching liquid, combine all the ingredients in a fish poacher or large skillet and bring to a boil. Reduce heat and simmer for 10 minutes.

3. Add the salmon to the poaching liquid and increase the heat to the point where there is just a slight ripple on the surface of the liquid. Adjust the heat so that the ripple is just maintained. Cover the pan and cook the salmon for 10 minutes. The fillets should be slightly opaque in the center.

4. With a slotted spatula, carefully remove the fillets from the liquid to 4 dinner plates. Top with dill sauce and serve with snap or shell peas and boiled new potatoes. Alternatively, remove the fillets to a large platter and chill for 4 hours. Serve them cold with dill sauce and the same warm accompaniments.

Makes 4 servings

Broiled Bluefin Tuna Steaks

Every once in a while a midcoast fishing tournament will make native bluefin tuna available in late August, the same time that coastal gardens begin to explode with the fruits of various vine plants. Marinated tuna steaks with Fresh Melon and Cucumber Sauce (see pages 92–93) make for a cooling and satisfying late summer repast.

Marinade:
1 small onion, thinly sliced
1 teaspoon fennel seeds
1 teaspoon minced fresh garlic
1/2 cup vegetable oil
1 tablespoon fresh or 1 teaspoon dried rosemary
1/4 cup cider vinegar
1/3 cup dry white wine
1 tablespoon fresh lemon juice
1/2 cup tamari or good-quality soy sauce
1/4 cup dry sherry

Tuna:
8 bluefin tuna steaks, about 10 ounces each and 3/4 to 1 inch thick
Lemon wedges and fresh parsley for garnish

1. To make the marinade, mix well all the marinade ingredients in a nonreactive container. Dip each tuna steak into the marinade and place the steaks in another nonreactive container. Pour the marinade over the tuna steaks. Marinate in the refrigerator for 12 to 24 hours.

2. Preheat the broiler or prepare an outdoor grill according to the manufacturer's instructions. Place the tuna on a baking sheet and discard the marinade. Broil or grill the tuna steaks 4 to 5 inches from the heat source for 4 minutes. Flip the steaks and cook 3 to 4 minutes longer, or until the fish is slightly pink in the center. Transfer the fish to a platter and garnish with lemon wedges and parsley. Serve at once with Fresh Melon and Cucumber Sauce, if desired.

Makes 8 servings

Mackerel Over an Open Fire

The mackerel run in Eastern Maine usually begins in early July and lasts well into August. Most of the fish caught by hungry trollers are tinker mackerel that weigh about three-quarters of a pound before being cleaned and dressed. Two to three fish per person usually suffice, fewer if the fish happen to be bigger. An open fire to which you add alder or birch twigs just before you cook the fish imparts the best flavor, but if this is not feasible, an outdoor charcoal grill will do fine. A hinged basket cooker is essential for turning the fish; otherwise the skin and flesh may stick to the grates of your grill.

8 tinker mackerel (about ¾ pound each), cleaned and dressed
Lemon wedges

1. Prepare an outdoor fire with assorted hardwoods: birch, oak, maple, apple, and cherry work nicely. Allow the fire to burn down to the point where there are only coals. While the coals are still hot, add alder or birch twigs, the greener the better. Alternatively, prepare coals in an outdoor cooker according to the manufacturer's instructions. When the coals are ready, sandwich the mackerel in the basket cooker.

2. Place the cooker 6 to 8 inches from the coals and grill for 5 minutes. Flip the basket and grill the other side for 5 minutes longer. Open the basket and with a sharp knife make a slit along the back of one of the fish. If the meat has lost its translucency, it is done.

3. Transfer the fish to a large platter and serve at once with lemon wedges.

Makes 4 servings

Potted Mackerel

When it comes to catching and cooking a summer morning's haul of mackerel, eyes are often bigger than mouths. This English-style fish pâté comes to the rescue as the perfect thing to make with leftover flaked mackerel delightfully infused with the smoke from its cooking fire.

¼ pound (1 stick) unsalted butter
2½ cups cooked, deboned, and flaked mackerel
1 small onion, minced
1 tablespoon fresh lemon juice
2 tablespoons brandy
¼ cup minced fresh dill
Salt and freshly ground pepper, to taste

1. Beat the butter in a mixing bowl with an electric mixer until creamy. Using a wooden spoon, work in the flaked mackerel and onion. Add the lemon juice, brandy, and dill, mixing well. Season the mixture to taste with salt and pepper.

2. Pack the mackerel pâté into a small crock or earthenware bowl. Cover and refrigerate for a few hours to mellow the flavors. Bring the potted mackerel back to room temperature before serving and accompany with crackers or thin rounds of bread that have been lightly toasted.

Makes about 3 cups

The great sardine man/icon who used to stand tall in Kittery welcoming all who crossed the state border to both vacationland and sardineland.

Chapter Four

Sardines and Other Small Fry

THE association of Maine with sardines has been embedded in my mind since childhood. I remember the long car trek from Connecticut to our grandparents' pine-shaded camp in Brooklin and how the gigantic statue of a yellow-slickered fisherman, extending a unique Down East welcome to each and every traveler who crossed the bridge spanning Portsmouth's Piscataqua River, portended our final destination. The towering sight of this friendly Mainer sporting a larger-than-life tin of sardines meant that the air would soon grow cooler and there would be only three and a half hours more of anticipatory riding listening to the omnipresent squeak of my mother's Styrofoam ice chest rattling over the monotonous Maine Turnpike and waging personal territorial space wars with my loving siblings in the back seat of our station wagon. While this folkloric icon has long since been moved from its welcoming perch in Kittery to the Stinson Sardine Company in Prospect Harbor, to this day I cannot cross the state border into Maine without immediately feeling that I am in sardineland.

It is this vivid memory that has fueled my curiosity about the subject of this chapter and made my hours of research especially rewarding. Ironically, I had never eaten a sardine before beginning this book. The novelty and excitement of discovering a pleasant taste in a food that is unquestionably healthful has made me an easy and enthusiastic convert to sardine cookery and encouraged a fascination with

the history of the sardine industry in the state of Maine.

Maine is the only state in the United States that markets canned sardines. By general definition, *sardine* is a generic term used to describe a number of different kinds of small saltwater fish that are prepared, cooked, and packed in a specific way. The Maine sardine is an Atlantic herring of the Latin classification *Clupea harengus*. The smallest Atlantic herring range from two to three inches in length and are dressed and canned as sardines, while the larger herring of six to eight inches are cut into bite-size steaks and packed as "fish steaks" or filleted and smoked to make kippers. Sardines are found in all seas with the exception of the frigid Arctic and Antarctic waters, making them one of the most important commercial fish in the entire world. It is known that native Maine Indians captured sardines with primitive weirs, or circular brushwood traps, strategically placed in shallow coves and coastal inlets. The first experiments of the new settlers in canning sardines failed, but an incident during the Franco-Prussian War of 1870 made sardine fishing in Maine into a viable industry.

A New York fish importer by the name of Henry Sellman became a major sardine pioneer, and this is his personal account of the industry's beginnings (as given in *Maine Sardine Industry History: An Anthology*):

The Franco-German war in 1870–71 was the approximate if not immediate cause of the origin of the American sardine industry, and it was brought about in the following manner: For about ten years previously there were imported from Hamburg, Germany, by a firm in New York, an article of merchandise known as "Russian sardines." The fish used were small herring taken on the coast of Norway, and were prepared as follows: After being suitably salted the heads and entrails were removed; the fish were then thoroughly washed, and, after draining in baskets, packed in layers in kegs, every other layer receiving a definite quantity of whole spices, such as cloves, pepper, mustard seed, bay leaves, allspice, red peppers, and capers. A pickle of slightly salted vinegar was added after the package had been filled up with fish. From a small beginning this article grew rapidly in favor, principally among the German population, and the demand for goods became so extensive that the importation amounted to not less than 50,000 kegs per annum. When in the early part of the Franco-German war, in consequence of the blockade of German ports by the French navy, the importation of the article from Hamburg had to be abandoned for the time being, the price of the article advanced fifty percent, in New York, owing to the small supply in the market.

It was under these circumstances that the writer conceived of the idea of finding a suitable fish taken in American waters for the purpose of producing the so-called Russian sardines in this country. The small smoked herring that are put up in boxes, and known in our markets as No. 1 and scaled herring, furnished a basis for investigation as to suitability of the fish under a different mode of curing and preparation for the purpose mentioned. As these fish were principally prepared at Eastport, Maine, an order was transmitted to Messrs. Griffin Brothers, of that place, for a sample shipment of small salted herring, with full instructions as to the manner of salting and preparing the same. The shipment came to hand in due time, and the quality of the fish proved satisfactory.

After this initial success, it did not take long for sardine production to grow and flourish. By 1880, Maine had eighteen sardine canneries concentrated for the most part in the Eastport-Lubec area. By 1900 more than seventy-five canneries had been established all up and down the coast. Unfortunately, such proliferation produced oversupply, which in turn led to a fall in prices that was temporarily devastating to the industry. The year 1910 marked the beginning of a forty-year period of new prosperity in the sardine

business. Because war usually brings an increased demand for affordable canned goods, both World War I and World War II further stimulated canned-fish production. The sardine industry peaked in 1950 with nearly four million cases of sardines being packed in forty-six different plants along the Maine coast.

Related and by-product industries developed in Maine as well, as a result of the successful sardine-packing businesses. Examples include the 1889 opening of a factory in Eastport for decorating lithographed sardine tins. A Portland firm began to supply solder for sealing tins, and "shooks," for making packing crates for sardines, were cut in local sawmills across the state. By-products from the Atlantic herring led to the opening of fishmeal and fertilizer plants, as well as pearl essence factories for converting herring scales into opalescent materials for lipstick, nail polish, buttons, and costume jewelry. In 1948 factories started making pet food from Maine herring as well.

Wartime demand was not maintained, and from 1960 on, the number of sardine canneries in operation has steadily declined. At present there are eight canneries in the state of Maine producing between 800,000 and 900,000 cases of sardines per year. The Maine Sardine Council was established as an independent state agency in Brewer in 1951, and it does a wonderful job of promoting and maintaining high-quality standards in the state's sardine industry. Of the council's array of educational literature, I'm particularly fond of an instructive comic book printed in both English and Spanish detailing the adventures of young Ricky and Debbie in Sardineland, or *Ricardo y Debora en La Tierra de Las Sardinas*, if one prefers. Like me during my childhood trips to Maine, the fictitious Ricky and Debbie quickly learn that Maine is synonymous with sardines. As the comic strip progresses, the two youngsters get to go on board a sardine fishing boat, or seiner, and experience the modern technology of today's industry. They learn how schools of herring are detected through a combination of depth recorders, sophisticated echo-sounding devices, and even light airplanes that track silvery flashes of fish scales in the water from the sky above.

Once a school of sardines is located, the fishing

The Port Clyde sardine-packing plant in Rockland.

boats employ large nets called purse seines to encircle the herring. A drawstring is then pulled to close the bottom of the net and thereby entrap the fish in a manner that fortunately prevents collateral injury to dolphins and other marine life. The comic strip follows the fate of the captured sardines as they are sucked through a hose that simultaneously removes all fish scales and pumps the catch into a mixture of ice and seawater in holding tanks on carrier boats that will dispatch the sardines to nearby canneries as quickly as possible. Ricky and Debbie are driven off into the sunset exclaiming that all the versatile and nutritious sardines in the country come from the beautiful state of Maine. I decided to sate the rest of my personal curiosity about the sardine industry with a firsthand look at the less adventurous and glamorous side of the business by taking a tour through the Port Clyde packing plant located along the picturesque shorefront of the economically depressed town of Rockland.

John Melquist, manager of the Port Clyde plant, greeted me cheerfully in front of the large, weathered red building. I learned that as the carrier boats arrive at the cannery, the herring are pumped briefly into new holding tanks for an hour or two before being taken by conveyors for washing, size sorting, and precooking. Next, a machine removes the heads and tails from the herring, though in the early days of labor-intensive canning this decapitation, shockingly enough, was carried out by children no more than ten or eleven years old. Child labor laws and new technology between 1900 and 1915 halted this dangerous practice, but to this day every single can of sardines is still *packed* by human hands, and those hands belong almost exclusively to hair-netted women. Male chauvinism, it would seem, has once

43

Sardines and Other Small Fry

and forever dictated that women are more deft with their hands than men. Indeed, a 1901 description of sardine factory occupations in Eastport describing packers as "all women" remains as valid today as it was back then.

Cans of snug, women-packed sardines continue on their conveyor-belt journey through the plant to male-operated machines that quickly inject into the tins the packing liquid, be it oil, spring water, or spiced sauces. Covers are finally applied, and the tins are sealed and subjected to one final cooking and sterilization. United States processing differs from the Norwegian competition in that Norwegians practice the added step of smoking their catch over an oak fire for an hour before the hand-packing of tins begins.

All sardine-canning operations in Maine are subject to federal regulations, although the state of Maine also monitors its own rigorous standards with

inspections. Laboratories at the Maine Sardine Council in Brewer are set up to inspect every case lot of sardines and rate them in accordance with twenty-one different quality factors, ranging from smell, to appearance in the tin, to taste.

"Packed like sardines into a tin" has long been a popular expression, but less well known is the fact that nutrition is packed as tight into a tin of sardines as the sardines themselves. A single 3¾-ounce can of Maine sardines provides at least 50 percent of recommended daily protein intake, 10 percent of daily iron needs, 40 percent of the recommended amount of calcium, and 15 percent of the daily requirement for vitamin D. Additionally, sardines are rich in Omega-3 acids that are believed by current studies to reduce the bad cholesterol in our bloodstreams and enrich the good cholesterol.

Such health benefits serve to heighten the joy of cooking with sardines. Many a Mainer will say the

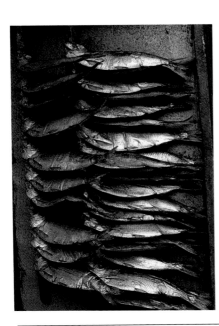

Smoked alewives are sold from roadside markets during the spring.

favorite way to enjoy sardines is right out of the tin or perhaps, more fancily, on toast with a squeeze of lemon. Jeff Kaelin, the director of the Maine Sardine Council, echoes this Maine bias toward unembellishment, though he was kind enough to turn me loose in a room containing all the files of recipes developed for the Maine Sardine Industry over the years. The recipes in this chapter reflect what I eagerly netted from the council's dusty but abundant files.

Before concluding this chapter, I must mention two more small fish or fry of size similar to sardines that are caught in nets and savored by Mainers. Alewives are a different sort of herring than those used for sardine canning, and they are quintessential Robert P. Tristram Coffin fare, as these days it is truly only the old-timers who fuss with these incredibly bony but tasty small springtime fish. Coffin wrote in *Mainstays of Maine:* "I don't know where the name [alewife] comes from exactly, but I know how to pronounce it. It is pronounced L–Y. That's the right and native way." After waxing eloquent about alewives for several ensuing paragraphs, Coffin goes on to explain:

There are lots of bones in alewives. They are webs of lacy bones. But their meat tastes so good that men eat them bones and all, and laugh at anatomy. They bite into their fat bodies, browned in cornmeal, and blow some of the bones out of the corners of their mouths. They swallow the rest. I think each of these mammoth herring has about a half million ribs. . . . By the way, sucking infants demand and yell for ale-

wives along with the rest, once they get a whiff of them fried, and they get them, bones and all. It is a great wonder any Maine man, woman, or child can ever get his shirt, skirt, or diapers off at night, he, she, or it eats so many alewives in the Spring. He, she, or it is so exactly like a pincushion, the alewives' ribs come through his skin so!

Today most Mainers sway toward the lazier preference for smoked alewives, smoking having disintegrated many of the bones, and it is common to see whole strings of golden smoked alewives hanging on sticks for sale along rural roadside markets come springtime.

More popular for fresh-caught eating than alewives are smelts. Although some smelts are ice-fished in winter months, most are caught romantically by moonlight or lantern in early-morning hours as they take a frantic spring swim upstream to spawn in warmer waters. Smelts are almost always eaten fried or grilled within hours of being caught, thereby making them frequent breakfast fare. A favorite description of spring smelting comes from neighbor and Blue Hill resident Esther E. Wood, who a while ago compiled a charming cookbook called *Country Fare — Reminiscences and Recipes from a Maine Childhood.* In the chapter entitled "Flipping Fresh," Miss Wood recalls:

My father liked fresh fish: "flipping fresh" was the way he expressed his choice. During my childhood we had fresh fish twelve months of the year.

Old-fashioned sardine tins.

In the spring we ate smelts. They were better than cheap; they were free for the dipping. Cousin Austin was the official dipper and he kept the frying pans of the neighborhood filled with fish for the duration of the fish-run.

Once Olive and I went with Austin when he went smelting. We left the house before sunrise. A waning moon gave light; the fragrance of lilacs in the door-yard filled the air. We cut across the rocky pasture to the store where the meadow brook poured its swamp water into the bay. There, at the flood of the tide, smelts were swimming upstream by the hundreds to lay their eggs. They pulsated in the water like silver feathers come alive. Austin used a dipper that his father had made by nailing an opened crocus sack to a barrel hoop. While he bent to dip the fish, Olive and I knelt and harvested them with our hands. Though some wiggled from our fingers, we soon had a ten-quart pail filled. When our pails were stocked, Austin called a halt. "No use to dip any more. Let's go home and get the folks up for breakfast. I want fried smelts for my breakfast."

"Me too," agreed his sister and I.

Mother cleaned the smelts, dipped them in beaten eggs, rolled them in corn meal and fried them in a spider greased with salt pork. They came to the table hot, golden, and flavorful. Leftover smelts were served cold for supper. Cold smelts and rhubarb sauce are natural companion foods for May suppers.

Fortunately, today, little has changed in the ease of capturing spring smelts or the method of cooking the copious catch, though conscience may dictate the use of vegetable oil over salt pork when pan-frying.

Maine Sardine Dip

This creamy spread is one of the most simple yet elegant ways to enjoy the flavor of Maine sardines. It is the perfect nibble to serve to break the ice at any coastal cocktail celebration accompanied by crackers and/or crisp garden vegetables as dippers. A garnish of lemon wedges and dill sprigs perks up the monotone hue of the sardines.

1 package (8 ounces) cream cheese, at room temperature
1 tin (3¾ ounces) Maine sardines packed in spring water, drained
3 scallions, trimmed and minced
1 tablespoon fresh lemon juice
1 tablespoon Worcestershire sauce
2 tablespoons brandy
2 tablespoons minced fresh parsley
2 tablespoons minced fresh dill
Salt and freshly ground black pepper, to taste
Lemon wedges and fresh dill sprigs to garnish

1. Beat the cream cheese and sardines together in a mixing bowl with a wooden spoon or an electric mixer. Blend in the scallions, lemon juice, Worcestershire, and brandy until combined. Do not overbeat, however, as the spread should retain a little texture. Mix in the parsley and dill. Season to taste with the salt and pepper.

2. Transfer the dip to a serving dish. Cover and refrigerate a few hours to mellow the flavors. Garnish the dip with lemon wedges and dill sprigs and serve with favorite cracker or vegetable dippers.

Makes about 2 cups

Spicy Sardine Spread

This saucy spread is a coarser and lustier cousin of the more refined Maine Sardine Dip. Serve on toast or crackers or use as a filling for a very satisfying Down East sandwich.

2 tins (3¾ ounces each) Maine sardines packed in oil, drained
½ cup chili sauce (Maine-made Mother's Mountain works nicely)
2 tablespoons prepared horseradish, drained
1 tablespoon capers, drained
1 clove garlic, minced
3 scallions, trimmed and minced
2 tablespoons fresh lemon juice
½ to 1 teaspoon hot sauce, such as Tabasco
¼ cup minced fresh parsley
Freshly ground black pepper, to taste

1. In a small mixing bowl, mash the sardines with the tines of a fork. Blend in the chili sauce, horseradish, capers, garlic, and scallions. Add the lemon juice and hot sauce to suit your palate. Mix in the parsley and season to taste with the pepper.

2. Transfer the spread to a serving dish and store, covered, in the refrigerator. The spread tastes best if brought back to room temperature before serving.

Makes about 1 cup

Sardine-Stuffed Eggs

These tangy deviled eggs use Maine sardines packed in mustard sauce.

6 hard-boiled eggs, peeled
1 tin (3¾ ounces) sardines packed in mustard sauce
½ teaspoon dry mustard
1 teaspoon curry powder
1 teaspoon Worcestershire sauce
4 tablespoons mayonnaise, preferably Hellmann's
Salt and freshly ground black pepper, to taste
Red pimiento strips and parsley sprigs to garnish

1. Halve the eggs lengthwise and remove the egg yolks, reserving the white shells. Mash the egg yolks and sardines together in a mixing bowl until well combined. Add the dry mustard, curry powder, and Worcestershire. Fold in the mayonnaise and season the mixture to taste with salt and pepper.

2. Mound the yolk mixture into the cavities of the reserved whites. Place 2 thin pimiento strips to make an X on top of each egg half and garnish with a small sprig of parsley. Serve at once or refrigerate until ready to serve.

Makes 12 stuffed egg halves

Sardine and Corn Fritters

Sardines packed with jalapeño peppers are a current favorite of Jeff Kaelin, director of the Maine Sardine Council. I used a sample tin that Jeff gave me to update this recipe, which I discovered in the council's food files from the 1960s. The fritters emerge very light and feathery and make a fun snack, brunch feature, or dinner side dish. While frying the fritters in bacon fat may negate all the great health benefits packed into a tin of sardines, it sure does make the recipe taste extra delicious.

3 large eggs, separated
1 tin (3¾ ounces) sardines packed with jalapeño peppers
1 cup frozen whole-kernel corn, defrosted
3 tablespoons minced onion
4 tablespoons unbleached all-purpose flour
½ teaspoon salt
½ teaspoon freshly ground black pepper
4 tablespoons bacon fat, butter, vegetable oil, or olive oil

A lusty bowl of pasta tossed with delicious Port Clyde Pesto.

1. Beat the egg yolks with an electric mixer until thick and lemon colored, 2 to 3 minutes. Mash the sardines and stir into the egg yolks along with the corn and onion. Blend in the flour until smooth. Season with the salt and pepper.

2. In a clean bowl and with clean beaters, beat the egg whites until stiff but not dry. Gently fold the egg whites into the sardine batter until just combined.

3. Melt the shortening of your choice in a large skillet over medium heat. For each fritter, drop about 2 heaping tablespoons of batter into the hot fat. Cook until golden brown on the underside, flip, and continue cooking another 2 minutes or so, until golden all over. Keep cooked fritters warm in the oven while cooking the rest of the batter. Serve the fritters hot.

Makes 16 fritters

Pasta with Port Clyde Pesto

The recipe for this unusual and innovative sardine-based pesto was first sighted in the Maine Organic Farmers and Gardeners Association's *A Bountiful Year Cookbook*. Jonathan and I were immediately enticed by the notion of this Maine variation on a classic Sicilian dish. We added a few elaborations of our own to the recipe to bring this sardine pesto to perfection and now enjoy the resulting pasta dish either piping hot during cold spells or slightly chilled in the summertime. The raisins add sweet but harmonious contrast to the pungency of the sardines and anchovies.

½ cup dark raisins
¾ cup dry white wine
¼ cup pine nuts or walnuts, lightly toasted
2 cloves garlic, minced
2 cans (3¾ ounces each) Maine sardines packed in oil
1 tin (2 ounces) anchovies packed in oil

Fried Smelts

Smelt fishing, or smelting, as it is referred to by Mainers, is a favorite pastime during the early days of spring. The most common method of preparing these tasty small fry is simply to "fry up a mess of smelts." Johnnycake (see page 60) and coleslaw (page 69) are good candidates to play supporting roles to make this a real Down East feast.

2 pounds fresh smelts
¼ cup cornmeal
¼ cup unbleached all-purpose flour
½ teaspoon salt
¼ teaspoon freshly ground black pepper
4 to 5 tablespoons vegetable oil
Lemon wedges

1. Clean the smelts by first removing their heads with a sharp paring knife. Slit the fish down the bellies and scoop out the entrails. Rinse the smelts under cold running water and pat dry with paper towels. Preheat oven to 200°F.

2. In a pie pan or medium-size bowl, mix together the cornmeal, flour, salt, and pepper. In a large skillet (preferably cast-iron), heat enough oil over medium heat to cover the bottom of the pan. Dredge the smelts in the cornmeal mixture and fry until golden brown on one side, 4 to 5 minutes. Remove the fish to a platter, being careful not to break them, and place them, uncovered, in the warm oven. Repeat the process, adding a little more oil to the pan when necessary, until all the fish are cooked.

3. Garnish the platter with plenty of lemon wedges for squeezing over the smelts and serve family-style.

Makes 4 servings

1 cup freshly grated Parmesan cheese
Grated zest of 1 lemon
½ cup (or possibly a little more) olive oil
1 bunch fresh parsley, minced
1 pound linguine or other favorite pasta, cooked according to package directions

1. Place the raisins and wine in a small saucepan over medium heat. Simmer 10 minutes to soften and plump the raisins. Remove from heat and set aside.

2. Place the pine nuts (or walnuts) and garlic in a food processor or blender and process to make a paste. Add the sardines and anchovies undrained, ¼ cup of the Parmesan cheese, and the lemon zest. Process until smooth. Thin the pesto with the ½ cup olive oil, adding a little extra if the mixture seems too thick. Transfer to a bowl and stir in half of the minced parsley and the reserved raisins, including any liquid.

3. Cook the pasta, drain it, and toss it with the sardine pesto in a large bowl, mixing well. Sprinkle with the rest of the minced parsley and serve at once accompanied by a bowl of the remaining Parmesan for passing. Alternatively, let the pasta cool to room temperature and then place it in the refrigerator until cold. The chilled pasta should be served within 24 hours.

Makes 6 servings

Pemaquid Light.

Campfire Smelts

Maine cookbooks abound with recipes for foods cooked in foil, outdoors, over hot campfire coals. Although this method works well for cooking whole large fish, such as salmon, haddock, and mackerel, it is much quicker with smaller fish, such as smelts. Conveniently, these tasty little fish start to run just in time for those first spring camping trips when melting snows have swelled the local coastal streams.

3 pounds fresh smelts
½ cup coarsely chopped onion
⅓ cup chopped fresh parsley (optional)
1 teaspoon salt
Freshly ground pepper, to taste
3 strips bacon, cut in half

1. Clean the smelts and drain on paper towels.
2. Cut 6 12-inch squares of heavy-duty aluminum foil. If you don't have heavy-duty foil, double up the squares. Lightly grease each square. Divide the fish evenly into 6 portions and place each portion on one half of each square. Sprinkle each portion equally with onion, parsley (if using), salt, and pepper. Place a half slice of bacon on each portion. Fold the other half of the foil over the fish and seal tightly by rolling the edges all around.
3. Place the fish packages in a bed of hot coals. Cook 15 to 20 minutes, turning two or three times.
4. To serve, remove the packages from the coals and cut a large crisscross in the top of each one.

Makes 6 servings

Chapter Five

Smokin'

LONG before I knew I would be writing a cookbook on Maine or that this cookbook would contain a chapter on smoking foods, I had dated a fellow who worked in a short-lived smokehouse operation on Nantucket Island. I used to say then that the smell of smoke on a man could drive a woman wild and that a company like Calvin Klein or Polo/Ralph Lauren ought to bottle the intoxicating essence as a cologne certain to make a fortune. A few years later, I began to use some utterly exquisite smoked seafoods in my Nantucket catering business from a place called Ducktrap River Fish Farm in Lincolnville, Maine. At the time I knew nothing more about the operation than that it was producing the best smoked salmon and smoked mussels I had ever tasted. Another few years passed, and Ducktrap and its handsome, Harvard-educated owner, Desmond FitzGerald, began to receive a lot of glowing press. And then, still another few years later, I had my first opportunity to meet the divine Des in person to interview him for this book. The idea for the cologne suddenly leapt back into consciousness in the charmed presence of the preppy proprietor. "Now, this is smokin'?" I sighed to myself.

But Des FitzGerald is more than just a pretty (and much married, I might add) face. He is the ingenious founder, owner, and visionary behind what has become a multimillion-dollar smoked-seafood business. His story has now been told many times in prestigious publications ranging from glossy *Connoisseur* magazine to the inky *New York Times*. Fame and fortune aside, we are proud to confirm,

Ducktrap's products are still the most superb we know.

In brief, Des's Maine story began in childhood with Down East family summer vacations away from the oppressive heat of his native Washington, D.C. While studying biology at Harvard, Des spent a summer working on a commercial salmon-fishing boat in Alaska. En route to Alaska, he had passed a month and a half at a friend's trout farm in California, an experience that was to leave an indelible impression. After graduating from Harvard, Des continued his education with studies in aquaculture at the University of Washington in Seattle, a graduate program that he likens to a "Berlitz Fish Program" of fishing all day and all night. After a year or so, the siren call back to the clean and crisp air of his youthful vacations in Maine began to sound. He

Des FitzGerald inspects sides of smoked salmon at his Ducktrap River Fish Farm operation in Lincolnville.

51

A plentiful array of smoked trout speckled with golden mustard seeds from Kohn's Smokehouse.

remembered the trout farm in California and how it seemed to him to offer a livelihood with the utopian combination of using biology and business acumen to work outdoors with wildlife. He returned to Maine with a dream of establishing a trout farm of his own and spent the next year looking for an ideal location.

Des was drawn to the midcoast section of the state because he loved its mixture of "lakes near the ocean with some mountains thrown in as well." His search ended with thirty acres of woodland where the Ducktrap River flows in Lincolnville. The river

was named for Indians who had once trapped ducks along the banks, and its still undeveloped potential appealed to the dreamer in FitzGerald. Des started his trout farm in the fall of 1978 with 60,000 brook trout fingerlings and expectations that they would be restaurant ready by the following spring. He confesses, "I had no marketing in mind then and, to be honest, I haven't since. I did a very casual marketing study by going around saying 'I'm going to grow trout; are you interested?'"

After enjoying the natural rhythms of feeding his trout for three 45-minute periods each and every day and loving to watch them flip and flash in their ample water supply, Des began to hear another voice in him saying "let's expand this a little bit and try to do something different." That something different began with experiments in smoking some of his trout and then some mussels when he became friends with Chip Davison, who had started the nearby Great Eastern Mussel Farms. One evening in a bar in Camden he met a woman who was living on a sailboat. She suggested that FitzGerald needed a logo for his business endeavors and that her company, Fly-by-Night Graphics, could supply one. An etched trout soon became the distinctive Ducktrap logo. Recently and reluctantly, Des accepted that trout farming could never be a viable business, but the trout logo will remain emblazoned on every one of Ducktrap's smoked seafood products as a reminder of where dreams may lead.

Des's first attempts at smoking took place in a homemade smoker rigged from an old and inoperative refrigerator. After much frustration in trying to achieve consistency of product, the defeated entrepreneur took off for Scotland and England to glean insight by studying traditional European smoking methods. Des learned a lot in a short time about smoking and now uses English-made smokers exclusively at Ducktrap. Having quality smokers geared entirely to smoking seafood has allowed Des to indulge his restless creativity in making innovations of his own. An example is Ducktrap's recipes for smoking scallops and mussels, of which there was no precedent in European techniques. The woods over which the seafoods are smoked make up a very important part of Des's flavor equation. Large European smokehouses smoke foods mostly over oak, while those in places like Brooklyn, New York, are relegated to using what is commercially available — mostly hickory and liquid smoke. Maine, by contrast, offers a great natural resource in wood, and FitzGerald takes full advantage of that by employing a blend of four different native woods: red oak and sugar maple as hardwoods and chokecherry and apple as fruitwoods. The proportions in which these woods are blended to smoke any given product remain a trade secret, but FitzGerald will disclose that a flavorfully powerful fish such as bluefish requires a lot of dominant, strong smoke from red oak while delicate shellfish such as scallops require the sweetness of lighter apple wood.

Ducktrap Farm smokes only seafood, and Des exercises a blend of environmental consciousness and integrity for freshness in selecting which seafoods will bear the Ducktrap label. Since wild Atlantic salmon are an endangered species, Des won't use them and instead opts for farm-raised salmon from the Canadian border. In fact, he explained that farm-raised salmon are "a wonderful reason to be in Maine right now," since there is a major flow of salmon over the border and he can nab his fish a fresh two and a half hours into its iced journey to Boston for immediate smoking on premise. Mussels come from forty feet below cold coastal waters around Jonesboro and are bravely dived for by Dave Thompson and his son. The deep-water mussels tend to be free of pearls and grit and much purer in flavor than those gathered in low tidal waters. Maine shrimp come from a purveyor in Portland who has mastered the tricky art of flash freezing these delicate crustaceans to preserve freshness and firmness. Des prefers the Maine shrimp over larger Gulf varieties because he likes all of his smoked shellfish to be of one-bite size. Currently, the best and most affordable scallops for smoking come from Argentina, and the day we visited Ducktrap, Des was experimenting with smoking catfish raised on farms in the South. Since Ducktrap already has twenty-five different products in its line, including a variety of smoked seafood pâtés, Des confessed that his employees let out "an audible groan" when the catfish arrived.

Desmond FitzGerald clearly loves what he is doing, and because he sustains a fascination for "what happens to seafood when it is enhanced by smoke," he has no plans to expand his operation into smoking nonseafood products. When asked about plans for the future, this "no-marketing strategist" replied, "I'm not interested in seeing Ducktrap reach any volume dollar-wise. I'm interested in seeing the product get better."

A Maine smokehouse operation that is devoted to smoking products other than seafood is Smith's Log Smokehouse in Brooks. Owners Andy and Kay Smith moved to Maine from Philadelphia during the back-to-the-land movement of the sixties. Andy Smith came from a long line of butchers in

This sign hangs by the original log cabin/smokehouse that Andy Smith built by hand during a recession in the logging business.

Philadelphia, with a grandfather, father, and six uncles all in some sort of meat-processing business. Smith, however, had left for Maine to rebel, and, refusing "to be any meat cutter," he became a vegetarian. He turned to logging for income, but a recession in the late seventies lured him back to the family business. Trying to be creative with a surplus of unsalable logs on his property, Smith decided to build an old-fashioned log cabin using only oxen and hand tools as aids. About the same time, a neighbor invited him to a livestock auction. As a vegetarian, Smith thought this strange but went along anyway. He ended up buying a couple of pigs, having a total change of heart, and turning his log cabin into a smokehouse fired by a woodstove. This was 1980 and the beginning of Smith's Log Smokehouse.

Today, Smith's Log Smokehouse features a sleek USDA-approved processing plant on the very grounds where Andy and Kay once tilled their vegetable garden. The original log cabin now serves as a combination smokehouse and product salesroom, and Smith has built up an honorable reputation for smoking meats by traditional curing methods that use no nitrates or chemicals unless specifically requested in a custom order. He also uses organically raised Maine meats as much as possible as bases for his delicious blackstrap-molasses-cured ham and bacon, smoked sausages, hard salamis, hot dogs, and smoked birds. The product that Smith is most proud of is also the Smokehouse's best-seller — beef jerky cured with honey and tamari. Andy says that it took him thirteen different attempts to get the jerky just right and that he persevered by keeping in mind a lesson learned during his logging days. He remembered a time when a skidder had broken out in the woods on the machine used to haul the logs. He observed a fellow logger applying some ingenuity to form a makeshift runner and resolve the crisis within forty-five minutes. Since then, Andy Smith has strived "to view major catastrophes as challenges."

The first product Smith developed for his meat line was scrapple, a staple in his native Pennsylvania. "Oh, I could go on and on about this item," he avers. "Pound for pound, it's your best meat buy when you think nutrition. A Pennsylvania Dutch dish, all the goodness is boiled out of pork bones, and to this broth is added wheat flour, cornmeal, buckwheat flour, and spices, with sage flavor predominant. This porridge is poured into pans to cool and harden. Your job is to slice it thin and fry till crispy on both sides. Serve with maple syrup or ketchup, with egg or potatoes. For breakfast or dinner." Once when describing a recipe to Jonathan for a favorite stir-fry of vegetables with chorizo, a spicy Mexican sausage, Smith seemed truly insulted when Jonathan asked if he drained the fat off the sautéed chorizo. Crestfallen, the burly, bearded Andy Smith replied, "We work so hard to get the unique flavor into our sausage with the fat, how dare anyone throw it away?"

Another Maine smokehouse that deserves mention is Kohn's Smokehouse just south of Thomaston in the small hamlet of Saint George. Kohn's smokes

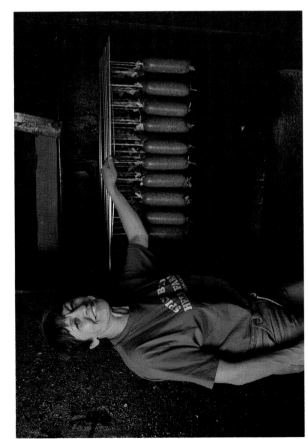

Ute Kohn pushes a bevy of cervelat sausages into the oven for a long, slow smoke.

Andy Smith, owner of Smith's Log Smokehouse located in the backwoods near Monroe.

both fish and meat. Its owner, Ute Kohn, moved to Maine from Germany in 1975 and immediately began smoking foods in a European manner using secret recipes from her husband's family-owned butcher shop in East Prussia. Ute's trademark flavors come from her application of European techniques, which rely on smoke rather than salt as the chief preserving ingredient, to local fare, which may one day be the catch off a fishing boat and another day a custom smoke order to satisfy a hunter's success. For wood, Ute thriftily utilizes the hardwood and fruitwood scraps from neighboring boat-building businesses.

One spring day when we visited, we found the owner busily transferring a hefty batch of cervelat to a smoking oven, where it would cure slowly for one and a half weeks. Another autumn visit found the wiry and industrious Ute so buried in custom orders for farmers and hunters that she couldn't see her way clear through the smoke to chat. Kohn's Smokehouse operates as a cottage industry and therefore cannot ship foods out of the state of Maine. Those finding themselves in the midcoast area would be wise to make the trek through the spectacular saltwater countryside on Route 131 to Kohn's to sample such specialties as smoked Maine lobster, mackerel, and Foggy Ridge Game Farm pheasant. Kohn is always fond of telling customers, "If it walks, swims, or flies, we smoke it."

When it comes to cooking with products from Maine smokehouses, Jonathan and I have found that there is not much we can do to improve on the perfection of the products in their natural state. Hence, we are apt to recommend putting together our Down East Antipasto platter as a way to savor a cross section of the native smokehouse plethora. When we do cook with these smoked goods, we tend to pair them simply with other Maine products, such as smoked mussels, in a salad with a local goat cheese, hard salami shredded into the filling for a baked Maine potato, blackstrap ham basted with orchard cider, and beef jerky strewn into an old-fashioned split pea soup.

The well-known American food expert Evan Jones once explained that the appeal of smoked foods comes from tasting "fusions of flavors of land, sea, and air." When that concept is applied in the specific context of Maine, it is no wonder that so much Down East delight is to be had from those foods that get put up in smoke.

Pastry Sticks with Smoked Salmon

The inspiration for this hors d'oeuvre comes from Ducktrap River Fish Farm's salmon snack suggestion sheet. A dill-flecked cream cheese pastry is cut into bite-size strips and topped with delicious pink slices of Ducktrap's Kendall Brook label presliced smoked salmon. Once baked, the strips emerge as a flaky and ethereal cocktail savory. The large yield of close to a hundred sticks makes this recipe a great one for the entertaining files. Extras can be frozen and reheated as need or the craving strikes.

Cream Cheese Pastry:

6 ounces chilled cream cheese, torn into small pieces
1 cup (2 sticks) unsalted butter, chilled and cut into small pieces
2 cups unbleached all-purpose flour
1/4 teaspoon salt
1/2 cup loosely packed minced fresh dill
2 teaspoons fresh lemon juice

Smoked Salmon Topping:

8 ounces presliced smoked salmon, preferably Ducktrap's Kendall Brook label
1 large egg beaten with 1 tablespoon water
Paprika

1. To make the pastry, place cream cheese, butter, flour, salt, and dill in a food processor fitted with the steel blade. Process until the mixture resembles coarse crumbs. Add the lemon juice and continue to process until the dough begins to form into a ball. Remove dough from the processor, shape into a disk, dust lightly with flour, and wrap in plastic wrap. Chill in the refrigerator for at least 2 hours.

2. When ready to make the pastry sticks, preheat oven to 350°F. Line a couple of large baking sheets with parchment paper.

3. Roll the cream cheese pastry out on a lightly floured surface to about 1/8 inch in thickness. Cut the dough into strips about 1/2 inch wide and 2 1/2 inches long. Arrange in rows spaced about 1/2 inch apart on the prepared baking sheets.

4. Cut strips of salmon slightly smaller than the pastry strips. Place a double layer of salmon strips on top of each pastry strip. Using a pastry brush, brush the strips all over with the beaten egg and water mixture. Sprinkle each strip lightly with some paprika.

5. Bake the strips until puffed and lightly browned, about 12 to 15 minutes. Serve hot from the oven or cooled to room temperature.

Makes about 100 bite-size strips

We like to serve our Down-East-Style Antipasto on a contrasting platter from one of Maine's many potters.

Down-East-Style Antipasto

This adaptation of an Italian classic poses little challenge to the cook, as all the ingredients can be procured in a finished state. In the winter of 1991, Jonathan took a rare break from the daily routine of running his restaurant, partly to work on this book and partly to recharge his batteries and research some fresh ideas for his menu. After visiting several cottage industries and smokehouses, he, not surprisingly, added this antipasto to his menu. At the restaurant it is usually served for two, but it can be easily expanded to serve four, as in this recipe. If you happen to have a platter from one of the area's famous potteries, such as Rowntrees or Rackliffe, by all means use it to serve up this medley of Down East treats.

6 to 8 large lettuce leaves
⅛ pound smoked Maine shrimp, preferably from Ducktrap
⅛ pound smoked Maine mussels, preferably from Ducktrap
⅛ pound presliced Kendall Brook smoked Atlantic Salmon, from Ducktrap
⅛ pound smoked bluefish fillet (we like Horton's from Waterboro)
4 to 5 slices grilled or toasted French bread brushed with olive oil
1 tin (3¾ ounces) Port Clyde Brand Sardines packed in olive oil or spring water
4 ounces Capriano goat cheese from York Hill Farm, thinly shaved with a cheese slicer
½ pound smoked salami from Smith's Log Smokehouse, thinly sliced
¼ pound dilly beans (see page 147 or store-bought)
Lemon wedges and fresh parsley sprigs for garnish

1. Lay the lettuce leaves on a large platter to cover.

2. Decoratively arrange all the ingredients on the platter. The sardines should be placed on top of the grilled or toasted French bread.

3. Garnish the platter with lemon wedges and parsley.

Makes 4 ample first-course servings

Warm Salad with Smoked Mussels and Chèvre

This salad is frequently on the menu at Jonathan's Restaurant. I find it magical in its balanced flavor combination of mellow sherry, smoky mussels, creamy goat cheese, and crunchy pine nuts. Both texture and temperature conspire to add excitement to this superb appetizer or luncheon salad.

Dressing:
1 cup olive oil
1/2 cup red wine vinegar
1/4 cup dry sherry
1 large clove garlic, minced
1 shallot, minced
1/4 teaspoon dried thyme
1/2 pound smoked mussels, preferably from Ducktrap

Salad:
1/2 pound fresh, assorted seasonal greens, such as variety lettuces, spinach, arugula, chard, mustard greens, or young beet greens
1/4 cup toasted pine nuts
2 to 3 tablespoons olive oil
1/2 pound fresh chèvre, preferably from York Hill Farm or Seal Cove Farm
Assorted sprouts for garnish
Freshly ground black pepper, to taste

1. Preheat the oven to 350°F.

2. To make the dressing, in a nonreactive saucepan combine the olive oil, vinegar, sherry, garlic, shallot, and thyme. Over medium heat, bring the mixture to a boil. Reduce the heat to low and add the mussels. Simmer for at least 5 minutes so the mussels can impart their smoky flavor to the dressing.

3. Meanwhile assemble the salads. Divide the greens evenly among 6 plates. Cut the chèvre into 6 equal pieces and place on an oiled baking sheet. Drizzle any remaining oil over the top of the chèvre. Sprinkle the pine nuts over the greens.

4. Just before serving time and when the dressing is still hot, place the chèvre in the oven and bake it until just warm and beginning to melt, 1 to 2 minutes. Remove the chèvre from the oven and place one piece in the middle of each bed of greens.

5. With a slotted spoon, remove the mussels from the dressing and divide them equally among the 6 plates.

6. Whisk the dressing and distribute it evenly over the salads so its heat just begins to wilt the greens.

7. Top each salad with sprouts and freshly cracked pepper, to taste. Serve at once.

Makes 6 servings

Seared Atlantic Salmon Fillets with Smoked Maine Shrimp

The symphony of pink colors in this dish recalls shades of spectacular sunsets over the Camden Hills.

Salmon:

3 tablespoons unsalted butter, melted
4 center-cut salmon fillets, 6 to 8 ounces each
1/4 cup off-dry white wine (Chenin blanc, Riesling, or Bartlett Coastal White work nicely)

Sauce:

2 tablespoons unsalted butter
1 medium shallot, minced
1/2 teaspoon saffron threads
1 cup Jonathan's Quick Fish Stock (see page 000)
1/2 pound smoked Maine shrimp, preferably from Ducktrap
2 fresh plum tomatoes, seeded and diced
1/4 cup heavy cream
1 teaspoon finely chopped fresh parsley

1. Turn oven broiler to high. Brush half of the melted butter on a baking sheet. Arrange the salmon on the baking sheet so the fillets are not touching. Brush the tops of the fillets with the remaining butter. Sprinkle the wine over the tops of the fillets.

2. Place the salmon on the rack very close to the heat source and broil until the top of the fish begins to brown, about 5 minutes. Move the broiling rack down one notch and continue to cook until done, about 3 to 4 minutes. Salmon fillets will just begin to break when the sides are gently squeezed with your fingertips.

3. Meanwhile, make the sauce. Melt the butter in a medium-size skillet and sauté the minced shallot and saffron for 1 minute over medium heat. Add the fish stock and turn heat to high. Bring liquid to a boil and reduce heat to medium. Add smoked shrimp and tomatoes and simmer 1 to 2 minutes. Add cream, bring to a boil, and reduce for 1 more minute. Add chopped parsley.

4. Place salmon fillets on individual plates and spoon sauce over fish. Serve at once.

Makes 4 servings

Twice-Baked Potatoes with Smith's Log Smokehouse Hard Salami and York Hill Farm's Capriano

York Hill Farm in New Sharon, Maine, produces the pungent Cheddar-like goat cheese named Capriano that gives these luscious, twice-baked potatoes their addictive flavor. Speckling the filling with hard salami from Smith's Log Smokehouse makes this recipe a true celebration of Maine foods.

6 large Maine baking potatoes, scrubbed and patted dry
2 tablespoons unsalted butter at room temperature
3 tablespoons sour cream
1/2 cup milk or half-and-half
2 ounces Smith's hard salami, shredded on the side of a hand grater or with the shredding blade of a food processor
1/4 pound York Hill Capriano, grated
Freshly ground black pepper, to taste

1. Preheat oven to 425°F. Bake the potatoes until soft, 45 to 50 minutes.

2. When the potatoes are done, immediately slice the top quarter off lengthwise and set aside for nibbling or discard. Scoop the hot pulp from all the potatoes into a mixing bowl, taking care not to rip the skins. With an electric mixer, beat the butter, sour cream, and milk into the potatoes until light and fluffy. Fold in the salami and cheese; season the mixture to taste with pepper.

3. Reduce oven temperature to 400°F. Spoon the potato mixture back into the shells. Place on a baking tray and return to oven to cook until the tops of the potatoes are golden brown, 8 to 10 minutes. Serve at once.

Makes 6 servings

Blackstrap Ham Baked with Cider and Mustard

Jonathan and I both agree: this ham is one of which life-time memories are made. Smith's Log Smokehouse begins by curing boneless, skinless ham like prosciutto and then soaks it in blackstrap molasses before finishing with a smoke of hickory and maple wood.

1 blackstrap ham from Smith's (6½ to 7 pounds)
2 cups sweet apple cider
1½ tablespoons coarse or stone-ground mustard
18 to 24 whole cloves
1¼ cups coarse bread crumbs
1¼ cups light brown sugar

1. Score the ham in a crisscross diamond pattern with ¼-inch-deep slits 1 inch apart. Insert a clove in each diamond. Place the ham in a 9 × 13-inch non-reactive baking pan. Pour 1 cup of cider over the ham and let it sit to come to room temperature. Let the ham sit for at least 1 hour.

2. Preheat the oven to 300°F. Mix the remaining cider with the mustard. Spoon one-third of the mixture over the ham. Bake the ham for 30 minutes and then spoon another third of the cider mixture over it. Bake for another 30 minutes.

3. In a small bowl, thoroughly mix the bread crumbs and the brown sugar. Pat the mixture over the ham in an even layer. Reduce the heat to 275° and bake for 1 more hour.

4. To serve, transfer the ham to a cutting board. Pour the remaining third of the cider-mustard mixture into the baking pan and mix thoroughly with the drippings and accumulated cooking liquids, scraping up any brown bits clinging to the bottom of the pan. Transfer the sauce to a serving platter. Slice the ham thinly on an angle. Place the slices on the serving platter on top of the sauce. Serve at once.

Serves 12 to 15

Spider Johnnycake

We sweeten our old-fashioned johnnycake with a touch of molasses to complement the blackstrap molasses cure on Smith's Log Smokehouse's fabulous ham. When not served with ham, this johnnycake makes a traditional Maine accompaniment to a thick and hefty bowl of pea soup.

2 tablespoons unsalted butter
1 cup cornmeal
1 cup unbleached all-purpose flour
½ teaspoon salt
2 teaspoons baking soda
1 teaspoon cream of tartar
2 eggs
1 cup buttermilk
2 tablespoons molasses
1 cup whole milk

1. Preheat the oven to 400°F. Melt the butter over medium heat in a 9-inch black spider, or cast-iron skillet. Set aside.

2. Sift together cornmeal, flour, salt, baking soda, and cream of tartar. Mound into a mixing bowl. Make a well in the center and add the eggs, buttermilk, and molasses. Pour in 1 tablespoon of the melted butter from the spider, leaving the remaining tablespoon to coat the spider. Quickly mix the dry and liquid ingredients just until well combined. Do not overmix.

3. Spread the johnnycake evenly in the buttered spider. Gently pour the cup of whole milk over the top of the johnnycake; do not stir. Bake the johnny-cake until set and golden, 20 to 25 minutes. Serve, cut into wedges, warm or at room temperature. Some may wish butter to spread on top.

Serves 8

Smokehouse Split Pea Soup

Fogs as thick as pea soup and thick pea soup itself are both features of the Maine coast. This version replaces the customary ham in the soup with the delicious and chewy beef jerky from Smith's Log Smokehouse. For extra crunch and savor the vegetables and jerky are added to the pot after the split peas have cooked.

1 pound split green peas
1 medium onion, minced
2 cloves garlic, minced
2 stalks celery, minced
2 carrots, peeled and minced
2 cups canned or fresh tomatoes, seeded and diced
3 packages (1.6 ounces each) Smith's Log Smokehouse beef jerky, cut into ¼-inch dice
1 teaspoon dried thyme
Salt and freshly ground pepper, to taste

1. The night before you plan to make the soup, sort through the peas, discarding any foreign objects, and then place in a bowl and cover with cold tap water. Let soak overnight.

2. Drain the peas the following day and place in a large soup pot. Cover with water to come 1 inch above the peas. Bring to a boil, skimming off any surface foam that rises to the top. Simmer the peas until tender, 45 minutes to 1 hour. Purée the peas and liquid in batches in a food processor or blender and then return the purée to the pot.

3. Stir the onion, garlic, celery, carrots, tomatoes, and beef jerky into the purée. Season with the thyme, salt, and pepper. Bring the soup to a simmer over medium heat and continue to cook until the vegetables are fairly tender but not mushy, 30 to 40 minutes. If the soup seems to be getting too thick at any point, thin with water to desired consistency. Serve the soup hot, ladled into big bowls, and accompanied in true Maine fashion with Spider Johnnycake (see page 60).

Makes 6 to 8 hearty servings

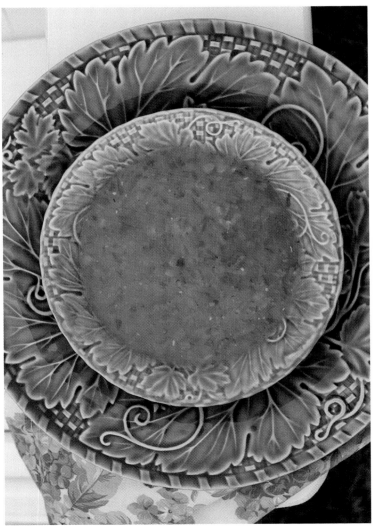

A rib-sticking bowl of Smokehouse Split Pea Soup.

Every Grange possesses an individual and unique poetic aura.

Chapter Six

Grange Suppers

IF we are correct in our observation that it is Maine's isolation which has helped to preserve it as a bastion of old-fashioned Yankee attitudes and practices, then it should come as no surprise that community and public suppers still reign as a strong tradition throughout the state. While rural Church Suppers are most likely to spring to mind as nostalgically embodying the faded memories of community potluck gatherings, we have decided to focus in this chapter on those public suppers sponsored by an equally popular state force and organization — the local Granges that make up the Maine State Grange Association.

Although the Grange is a national organization dating back more than 120 years, we are happy to report that it maintains particularly strong and visible roots in Maine. The National Grange was founded at the close of the Civil War as America's first farm organization in order to alleviate the desperate conditions of farmers south of the Mason-Dixon line. Subordinate Granges soon sprang up in states both North and South, with the first Maine Grange being the Eastern Star Grange founded in Hampden in October 1873. By 1900, there grew to be as many as 266 Subordinate Granges across the nation.

In its earliest days the Grange served a clear and effective purpose of representing the voice and needs of American farmers with a unified front. The Grange also sponsored cooperatives and stores to provide group purchasing power to members and an outlet for the sale and trading of members' agricultural goods. The largest Grange store business in

Maine was located in Houlton, and it contained a smithy, a flour mill, and a potato starch factory, which combined to ring up sales as high as $3,000 per day. Blue Hill writer Esther E. Wood included a fond and vivid description of Grange store trading during her father's day in her nostalgic *Country Fare:*

In my early-twentieth-century childhood, Father continued his forebears' practice of exchanging our butter, eggs, and vegetables for groceries and grain. It was my privilege to be his companion when he went to the Grange Store once a week to "do the trading." In Father's pocket was a list of our needs thriftily made out by my mother, who watched us drive the buggy out of the yard and called in farewell, "Now be sure to buy only what you need."

The Grange Store carried many items. For instance, on January 5th, 1905, my father bought: onions, 25 cents; lamp globe, 10 cents; pants, $3; nutmeg, 5 cents; cocoa, 25 cents. The pages of the old storebook show that Mr. Long also sold lace, cloth, envelopes, soap, butter, cheese, rope, wicks, paint, turpentine, underwear, hose, shoes, blankets, and patent medicine.

We brought our own containers for certain purchases: jugs for molasses and vinegar which were drawn from great hogsheads in the back room; wooden firkins for sugar; two-quart jars for the pickles. We had a market basket — one with a handle — into which we put tins of coffee and tea, bags of raisins and crackers, and wrapped chunks of cheese and salt pork.

Most of Mr. Long's goods were unpackaged. Crackers were sold scooped from big boxes or barrels; raisins and soap were boxed. Pickles were sold from brine-filled casks, always tempting a customer to help himself. Open cracker containers were also a constant invitation to a free snack.

Today, sadly, there are no longer any Grange stores, the last Maine stronghold having closed in North Jay in 1974.

Agricultural origins of the Grange aside, nowadays a curious back-roads traveler is most likely to glean a first impression of the Grange through stumbling upon a building or hall where local meetings are held. These structures are unassuming and quite often a bit dilapidated, yet they somehow humbly manage to offer an irresistible charm to those with keen photographer's or painter's eyes and sensibilities. Granges may plainly bear the name of the township where they are situated, but for us it is the Granges with poetic names that are the true finds. Some of our favorite Grange names include Halcyon, Tranquillity, Harvest Home, and Ocean View. While researching this book, photographer Cary Hazlegrove and I often became so excited in our quest to capture the individual personalities of these quirky country edifices that we contemplated making a bumper sticker for our car saying — "We brake for Granges!"

To non-Grange members such as ourselves, the appeal can be only a superficial one of cherishing an architectural detail or salivating over potluck possibilities, but to a Grange member both the building and the organization mean much more. The *Maine State Grange Handbook* clearly instructs that the goal of membership in every Grange "should be to improve the quality of life in Rural America." An agricultural committee carries on the original heritage of the group by giving yearly recognition awards to farm families that still earn at least 75 percent of their income directly from the farm, but much of the Grange activity in recent years has been redirected toward community service. The *Handbook* states that "each Grange is encouraged to assume a productive leadership role in community improvement, community service, and community development, thereby contributing much to a stronger and better way for all." The Grange is also known for placing strong emphasis on education and youth activities. Throughout the year, the Grange sponsors numerous youth contests in fields such as cooking,

woodworking, poster making, vegetable growing, and leadership. Women make up a strong faction of Grange membership, and there are other contests in needleworking, quilting, tatting, and cooking.

A typical Grange cooking contest is likely to consist of four different divisions — women's, men's, junior Grange girls, and junior Grange boys — with all contestants being required to prepare the very same printed recipes. The recipes are generally tried-and-true old-fashioned ones, such as hermits, blueberry cake, or cranberry bars, which are judged on appearance (30 percent), flavor (35 percent), and texture (35 percent).

Grange potluck suppers are held throughout the year to raise money for the maintenance of the individual Grange, and they are not nearly as regimented as the state-run recipe contests. This is not to say, however, that the food at every Grange Supper is always terrific. Jonathan had serious doubts about including this chapter at all after attending one of the popular Grange autumn Harvest Suppers a year or so ago. I, fortunately, have fared better in my Grange grazing.

My first Grange Supper was at the Dirigo Grange in Freedom. The word *dirigo*, by the way, is Latin for "I lead" and appears as part of the Maine State motto on flags and legal seals. The Dirigo Grange Hall has neither heat nor running water, so members had been anxiously awaiting the arrival of warmer spring weather to hold their first supper and meeting of the year. This particular Supper was not a public one to raise funds but was an occasion for the members to get together to discuss programs and agenda for the coming year. Our friend Phyllis Schartner from neighboring Thorndike had invited me along as her guest after a fiddleheading expedition earlier in the day. Phyllis was especially looking forward to the event, since the new Maine State Agricultural Queen was rumored to be making an appearance. Most of the women members brought either savory casseroles or sweet pies to the Grange, and there was no charge this opening night for the Supper. Phyllis baked one of her famous fruit pies, but unfortunately her dog ate it at home as she was about to leave for the Grange. There were still pies aplenty, however, I soon discovered as we arrived at the Grange Hall close to 5:30 P.M.

Laura Stevens of the Dirigo Grange takes on the happy task of guarding the evening's pies.

The door to the Dirigo Grange in Freedom is open for the first supper of the season.

and set out on a table covered with a cheerful plastic tablecloth. The casseroles were not fancy, but good and substantial offerings centered around macaroni (not pasta), ground meats, chicken, and tuna, with vegetables such as peas, onions, and seasonal fiddleheads serving as embellishments. There were, of course, baked beans and bowls of crisp coleslaw. Laura Stevens had made the baked beans for that evening according to her favorite recipe using Jacob's Cattle beans mixed with brown sugar, mustard, and salt pork, but no onion. The beans had been slow-cooked for at least ten hours, she proudly disclosed.

Some community and Grange Suppers are centered entirely around baked beans. Most others have at least a token pot or two of beans on premise. Every Mainer seems to have a slightly different

At that moment, most of the activity was centered in the spacious but ill-equipped kitchen. All sorts of portable casseroles, wrapped snugly in thicknesses of newspaper to retain warmth, were grouped on the chipped Formica countertops. Women were busily slicing pies of old-fashioned flavors such as custard, butterscotch, chocolate cream, and lemon meringue. The ample slices were put on paper plates, which were then arranged in assorted flavors on trays for passing to each long table after the buffet supper. Many of the women were outfitted in their best dress-up clothes and had belonged to Dirigo or another neighboring Grange for most of their lives. They were an amiable and chatty lot who enjoyed talking recipes and reminiscing with me.

At six o'clock all the casseroles were unwrapped

theory as to what makes the best baked beans, with most of the debates centering on whether to sweeten with brown sugar, molasses, or maple syrup, and whether or not to include onion, chopped or whole, in the pot. There is, however, general consensus on the best type of bean for baking. By my unofficial estimate, Jacob's Cattle are the baking bean of Down East choice, though both Yellow-Eyes and Soldiers run a respectable second. Smaller and wimpier navy and pea beans are most definitely for Bostonians. The tending of the bean pot borders on an art form with most Mainers, as they claim that the water must be added to the beans ever so prudently and gently during the long cooking period to ensure that the bean skins remain unsplit and intact. Kenneth Roberts wrote one of the all-time great odes to baked beans in his book, *Trending into Maine*, praising his grandmother's beans thus: "Her Yellow-Eye beans, watered while baking as sedulously as an orchid-lover would tend his rarest bloom, defied description."

Laura Stevens's beans at the Dirigo Grange did not disappoint, nor did any of the accompanying homey casseroles. After I had eaten more than my fill and was struggling to finish my piece of rich and sweet butterscotch pie, an elderly male member approached me voicing concern as to whether I had gotten enough to eat. As I assured him I had and thanked him for the generous hospitality of the Grange, he replied, "If you didn't get enough, then it's your own fault!"

I have also attended bean and casserole suppers close to my parents' South Blue Hill home at Central Hall, a handsome, faded yellow, square and shingled building dating from 1901. The structure had from time to time served as a Grange Hall, but the building is currently maintained by the volunteer labor of the Ladies Public Improvement Society, headed by our local postmistress, Dolly. Just this past May, I walked up our long driveway to attend a Supper down the road slated to begin at 5 P.M. I arrived tardily a few minutes after 5 to find the Hall filled to capacity and to be told by the ticket seller to wait for the second seating! For a brief moment, I felt the pang of being denied a choice reservation at a slick city restaurant. As I dawdled outside the entry, a whole new crowd gathered to wait the thirty minutes along with me for this second seating. Our appetites were soon encouraged further by the first seating's sighs of contentment and groans of "I ate too much" as they spilled back out into the bright daylight of an early May evening.

Once seated, I found that this Supper offered much the same style of casserole fare as the Dirigo Grange, only all the food was passed in its dishes family-style from table to table. At the end, pies were served in true Grange fashion — assorted flavors sliced and arranged on paper plates set on trays and distributed by women volunteers. This not being a supper preceding a Grange meeting, the attending crowd was more varied — a blend of locals, families with young children, and retired summer people. Much of the discussion at my table of a dozen or more people centered on other community suppers in the area, recollections from the previous Saturday Supper, and tips on the best upcoming events. Luck had it that Central Hall had a few more suppers scheduled throughout the summer, plus some rummage and food sales to raise some badly needed extra money for major repairs to the building.

A few months after this May Supper, I was overjoyed to see the apparent success of the Ladies Public Improvement Society as I witnessed Central Hall being raised up to receive a new foundation. The *Ellsworth American*'s honorable newspaper editor and poet James Russell Wiggins was also struck by the sight as he published this, his weekly poem, next to a preimprovement photograph of the old Central Hall:

One by one, the Grange halls go
The way of early autumn snow;
Each was a force once widely felt
But modern times have made it melt.

It filled one generation's need,
And shaped young lives by word and deed.
The Grange survives, its old age showing
And how we wish it still was growing.

A lot of folks who still stand tall
Got a running start in an old Grange hall
Some monuments of rural life
Are victims of our urban strife.

The recipes that follow bring the best tastes from our Grange experiences home.

Rhoda Smith's Raw Cucumber Relish

Rhoda Smith makes this unusual cucumber relish to accompany baked beans served for suppers at the Grange in Brooks. She says that overripe cucumbers yield the best-tasting relish — a boon to gardeners with cucumbers growing out of their ears!

24 overripe cucumbers, peeled
6 medium onions, peeled
Salt for sprinkling the cucumbers
1 quart, "more or less," apple cider vinegar
2 cups yellow mustard seeds
½ cup whole black peppercorns
3 cups granulated sugar

1. Using the large-holed side of a hand grater, grate the cucumbers and onions into a large bowl. Sprinkle with the salt and let stand 2 to 3 hours.

2. Drain off and reserve all the resulting juices from the cucumbers. Measure the liquid and then discard. Replace with exactly the same amount of cider vinegar, stirring to combine with the cucumbers. Mix in the mustard seeds, peppercorns, and sugar. The relish is ready to serve immediately, or it may be put up in glass containers and stored in a cool place.

Makes about 3 quarts

Dirigo Grange Onion Casserole

Cary Hazlegrove and I attended our first potluck Grange Supper together at Dirigo Grange in Freedom. After sampling our fair share of every single casserole on the ample buffet table, we both agreed that our hands-down favorite was this creamy white onion casserole. When we inquired among fellow diners about the person responsible, we were promptly told that Lona Ingraham always brings the onion casseroles to Grange Suppers. When we approached the sweet and modest Mrs. Ingraham, she seemed embarrassed by our accolades. But as the supper was winding down, Lona came to my note-taking corner and shyly confided her popular side-dish recipe to me. It makes a great accompaniment to a pot of baked beans or a hearty roast.

4 large yellow onions (about 2 pounds), peeled and thinly sliced
2 tablespoons butter
2 tablespoons unbleached all-purpose flour
¾ cup milk
Salt and freshly ground pepper, to taste
2 ounces sharp Cheddar cheese, shredded

1. Bring a large pot of water to a boil. Add the onions and boil until quite tender, about 15 minutes. Drain well.

2. Meanwhile, melt the butter in a heavy saucepan over medium heat. Stir in the flour to make a smooth paste and cook, stirring constantly, for 2 minutes. Gradually whisk in the milk to make a thick white sauce. Season to taste with salt and pepper.

3. Add the onions to the sauce, stirring to coat them thoroughly with sauce. Add the cheese and cook until melted. The onions may be served at once from the pot or transferred to a 1½-quart casserole and baked in a 325°F oven for 30 minutes. (We prefer to bake the casserole, as we think it concentrates the rich flavor of the onions all the more sweetly.) Serve hot.

Makes 10 to 12 servings

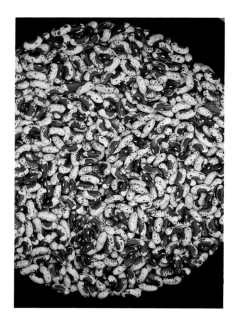

Maine Baked Beans

A state that hosts numerous Public Suppers centered solely on baked beans takes its beans seriously. We solicited the opinions of many different bean bakers to come up with the following recipe, which features Mainers' favorite bean — Jacob's Cattle. We also follow the advice of writer Kenneth Roberts of "judiciously adding a trickle of boiling water" at intervals during the long and slow baking period to keep the bean skins from splitting open.

2 pounds Jacob's Cattle beans
1 medium onion, coarsely chopped
⅓ cup molasses
⅓ cup brown sugar
1½ teaspoons ground ginger
2 teaspoons dry mustard
1½ teaspoons salt
¾-pound piece of salt pork, scored
5 to 6 cups boiling water

Baked beans in three stages: (1) Jacob's Cattle beans are soaked in water overnight; (2) the next day the beans are combined with onions, molasses, salt pork, and seasonings; (3) the finished pot of beans emerges with an enticing top crust from being uncovered during the final hour of slow cooking.

1. On the day before you plan to bake the beans, place them in a large bowl and cover amply with cold water. Let soak overnight. The following morning, drain the beans, place in a pot, and cover with fresh water. Bring the beans just to a boil and parboil until the scum rises to the surface. Skim off the scum and drain the beans once again.

2. Preheat the oven to 250°F.

3. In a bean pot or large ovenproof casserole, combine the drained beans, onion, molasses, brown sugar, ginger, mustard, and salt. Embed the scored piece of salt pork on top of the beans in the center of the casserole. Pour in enough boiling water just to cover the beans.

4. Cover the beans and bake for 5 hours. Uncover the beans every hour or so and add enough boiling water to replace that which has boiled away. Take care not to overwater the beans. After 5 hours, uncover the beans and bake for another hour uncovered in order to crisp the salt pork and form a top crust on the beans. Serve the beans hot with coleslaw and assorted pickles and relishes.

Makes 8 to 10 servings

Crisp Coleslaw with Boiled Dressing

Coleslaw is a common accompaniment to both baked bean suppers and lobster bakes. There is nothing complicated about Maine coleslaw, though people are quite particular about how it is made. In a famous essay, "The Perfect Church Supper," C. M. Webster described the importance of coleslaw thus: "Then [Father] asked for the cole slaw. A minor crisis was at hand. Had mayonnaise been used? No, only vinegar, cream (not milk), and sugar, and not too much vinegar. The critic ate a little of it; took another helping of yellow-eyes, and began to relax."

Our version uses the old-fashioned required boiled dressing, though we do cheat a bit with a small addition of commercial mayonnaise because we believe it adds to the final binding and creaminess of the coleslaw. If you take the time to soak the shredded cabbage and carrots in ice water for half an hour before assembling the salad, the coleslaw will be extra crisp.

Boiled Dressing:
¼ cup cider vinegar
¼ cup granulated sugar
1 tablespoon dry mustard
1 teaspoon celery seeds
½ teaspoon freshly ground black pepper
2 large eggs
½ cup light cream
½ teaspoon paprika
Salt, to taste

Salad:
1 medium to large head green cabbage, cored and finely shredded
2 large carrots, peeled and shredded
1 small onion, finely minced
3 to 4 tablespoons mayonnaise, preferably Hellmann's

1. To make the boiled dressing, combine the vinegar, sugar, mustard, celery seeds, pepper, and eggs in the top half of a double boiler. Whisk until smooth. Whisk in the cream and cook over simmering water, stirring constantly until thickened, 7 to 8 minutes. Remove from heat and season with the paprika and salt. Let cool to room temperature. (Note: The dressing may also be made ahead and stored in the refrigerator for up to a week.)

2. For the coleslaw, place cabbage and carrots together in a large bowl. Cover with cold water and top with several ice cubes. Let sit for ½ hour. Drain thoroughly.

3. Mix together cabbage, carrots, and onions in a large bowl. Add all the boiled dressing, stirring to coat the vegetables thoroughly. Blend in a few tablespoons of mayonnaise to complete the binding. Taste slaw for seasoning. Chill for a couple of hours in the refrigerator to blend the flavors. Serve cold.

Makes 12 to 15 servings

New England Boiled Dinner

The boiled dinner remains big in Maine. With the first sign of crimson color infringing on the blueberry barrens, Granges across Maine begin holding Harvest Suppers that more or less take the form of old-fashioned boiled dinners. Because Grange Supper chefs must feed vast numbers of people quite economically, they often employ canned commercial shortcuts that we personally find a little insulting to the roots of this great New England tradition. Jonathan and I have tapped into the wonderful rural spirit of Grange Harvest Suppers but devised a scaled-down family-style boiled dinner that we find more satisfying.

While corned brisket of beef takes center stage at most boiled dinners, Mainers are uniquely fond of doing similar dinners using dried salted codfish topped with crispy salt pork bits as a fish focal point. Jonathan and I like the idea of a merger, and on our platter we offer both meat and fish surrounded by the usual cabbage wedges, potatoes, rutabaga, carrots, and bright earthy beets.

Many New Englanders prefer cooking a brisket that is gray cured without the chemical preservatives of a red corned beef. You may use either type in our recipe, which, incidentally, is planned to supply plenty of leftovers for concocting a breakfast batch of Yankee red flannel hash.

69

Grange Suppers

Our version of a New England Boiled Dinner or Harvest Supper features both beef brisket and salt cod along with the usual array of earthy and colorful vegetables.

2 pounds dried salt cod
1 corned beef brisket, 4 to 5 pounds
1 rutabaga (2 pounds), peeled and cut into ³/4-inch chunks
2 to 3 pounds carrots, washed and cut into 2-inch diagonal chunks
2 pounds small red-skinned potatoes, scrubbed
1 medium head (about 2 pounds) green cabbage, cored and cut into 6 wedges
2 bunches medium-size beets, tops trimmed to ¹/2-inch stems and bottom roots left intact to prevent bleeding
¹/4 pound salt pork, blanched for 5 minutes in boiling water and then cut into a ¹/4-inch dice
2 tablespoons chopped fresh parsley
Assorted mustards, horseradish, and/or pickles to garnish

1. One day before cooking, place the cod in a large bowl and cover with cold water. Soak the cod in the refrigerator overnight, changing the water at least three times.

2. The following day, place the brisket in a large stockpot and cover with 24 cups of cold water. Bring to a boil, reduce heat, and simmer the brisket until almost tender, 2¹/2 hours.

3. Add the rutabaga and carrots to the pot and continue to simmer for 30 minutes. At the same time, place the beets in a separate pot, cover with water, and simmer until tender, usually about 45 minutes. After 30 minutes, add the cabbage wedges and potatoes to the brisket pot and continue simmering until all the vegetables are tender but not mushy, 20 to 25 minutes longer.

4. While all the vegetables are cooking, prepare the salt cod. Drain from the soaking liquid and rinse again. Place cod in a single layer in a large skillet. Ladle some stock from the brisket pot over the cod to cover. Cover the skillet and bring to a boil over medium-high heat. Let simmer 2 to 3 minutes, shut off heat, and keep covered until ready to serve.

5. Finally, brown the salt pork pieces in a small skillet over medium heat, watching carefully to prevent burning. When pieces are crisp, usually within 6 to 8 minutes, drain the pieces on paper towels and discard the fat in the skillet.

6. To serve the boiled dinner, drain the beets and slip off the skins and roots. Slice and arrange in a section of a large platter. Remove the other vegetables from the brisket pot with a slotted spoon and arrange around the platter. Remove the brisket from the pot, carve into thin slices across the grain, and place slices in the center of the platter, leaving some room for the salted fish. With a slotted spatula, carefully remove the fish from the liquid and place on the platter. (You can return the cooking liquid for the fish back to the brisket pot.) Ladle 1 to 2 cups of broth over the entire platter. Sprinkle the salt pork bits over the fish and the chopped parsley over the potatoes. Serve family-style accompanied by favorite condiments.

Makes 8 to 10 servings with leftovers

Deer Isle Gingerbread

Gingerbread has been a popular New England dessert since Colonial times, and Maine cookbooks today still contain numerous regional and family heritage gingerbread variations. We like the delicateness of this Deer Isle version, which retains an authentic old-fashioned flavor from using lard as the shortening in the recipe. You may substitute margarine if you are cholesterol conscious. The easy portability of gingerbread makes it a popular dessert choice for bringing to community suppers.

1 cup dark molasses

½ cup light brown sugar, packed

½ teaspoon ground cloves

2 teaspoons ground ginger

1 tablespoon ground cinnamon

1 cup boiling water

2 teaspoons baking soda

1 cup lard, melted

1½ cups unbleached all-purpose flour

½ teaspoon salt

2 eggs, beaten

1. Preheat oven to 325°F. Grease a 9 × 13-inch baking pan and set aside.

2. Stir molasses and brown sugar together in a large mixing bowl until smooth. Blend in the cloves, ginger, and cinnamon.

3. Combine the boiling water and baking soda, stirring to dissolve. Add this to the molasses mixture. Stir in the melted lard. Combine flour and salt and add to the batter, stirring until smooth. Blend in the eggs.

4. Spread the batter evenly in the prepared pan. Bake until the gingerbread springs back when lightly touched in the center, 30 to 35 minutes. Cool and cut into squares. The top of the gingerbread may be dusted lightly with sifted confectioners' sugar if desired.

Makes 12 to 15 servings

Community Supper Blueberry Cake

This recipe crops up under one title or another in almost every Maine cookbook. Marjorie Standish, onetime food columnist for the *Maine Sunday Telegram* and author of the well-liked *Cooking Down East* cookbooks, wrote that it was the most popular recipe ever printed in her newspaper column. Mainers say that the simple yellow cake melts in your mouth, and it is the first choice to cap festivities at many a summer community supper.

½ cup unsalted butter or margarine, softened

1 cup plus 2 tablespoons granulated sugar

¼ teaspoon salt

1 teaspoon vanilla extract

2 large eggs, separated

1½ cups unbleached all-purpose flour

1 teaspoon baking powder

⅓ cup milk

1½ cups fresh wild blueberries, tossed with 1 tablespoon flour

1. Preheat oven to 350°F. Butter an 8 × 8-inch cake pan.

2. In a mixing bowl, cream the butter and ¾ cup of the sugar together with an electric mixer until light and fluffy. Beat in the salt and vanilla. Add the egg yolks and beat until smooth.

3. Sift the flour and baking powder together and add to the creamed mixture alternately with the milk. In a small separate bowl, beat the egg whites with ¼ cup sugar until stiff but not dry. Gently but thoroughly fold into the cake batter. Fold in the blueberries.

4. Spread the cake evenly in the prepared pan. Sprinkle the remaining 2 tablespoons of sugar evenly over the top of the cake. Bake until the cake springs back when lightly touched in the center, 50 to 60 minutes. Serve warm or at room temperature cut into 8 squares.

Makes 8 servings

Dot's Chocolate Bars

Dot's Bars are a rich cross between chocolate pudding and brownies and a favorite dessert at Grange Suppers across the state. The inventor, Dorothy Shores, works at the State Grange Office in Augusta, and her recipe has appeared in both the *Maine State Grange Cookbook* and the *Best of Maine Church Suppers Cookbook*. I met Dorothy at the Dirigo Grange in Freedom, where she was delighted to be asked to share her recipe in yet another cookbook.

The recipe has a folkloric community-cookbook quality to it with its instructions to mix all ingredients in the order given. While there is no culinary reason why all the oil and the cocoa in the recipe couldn't be mixed at once, it is more fun to join in the spirit of the recipe and follow the quirky directions. We like the bars best when refrigerated before cutting.

⅔ cup vegetable oil
¾ cup cocoa powder, sifted if lumpy
¼ cup vegetable oil (yes, this is correct)
2 eggs

2 cups sugar
2½ cups unbleached all-purpose flour
1 teaspoon baking powder
1½ cups cold water
1 teaspoon vanilla

Topping:
1 cup semisweet chocolate bits
1 cup coarsely chopped walnuts

1. Preheat oven to 350°F. Lightly butter a 10 × 15-inch baking pan.

2. In a large mixing bowl, mix together all the bar ingredients in the order they are given, stirring well after each addition. Spread the batter evenly in the prepared pan. Sprinkle the chocolate bits and walnuts evenly over the top.

3. Bake the bars until just barely set, 20 to 25 minutes. Cool and then refrigerate until cold. Cut into squares and serve.

Makes 24 bars

Chapter Seven

Wild Things from Field and Forest

FOR many a Yankee the first sign of spring comes in the form of a color — a greening patch of lawn emerging from its icy brumal cover or the surprise discovery of a bold cluster of deep purple crocuses. For others it is a scent — an encompassing whiff of a sweet, sweet hyacinth or the subtler fragrance of a sun-nurtured hardy daffodil bobbing in an April breeze. In Maine, however, spring is more than anything else a sound — the ongoing symphonic gurgle of unfathomable inches of snow melting.

Rejoicing in spring as a sound does not also automatically mean that it is a real season. Most of the time, with the notable exception of 1991, we side with the writer Caskie Stinnett, who has too often "been bewitched by the promise of spring in Maine" only to be betrayed in the end, "just as a lover is betrayed by a fickle mistress."

Astonishingly enough, it is out of this concerto of running water, mud, increased sunshine, and hope that come two of Maine's most delicious and justly famed wild foods. First to arrive are fields of dandelion greens, stretching as far as the eye can see and reminding all residents that there is a shade of green to the state other than evergreen. In fact, the curmudgeonly, passionate Down East food fiend Robert P. Tristram Coffin wrote in *Mainstays of Maine* that it was dandelions that put the green back into man after a long, gray, barren winter. Coffin further believed that dandelion greens should never be eaten as a side dish or salad, but that the "small green pas-

ture octopuses" should be "sliced out of the earth, crowded into an ancient iron kettle with half a pound of salt pig," and then "boiled right up and down for three or four hours." Vitamins and dietitians should be damned, he said, as a good Maine man would want to eat five full plates of greens and still cry for more when effete nutrients boiled away with steam and allowed the greens to melt as tender as butter. Dandelion greens, concluded Coffin, along with alewives, smelts, and young clams, "make the Maine man over new each Spring."

Cookbook author Marjorie Standish also espoused long-cooked dandelion greens and wrote of generations of Maine families who enjoyed May dinner feasts of salt pork, potatoes, and dandelion greens cooked for a slow period of two and a half to three hours. The potatoes turned green from the dandelions, and all took on that favored Maine flavor of salt pork.

Heretics that we may seem to old-time Mainers, Jonathan and I confess that we prefer our dandelion greens with most of their vitamin A, iron, calcium, and potassium left intact — that is, tarnished by the cooking heat of no more than a warm and wilting splash of bacon dressing over the raw greens. Taking our lead from the French, who first named the plant *dent de lion*, or "tooth of the lion," we favor these wild leaves in a salad that is similar to French salads of bitter greens, crisp pork lardoons, and garlic croutons. In this country the Pennsylvania Dutch are known for a similar salad with the addition of a sweet counterpoint to the smokiness of the bacon and astringency of the vinegar. The secret to making a delicious wild-dandelion salad is to harvest the greens when they are young and tender, with no sign of a golden blossom. In other words, be ready to

Fields of brilliant yellow dandelions make the spring landscape sparkle after a long Maine winter. The tender and edible greens are best gathered before the fluffy golden flowers bloom.

forage through the fields shortly after the last lingering frosts of cruel April.

Once the prolific dandelion weeds begin to blossom and turn the landscape a happy shade of sunshine yellow, it is time to go into the woods in search of another delectable wild treat — fiddleheads. Mainers say that you can count on the edible fern fronds being ready for picking within a week, one way or the other, of Mother's Day. And then the season lasts only a scant two weeks. By definition, fiddleheads are greens that are the unfurled growth of a sprouting ostrich fern. The name comes from the poetic resemblance to the head of a fiddle. The ferns are found in abundance along many New England and Canadian rivers and streams and in moist woodlands.

I had been warned that fiddlehead foragers were a secretive lot when it came to sharing picking spots, but our indefatigable friend Phyllis Scharner, of Thorndike strawberry and orchard renown, enthusiastically offered to lead us on a fiddleheading expedition along streams in neighboring Albion. Despite years of cherishing the fleeting savor of fiddleheads purchased at semiexorbitant prices in fancy markets outside the state of Maine, nothing could have prepared me for the thrill of gathering my own fiddleheads for the first time. The day itself was one out of the tourist brochures. But it was the grace of each and every fiddlehead frond in infinite variations and stages of unfurling that overwhelmed me with an appreciation for the innate and glorious choreography of nature. Not wanting to disturb the delicate beauty of the dancing fiddleheads before me, I filled my brown paper bag only partially full with fiddleheads from peripheral places too shady or muddy for Cary, our photographer, to capture. Those fiddleheads that are ready to harvest have stems from two to five inches long and retain crosiers that are still rolled as tightly as a scroll. The verdant stalks are

snapped two inches or so below the curled fronds and then carted homeward with the great anticipation of soon cooking and eating the very essence of spring.

Because the picked stems of the fiddleheads naturally discolor brown with oxidation like a cut apple exposed to the air, the ends should be trimmed with a sharp knife in preparation for cooking. Fiddleheads are also flecked with a brown membrane similar to an onion's skin. This should be removed by rinsing and/or soaking the greens in several changes of cold water, depending on how stubborn or thick the brown skin is. Since this is the most arduous part of fiddlehead preparation, many makeshift roadside stands sprout like fiddleheads themselves during the month of May, selling cleaned greens. The most common way to enjoy fiddleheads is simply steamed

Fiddleheads unfurling dance along the banks of woodland streams and rivers each May.

Wild Things from Field and Forest

or boiled and then topped with melted butter and sometimes a spritz of lemon juice or vinegar. Our recipes reflect conversations with other fiddlehead aficionados, research in Maine cookbooks, and attendance at the Maine State Fiddlehead Festival sponsored annually by Unity College and the Maine Trappers Association. While culinary ingenuity and innovation know no bounds at this folksy spring festival, suffice it to say we tend to prefer our fiddleheads in savory dishes such as quiche to sweet concoctions such as cupcakes and cookies.

Before leaving the wilds of spring for those of summer, I must make mention of rhubarb. While rhubarb most certainly isn't of the same ilk as fiddleheads, it has been planted so long as a cultivated plant in Maine that it often appears to be wild. Indeed, many a rhubarb patch comes as a bonus with the deed to an old Maine house or saltwater farm. Even Robert P. Tristram Coffin admitted, in practically the same breath as his previously cited dande-

lion diatribe, that "rhubarb is a spring essential," and though a tame plant, "it tastes as wild as a woodchuck."

There are, naturally, many recipes for rhubarb pies in Maine cookbooks, but stewed sauces, jams, juices, tea breads, and fools also dot the pages of dessert collections. We think that one of the best and most satisfying uses for rhubarb is baked into a homey and old-fashioned New England crisp. One Maine cookbook I came across offered three similar crisp-style recipes under the names of Rhubarb Rumble, Rhubarb Crunch, and Rhubarb Pudding. We offer one straightforward crisp recipe that harbors all the warmth and comfort of a pie but is easier to make. Its preparation allows ample time to pursue the never-ending chores that tend to consume those Maine days falling between the last of the Nor'easters and the onset of June's vicious black-fly bane.

It is unfortunate that black flies and lady's slippers

The discovery of a pretty batch of pink lady's slippers often comes as an added bonus to the quest for wild things.

Chanterelle mushrooms, with their vibrant apricot hue and fanciful trumpet shape, appear to be surreal as they sprout under the filigree of thick summer forests.

are associated together in my mind. This is so because a neighbor of my parents was kind enough one June day to lead Cary and me into her woods to photograph her sensuous pink cache of lady's slippers in full bloom. We two shorts-clad women soon learned the hard way why our escort was protectively clothed from head to toe in fine netting that seemed to us more appropriate to a walk on the moon than a nature walk in the Maine woods. As fly bites turned to welts as red as a steamed lobster, Cary and I vowed to schedule no further interviews or photography sessions during the month of June in a vacationland turned hostile.

I relate this story because I have heard that morel mushrooms can be found growing wild in the Maine woods late in the spring. I cannot personally verify this because my fear of black flies temporarily suspends all mycological curiosity during prime morel-hunting season. Rather, I am content to wait for the nearly surreal chanterelle mushrooms that sprout in the fly-free woods of late July and August.

I remember first appreciating the trumpet-shaped and vibrantly apricot-hued chanterelle mushroom as a teenager in the birch woods of my grandfather's island in Blue Hill Bay. Last summer we were lucky enough to find some growing in the woods just across the street from my parents' South Blue Hill house. Usually, when it comes to summer in Maine, there isn't much that can lure me inland away from the mussel beds and clam flats of the coast, but stalking chanterelles ranks right up there with picking wild blueberries and raspberries on dry land.

The excitement of gathering such exquisite mushrooms calls for almost immediate enjoyment. Chanterelles definitely fall into the popular "less is more" philosophy of Maine cooking, and we like them quite simply sautéed in butter and then lavished over toast. We champion the sentiment expressed in the epilogue to British author Jane Grigson's book, *The Mushroom Feast*: "But when all's said and written, there is nothing better than field mushrooms that you have gathered yourself, on toast, for breakfast."

Warm Spring-Dandelion Salad

Those who enjoy gathering foods from the wild find all sorts of innovative recipes for the common and often baneful dandelion weed. Some fry the golden blossoms into fritters or distill them into folksy wine, while others make a pickle similar to capers from the first tiny and taut buds. A few adventuresome souls dig up the plant's deep roots and attempt to roast them as a coffee substitute. Organic gardener and bon vivant Stanley Joseph of Cape Rosier reported trying such as a caffeine substitute one time, only to return posthaste to the evils of real coffee.

Our favorite way to enjoy dandelions is to harvest the tender leaves before the fringed blossoms appear and toss them in a traditional, warm, sweet-and-sour bacon dressing. Most recipes call for sugar as the sweetener in the dressing, but we prefer maple syrup since it too comes from the wild and is often tapped slightly before the onset of dandelion season. The garnish of finely minced hard-boiled eggs imparts a pleasing dandelion-yellow spatter to the wilted salad.

8 slices bacon
3 tablespoons minced onion
¼ cup cider vinegar
¼ cup pure maple syrup
Salt and freshly ground black pepper, to taste
8 cups tender, young dandelion leaves, washed and dried
2 hard-boiled eggs, peeled and finely minced

1. Cut the bacon slices into a ¼-inch dice and fry over moderate heat in a medium-size skillet until crisp. Remove the bacon with a slotted spoon and drain on paper towels. Leave ½ cup bacon fat in the skillet and discard the rest.

2. Add the minced onion to the hot bacon fat in the skillet and sauté until softened, about 3 minutes. Whisk in the vinegar and syrup. Bring to a simmer and season to taste with salt and freshly ground pepper. Keep warm over medium-low heat.

3. Place the dandelion greens in an ovenproof serving bowl and warm in a preheated 300°F oven until the greens just begin to wilt, about 5 minutes. Remove and toss with the warm dressing. Mix in the reserved crisp bacon and the minced egg. Serve at once.

Makes 4 to 6 servings

Graceful green fiddleheads taste all the more glorious when highlighted with a dusting of Parmesan cheese.

Favorite Fiddleheads

Mainers like to flavor all manner of cooked greens with the smokiness of salt pork and tang of vinegar. This recipe taps into that predilection but adds a few twists. An ounce or so of salt pork is simmered in a pot of water to scent the fiddlehead cooking liquid. Once the fiddleheads are cooked, turning vibrant green and tender, they are drained and tossed with lemon butter and coarse bread crumbs toasted with mustard. The mustard stands in for the sharpness of the more customary vinegar. A light and last-minute dusting of Parmesan cheese completes the simple harmony of the dish.

1 2-inch strip salt pork, 1 to 1½ ounces
6 tablespoons (¾ stick) unsalted butter
1½ tablespoons Dijon-style mustard
1½ cups coarse fresh white bread crumbs
2 pounds fiddleheads, cleaned and trimmed

1 tablespoon fresh lemon juice
Salt and freshly ground pepper, to taste
1/4 cup freshly grated Parmesan cheese

1. Fill a large saucepan half full with water and add the salt pork. Simmer over medium heat for 15 minutes.

2. Meanwhile, melt 4 tablespoons of the butter in a small skillet over low heat. Whisk in the mustard and then add the bread crumbs, tossing to coat evenly with the mustard butter. Sauté the mixture, stirring frequently, until the crumbs are slightly crunchy and toasted, about 10 minutes.

3. Bring the salt pork and water to a full boil and add the fiddleheads. Cook until the fiddleheads are crisp-tender, about 5 minutes. Drain, discarding the salt pork, and toss the fiddleheads with the remaining 2 tablespoons of butter and the lemon juice. Toss with the mustard bread crumbs and season with salt and pepper, to taste. Transfer to a serving dish and dust the top with the Parmesan cheese. Serve at once.

Makes 6 to 8 servings

Fiddlehead Soup

This textural soup is laden with the colors and crunch of spring. Some of the fiddleheads are puréed to make a pale green soup base while the rest are left whole to mingle gracefully with flecks of leeks and carrots and chunks of potatoes in a warming soup that is truly a salute to the season.

4 tablespoons (1/2 stick) unsalted butter
2 fat leeks, washed, trimmed, and minced
2 carrots, peeled and minced
1 clove garlic, minced
1 teaspoon dried tarragon

4 1/2 cups water
1 cup dry white wine
3 medium potatoes, peeled and cut into 1/2-inch cubes
3 cups fiddleheads, cleaned and cooked until tender
1 1/2 cups half-and-half
Salt and freshly ground pepper, to taste

1. Melt the butter over medium heat in a stockpot. Add the leeks, carrots, and garlic. Sauté until quite soft, about 10 minutes. Add the tarragon and cook a minute more.

2. Pour the water and wine into the pot and add the potatoes. Place half of the cooked fiddleheads in a blender or food processor and purée until smooth. Stir into the soup. Simmer the soup uncovered, stirring occasionally, until the potatoes are tender, about 30 minutes.

3. Add the remaining cooked fiddleheads to the soup along with the half-and-half. Season the soup with salt and pepper and continue to simmer about 10 minutes more to warm throughout and mellow the flavors. Serve hot ladled into soup bowls.

Serves 6 to 8

Fiddlehead Quiche

Fiddlehead aficionados say that most recipes designed for asparagus or spinach work well with fiddleheads. This savory and elegant quiche is a perfect example. Taking a little extra time to creatively arrange the fiddlehead coils on top of the quiche custard produces a finished tart of enticing visual appeal.

Quiche Crust:
1 3/4 cups unbleached all-purpose flour
1/2 teaspoon salt
12 tablespoons (1 1/2 sticks) chilled unsalted butter
1/3 cup ice water

Filling:

4 eggs

1 cup evaporated milk

3 tablespoons minced scallions or chives

Pinch of nutmeg

Dash of cayenne pepper

Salt and freshly ground pepper; to taste

1½ teaspoons Dijon-style mustard

1½ cups shredded Swiss cheese

4 slices bacon, cooked crisp and then crumbled

2 cups fiddleheads, cleaned and cooked until just crisp-tender

1. To make the crust, place flour and salt in a food processor fitted with a steel blade. Cut the butter into small pieces and add to the flour. Blend in the processor until the mixture resembles coarse crumbs. With the machine running, add the ice water and process until the dough just begins to form into a small ball. Shape the dough into a flat disk, wrap in plastic wrap, and refrigerate until ready to use.

2. Preheat the oven to 375°F. Roll the crust out into a thin circle to line a 9-inch pie dish. Trim and crimp the edges of the crust decoratively. Prick the bottom of the crust all over with a fork. Bake for 6 to 7 minutes to partially set the crust. Remove from oven and set aside briefly.

3. For the filling, beat together the eggs, evaporated milk, scallions, nutmeg, cayenne, salt, and pepper until well combined. Brush the mustard thinly over the bottom of the quiche crust. Scatter half of the shredded cheese and all of the bacon over the bottom of the crust. Layer half of the cooked fiddleheads on top and pour in all of the egg mixture. Top with the rest of the cheese and arrange the remaining fiddleheads in concentric circles over the top.

4. Bake the quiche until the center is set, 40 to 45 minutes. Let rest for 10 minutes and then cut into wedges to serve.

Makes 6 to 8 servings

Roast Spring Chicken with Fiddleheads

Lots of onions and fiddleheads roasted in the pan alongside the chicken make this a homespun yet fabulous one-pan meal.

1 roasting chicken (about 5½ pounds)

Half a lemon

2 tablespoons dry mustard

2 tablespoons ground ginger

1 teaspoon salt

1 teaspoon freshly ground black pepper

8 small to medium yellow onions, peeled and quartered

1½ cups chicken stock, preferably homemade

1 pound fiddleheads, cleaned and trimmed

1. Preheat the oven to 425°F.

2. Rinse the chicken and remove the giblets (save for another use if desired). Squeeze the juice from the lemon all over the chicken and then place the lemon in the bird's cavity.

3. Combine the mustard, ginger, salt, and pepper; pat the mixture generously all over the chicken. Place the chicken in a large roasting pan and scatter the onions around it. Roast for 30 minutes.

4. Reduce the oven temperature to 375° and pour the chicken stock over and around the chicken. Continue roasting for another 30 minutes, basting occasionally.

5. Add the fiddleheads to the pan, stirring to coat them with the roasting juices. Continue to roast, stirring the vegetables occasionally, until both the fiddleheads and chicken are tender, another 30 to 40 minutes. Carve the chicken and cover the slices with the pan vegetables and juices.

Makes 4 servings

Rhubarb Crisp

A tart, pink rhubarb base spiced with ginger, cinnamon, and cloves is topped with a buttery, brown-sugar streusel laden with the crunch of toasted walnuts. Serve warm from the oven with a generous scoop of vanilla ice cream as a reward for a day of completed spring chores.

6 cups diced rhubarb
3/4 cup granulated sugar
1 teaspoon ground ginger
1 teaspoon ground cinnamon
1/4 teaspoon ground cloves
2 tablespoons cornstarch
1/2 cup orange juice

Topping:
1 cup unbleached all-purpose flour
1/2 cup brown sugar, lightly packed
1 teaspoon ground cinnamon
1/2 teaspoon ground nutmeg
Pinch of salt
6 tablespoons unsalted butter
1 cup coarsely chopped walnuts, lightly toasted

1. Preheat oven to 350°F.
2. In a mixing bowl, toss the rhubarb together with the sugar, ginger, cinnamon, and cloves. Dissolve the cornstarch in the orange juice, add to the rhubarb, and toss to coat. Spread the rhubarb mixture into a shallow 2- to 2½-quart baking dish.
3. To make the topping, place flour, brown sugar, cinnamon, nutmeg, and salt in a small mixing bowl. Cut the butter into small pieces and blend into the flour mixture with your hands or a pastry cutter until crumbly. Mix in the walnuts and then scatter the topping evenly over the rhubarb.
4. Bake the crisp until the top is golden and the rhubarb is bubbling, 45 to 55 minutes. Serve warm.

Serves 8 to 10

Simply Sautéed Chanterelles

Fresh garlic is too overpowering to cook with the mushrooms. The garlic powder gives just the right hint of flavor to these fabulous mushrooms.

2 tablespoons unsalted butter
Half a medium onion, minced
1/2 pound fresh chanterelles, wiped with a paper towel to remove dirt and stray bugs
1/4 teaspoon garlic powder
Salt and freshly ground black pepper, to taste
2 thick slices best-quality white or other favorite toasting bread, toasted
2 tablespoons minced fresh parsley

1. Melt the butter over medium heat in a medium-size skillet. Add the onion and sauté until softened, 5 minutes. Coarsely slice the chanterelles and add to the skillet. Sprinkle with the garlic powder and then cook, stirring frequently, until all the liquid exuded by the mushrooms has evaporated, 12 to 15 minutes. Season to taste with salt and pepper.
2. Place each slice of toasted bread on a serving plate. Divide the sautéed chanterelles evenly over the two slices. Sprinkle each with parsley and serve at once for an unforgettable beginning to a summer morning.

Makes 2 servings

A splendid spring overview of the seaside garden in South Blue Hill that nourishes our family and customers at Jonathan's Restaurant alike.

Chapter Eight

Saltwater Farms

A seacoast farm, such as this, extends far beyond the boundaries mentioned in the deed. My domain is arable many miles offshore, in the restless fields of protein. Cultivation begins close to the house with a rhubarb patch, but it ends down the bay beyond the outer islands, handling for cod and haddock with gulls like gnats around your ears, and the threat of fog always in the pit of your stomach. . . .

I think it is the expansiveness of coastal farming that makes it so engrossing. . . .

E. B. WHITE
"Salt Water Farm"

THE gentle morning rain of early June is most welcome, for the tiny seedlings that have emerged in the garden that supplies Jonathan's Restaurant in Blue Hill are quite thirsty. This garden covers about a quarter of an acre on a six-acre plot of shoreland owned by our family. It is high on a hill adjacent to an old barn that serves as a spacious home for a 1953 Farm All tractor, an array of garden tools, two small boats, and a family of swallows that returns year after year. June provides a virtual sensory smorgasbord for this and every other saltwater farm on the coast of Maine. The sea of lupine, dressed in its brightest pink and indigo blue colors, descends to a grove of tall spruce trees. A cluster of poplar trees with their pale green leaves contrasts with the dark evergreens, especially on a gray morning. A chorus of songbirds is complemented by the staccato of a downy woodpecker doing his thing to a dead, hollow elm tree on the other side of the barn. The gurgling of lobster-

boat engines firing up for a long day of work is followed by a dull, comforting purr that can be heard for miles across the absolutely still bay. The lonely cries of seagulls hovering over these boats are frequent. The smell of low tide is unmistakable, but the intoxicating aroma of white and purple lilacs predominate on this day.

The irresistible urge to walk through the rows of the garden to see how everything is doing surely will result in a few black fly bites, soaked sneakers, and wet cuffs, but this inconvenience will be eminently tolerable when it is discovered that no cutworms got the tender young pepper plants overnight and that the seedlings, quite droopy just the day before, have perked up and are smiling their thanks. Poking into the ground to see if the first radishes are ready for harvest results in a handful of seedlings that really are too small, but they taste good anyway. The first planting of savoy spinach is ready, however, and will undoubtedly find its way into the salads of the restaurant tonight. This is just one morning at our garden in South Blue Hill. Sun-drenched or fog-laden, each one is different and equally as soothing to the soul.

Ours is not the typical saltwater farm, but neither is any saltwater farm typical, for the term is very broad. Across the street is a much smaller garden with chickens and geese roaming the yard. In its own way, it too is a saltwater farm. Down the road a notch in North Brooklin is a stately home surrounded by dramatic flower gardens, small, fragmented vegetable patches that crawl right to the kitchen door, donkey stalls, and coops of esoteric game birds. A pen attached to the main barn houses a litter of six-week-old German Shepherd puppies. The interesting medley of sounds and aromas, dis-

sonant and clamorous as they are, nevertheless blends comfortably with the spectacular views of Mount Desert Island and its worn but majestic peaks. This is the home of Mary Margaret and Fairfield Goodale, married for forty-six years and transplanted from the frenetic metropolitan life-style of Boston. The Goodales employ a hired hand or two, but Mary Margaret is up at dawn every morning tending to her squabs and donkeys, harvesting eggs, moving the sheep to another pasture, and doing the things that people do on a working farm. She is happy and very much at peace with herself.

Down the road another dozen miles or so is Amen Farm, owned by Helen and Roy Barrette, also transplants. Roy is a well-known essayist on a wide variety of subjects and for twelve years wrote a column entitled "The Retired Gardener" for the *Ellsworth American*, a local newspaper. Now in his mid-nineties, he continues to be vibrant and mentally sharp, and to contribute an occasional column to the *American*. Because of the physical limitations brought on by age, the Barrettes are unable to work Amen Farm as they once did, but the exotic plants and flowers, vegetable gardens, and pristine surroundings of this special place still remain. In the introduction to his book, *A Countryman's Journal*, Roy wrote:

We did not come here to escape anything, but to find something. Our family was grown and married, we were healthy and reasonably well off, and I had

skills that could be employed here as well as anywhere else, so we were free to do as we wished. What we desired was what a great many people seek in these latter days of the twentieth century, an opportunity to rediscover some of the virtues of a more stable, simpler society. While everything has not developed as we expected, enough has so that we are more than glad that we came here and enormously grateful for our good fortune. We found that the twentieth century intrudes no matter where one lives, but there are good as well as disturbing aspects to that fact. We have learned that while there are some who envy us our life here, there are more who, although they think it is wonderful to visit for a few months in summer, view the idea of "year-round isolation" with feelings ranging from apprehension to astonishment that we would deliberately elect it. As for us, whether the day dawns blue and brittle cold, or damp and foggy with a smoky southwester, we sing our morning hymn of gratitude.

We discovered that a similar "morning hymn of gratitude" is sung by many a saltwater farmer. Jean Hay of Hay's Farm Stand and Paul and Mollie Birdsall of Horsepower Farm are cases in point. In 1978 Jean operated what could be characterized as a small produce market in an old blacksmith shop alongside a millstream. It was named the Peasant Gourmet. She decided not to open it the next season, sensing that the clientele was after something that was "too gourmet, and not enough peasant." After a few years of writing for a newspaper, Jean returned to what now seems to be her true calling. Her small farm stand is surrounded by vast gardens and small pastures occupied by a variety of farm animals, including goats, pigs, and geese, which are cleverly employed to assist with the weeding of long rows of onions. Every practice on this saltwater farm is in strict compliance with the written as well as unwritten principles of organic gardening. No chemical fertilizers or pesticides are used; animals are systematically rotated from pasture to pasture; cover crops are planted in patches to restore the soil; the belief that "what you take from the earth must be put back" is strong.

Jean is a dedicated farmer, and the fruits of her labor can be enjoyed by all when her farm stand opens its doors for business each morning around 10 A.M. The display case for the multicolored heads of lettuce that still harbor morning dew is an old metal sink. Sheepskins for sale drape the split-rail fence outside the stand. Old Goat's Soap tucked away on a shelf inside always garners a comment or two from customers. The first young carrots, washed and displayed with their long green tops, are beautiful in their imperfection. The selection of produce varies as the season progresses, and the vegetables are always of top quality. Fresh raspberries occupy pride of place in July, and although they really need no embellishment to be enjoyed, there are few who would turn down an accompanying bowl of homemade ice cream. Bushel baskets of peppers and tomatoes, still warm from the sun, exude irresistible earthy aromas in August. Corn, squash, beans, cucumbers, and just about anything else that grows fill the stand in September, the most bountiful of

months for saltwater farms in Maine. The cooler nights of late September continue to be followed by warm days, which serve to ripen the fall and winter storage crops. The stand takes on an orange hue in October as pumpkins, lots of pumpkins of all sizes, overflow the small area. Jean's place, along with other small organic farm stands that can be found up and down the coast, provide us with the opportunity to eat foods that are harvested when they are in peak condition. We know the world is a better place with Jean Hay and her kind in it.

When asked why they moved to Maine in 1973, Paul Birdsall said that he could not stay awake at the wheel when driving back and forth from his pressure-filled job in south-central Connecticut. When asked, "Why horses instead of tractors?" Paul immediately responded, "Don't get me wrong. I appreciate a good piece of machinery, but the combustion engine and I do not get along well." Horse-

Magnificent flowers fringe the entrance to Stanley Joseph and Lynn Karlin's vegetable garden in Cape Rosier.

Paul Birdsall and his trusty equestrian team at Horsepower Farm.

power Farm in North Blue Hill is subject for an entire book of its own, and passing mention in this chapter could never do justice to the dedication Paul and Mollie have given to this venture. The Birdsalls have made a solemn commitment to organic farming and gardening; it is their life, and it will be forever. Paul presides over a team of workhorses that plow, till, harrow, and seed the expansive fields of Horsepower Farm. In the winter, these statuesque animals are the vehicles for old-fashioned sleigh rides.

Recreation aside, Horsepower Farm is serious business. Paul is occupied with the tasks of managing the fields and the horses, while Mollie's domain is the market garden, which provides local restaurants and small stores with organic produce, ranging from the first tender peas of spring to the root and storage vegetables to be put away for the long winter. Farmhands supplied through the Maine Organic Farmers

and Gardeners Association (MOFGA) and other agricultural apprentice programs assist with many of the daily chores, including care of the farm animals, which also include chickens and sheep. Lamb and mutton from a herd of some thirty sheep are sold locally. As the fields rest under a cover of snow for the winter, Paul and the horses do not, as they go deep into the woods to cut and haul wood. Once again there is an adherence to a life-style that can command only the highest admiration and, from many, an envy of their courage to make such a commitment.

In a different vein are Stanley Joseph and Lynn Karlin of Cape Rosier. Stan is a disciple of "back-to-the-land" gurus Scott and Helen Nearing. Inspired by their 1954 book *Living the Good Life*, Stan set out to meet the homesteading Nearings and wound up purchasing their land and home in 1980. The Near-

Funny Farm proprietor Stanley Joseph at home on Cape Rosier.

Midsummer is a lush time at Stan Joseph's garden, which is enclosed by a stone wall originally built by "good life" guru Scott Nearing.

ings' "good life," so to speak, was simple, systematic, and austere. Stan and Lynn have tempered that austerity, and the farm on which they live has evolved into what is now a secluded paradise. The principles of organic farming are firmly intact, but whereas Scott Nearing tilled his fields with a wheel hoe, Stan uses rototiller and tractor. Many of the gardens are given over to flowers, although there is ample cultivation of food; these are spectacular flower gardens. Behind a stone wall are vegetable gardens that provide local restaurants and markets with organic produce. Plenty of space is also given to the cultivation of chives, which are dried and used to decorate wreaths to be sold in December. High-bush blueberries covered with huge nets have been one of the cash crops of the farm for several years. A homemade Finnish sauna with a sod roof occupies a small island in the pond behind the farmhouse and is used fre-

quently by friends and neighbors. Too many cats to count stroll around the farm. While there is a fairytale feeling to this farm, a tour of the grounds with Stan and Lynn makes it apparent that they have accented a basic and realistic life-style with out-of-the-ordinary pleasures and pastimes. The result is a harmonious whole. It is unquestionably a lot of work to maintain this personal utopia, but as Stan said to us more than once on our several visits, "It feels good to work here."

The recipes that follow take advantage of the seasonal harvests that come from saltwater farms and in all cases work best with flavorful fruits and vegetables in peak condition. We continue in this chapter to be of the distinctly Maine food notion — the less you do to it, the better it is — save for a few current inspirations from the summer catering files of Jonathan's Restaurant.

Pea Wars and Winners

THE quest for biggest pumpkin or the first red tomato often gives rise to friendly competition between neighbors. In Maine, where the growing season is short and the ground is often unworkable until mid-April, it is the thought of fresh peas on the Fourth of July that will nudge the home gardener away from the comfort of a woodstove and into the mud flats. Peas grow well in cool weather and do not seem to mind the soggy spring that holds on to frosty nights well into May.

For years Jonathan has unsuccessfully attempted to harvest his gardens before those of a friend and neighbor who lives a couple of miles down the road. Finally realizing that this "pea scoundrel" knew something he did not, he initiated The First Annual Hancock County Pea Contest in hopes that someone could come up with a harvest before his rival. At this writing the contest is five years old. The rules are simple: (1) the variety must be sugar snap, primarily because the six-foot vines require staking, thus eliminating many lazier would-be entrants, and also because they are tasty and versatile — they can be used as either a shell or edible-pod pea; (2) all seeds must be sown directly into the ground; (3) no commercial growers are permitted in the contest; (4) the peas must be grown in Hancock County; and (5) the first gardener to deliver two dozen mature sugar snap peas will be the recipient of dinner for two at Jonathan's Restaurant. (Jonathan will also happily buy a glass of wine for anyone who can beat the "pea scoundrel," whose name happens to be Bob Stafford.)

Bob Stafford has won the contest several times, and one year he even cut a sailing trip short to rush home to harvest his peas. Recent years have produced new winners, the latest being Lawris Closson of North Blue Hill. Lawris at seventy-nine years of age still goes haying and blueberry raking during the dog days of August and at any given time will have farm animals being readied for the freezer. Upon hearing of Jonathan's contest, he vowed to win. He did in 1991, bringing two dozen perfectly shaped sugar snap peas to Jonathan on June 21, ten days before anyone else and when Jonathan's vines were just beginning to flower. On delivery of his winning peas, Lawris had the following conversation with Jonathan:

Lawris: Those what you looking for?
Jonathan: They're winners, Lawris.
Lawris: What's the prize, again?
Jonathan: Dinner for two; anything you want.
Lawris: Don't know who I'd get to go with me. Guess I'll just have to come twice.

The Meaning of MOFGA

MOFGA stands for Maine Organic Farmers and Gardeners Association. Through our travels and research we have found that MOFGA is more a way of life than an association. Its mission is clearly stated in its brochure: MOFGA works to

- grow safe and healthful food and make it available to all
- recycle natural resources on the farm and in the garden
- protect the diversity and integrity of plant and animal life
- promote small farming and support rural communities

Farmers such as Jean Hay and Paul and Mollie Birdsall along with 2,000-plus other members of MOFGA keep this association strong with their dedication to a way of life that is emulated not just in Maine but across the country. The celebration of this life-style culminates in what South Portland barbecue king Jonathan St. Laurent refers to as "Maine's annual party" — the Common Ground Country Fair, held each year in late September at the Windsor Fairgrounds.

MOFGA presides over farm apprenticeship programs, education and extension services, certification of farms that adhere to the tenets and principles of organic farming, and an award-winning bimonthly newsletter. It also sponsors local seminars, conferences, and other activities statewide that are in tune with the MOFGA philosophy. The "MOFGA Certified Organic" label offers assurance that no synthetic fertilizers, chemicals, or pesticides that may contaminate the soil, product, or environment have been employed in the production of food whether it be animal or vegetable. It is a strong and growing organization that has greatly influenced us in our views and approach to writing about Maine food and the people who are growing and selling it.

Maine Potato Salad

The sort of potato salad that is most common in Maine is creamy and white and enriched with chopped pickles and sliced hard-boiled eggs. The recipe that follows captures the flavor of the salads served to accompany many a lobster bake or chicken barbecue.

6 large Maine potatoes, peeled
½ cup chopped dill pickles
4 large stalks celery, diced
½ green bell pepper, seeded and diced
1 small red onion, minced
½ cup minced fresh parsley or dill
1 cup mayonnaise, preferably Hellmann's
1 cup sour cream
1½ tablespoons prepared mustard
1 tablespoon cider or white vinegar
1 teaspoon celery seeds
Salt and freshly ground pepper, to taste
5 hard-boiled eggs, peeled and thinly sliced

1. Place the potatoes in a large pot, cover with water, and boil until tender. Drain well and let cool to room temperature.

2. Cut the cooled potatoes into 1-inch chunks and place in a large mixing bowl. Add the pickles, celery, bell pepper, onion, and parsley; mix well. In a separate small bowl, whisk together the mayonnaise, sour cream, mustard, vinegar, and celery seeds. Toss the dressing with the potatoes and then season all to taste with salt and pepper.

3. Gently fold the sliced eggs into the salad. Transfer to a serving bowl and refrigerate until ready to serve.

Makes 8 to 10 servings

Unusual blue potatoes are mixed with more common red-skinned and white potatoes to yield a delicious patriotic potato salad.

Red, White, and Blue Potato Salad

Living in Maine has turned former craft-gallery owner André Strong into an avid potato farmer on his homestead between North Blue Hill and Bucksport. André loves experimenting with both old varieties of Maine potatoes and esoteric strains that his mother sends him from her native France. André showcases his unusual blue potatoes in this patriotic potato salad served in celebration of both America's Fourth of July and France's Bastille Day on July 14th. The recipe that follows is our close approximation of André's impassioned creation.

1 pound each red, white, and blue new potato varieties,
    unpeeled but scrubbed
½ pound smoked bacon, sliced
1 medium red onion, minced
½ cup cider vinegar
½ cup dry white wine
3 tablespoons olive oil
Salt and freshly ground black pepper, to taste
4 stalks celery, minced
3 tablespoons minced fresh tarragon
3 tablespoons minced fresh parsley

1. Place all the potatoes in a pot and cover amply with water. Bring to a boil and simmer until the potatoes are fork-tender, 25 to 30 minutes. Drain well.

2. While the potatoes are cooking, brown the bacon in a large skillet until quite crisp; remove from the skillet and drain on paper towels. Add the onion to the bacon fat in the skillet and sauté until soft-ened, about 5 minutes. Swirl in the vinegar, wine,

91

Saltwater Farms

and olive oil. Season the mixture with salt and pepper and keep warm over low heat.

3. Cut the hot potatoes into coarse chunks and toss with the celery in a large mixing bowl. Pour the warm bacon dressing over the potatoes, stirring to coat thoroughly. Mix in the tarragon and parsley. Crumble the bacon into small pieces and add to the salad. Transfer to a serving bowl and serve warm or at room temperature.

Makes 8 to 10 servings

Cucumber Salad with Dill and Yogurt

From late July until the first frost in early October, cucumbers and dill are proliferate in coastal Maine gardens. This simple recipe is a perfect foil for a spicy Pulled Pork Sandwich (see page 114). We like to leave the skins on the cucumbers for a nice color contrast, but if you are using the waxed store-bought variety, make sure you peel them completely.

4 large cucumbers (peeled if necessary), thinly sliced
1 small red onion, peeled, halved, and sliced thinly into crescents
1 tablespoon salt
4 tablespoons cider vinegar
1/2 cup coarsely chopped fresh dill
1 cup plain yogurt
8 large leaves of loose-leaf lettuce

1. Place the sliced cucumbers and onions in a large nonreactive bowl. Toss thoroughly with the salt. Allow the cucumbers and onions to sit for 20 minutes.

2. Add the vinegar and let the vegetables sit for another 20 minutes. Drain the liquid and discard.

3. Add the dill and yogurt and chill for 1 hour. Place the cucumbers on lettuce leaves and serve at once. (Note: Fresh mint substituted for the dill produces a different but equally delicious side dish.)

Makes 8 servings

Fresh Melon and Cucumber Sauce

Coastal Maine has a rather short growing season. In late August and early September, everything seems to be ready at once. Each year our garden boasts a few melons at this time, and although they do not reach the dimensions of the oversize cantaloupes and honeydews that we see in grocery stores, the taste of a fresh homegrown muskmelon is very satisfying. At this time cucumber plants are producing at full force, mint patches relentlessly continue their invasion into garden space designated for other uses, and cilantro (coriander), having reseeded itself from previous plantings, is popping up all over the garden. This sauce is a wonderful cool topping for fish hot from the grill.

1 muskmelon, about 3/4 pound, or 1/2 cantaloupe of the same weight
1 medium cucumber, peeled, seeded, and coarsely diced
2 tablespoons minced red onion
1 tablespoon lightly chopped fresh mint leaves
2 teaspoons lightly chopped fresh cilantro leaves
1/4 cup dry pear wine or dry vermouth

Remove the flesh from the melon and chop it coarsely. Add the remaining ingredients, mix well, and refrigerate for 2 hours. Serve over grilled fish.

Makes about 4 cups

Five-Vegetable Slaw

This colorful slaw, abundant with garden-ripe vegetables, garnishes many a plate at Jonathan's Restaurant during the summer months.

4 cups shredded red cabbage
4 cups shredded green cabbage
½ pound carrots, shredded
1 pound mixed yellow and green summer squash, shredded
1 red onion, halved and sliced thinly into crescents
1 tablespoon salt
1 cup cider vinegar
½ cup raisins
1 tablespoon curry powder

1. Place the red and green cabbage, carrots, squash, and onion in a large mixing bowl. Toss the vegetables with the salt and let them sit for 30 minutes. The salt will extract moisture from the vegetables.

2. Drain the vegetables in a large colander and return them to the bowl. Add the vinegar to the vegetables and mix well. Allow the slaw to set for another 20 minutes. Drain again. Add the curry powder and raisins and mix well. Allow the slaw to mellow in the refrigerator for at least 1 hour. Serve when ready.

Makes 8 to 10 servings

Horsepower Farm Zucchini Casserole

Maine farmers are no exception when it comes to that universal penchant for growing more zucchini than can possibly be consumed in a summer. This recipe is what Mollie Birdsall of Horsepower Farm likes to make to put a dent in her crop. She says she will sometimes add Maine crabmeat to the garden-fresh blend to take the dish from side accompaniment to main course.

3 tablespoons vegetable or olive oil
2 scallions, trimmed and minced
2 cloves garlic, minced
2 medium zucchini, thinly sliced
1 bell pepper, seeded and minced
1 large carrot, peeled and grated
Salt and freshly ground pepper, to taste
1 cup plain yogurt
½ cup plus 2 tablespoons freshly grated Parmesan cheese
3 tablespoons minced fresh parsley or basil
¼ teaspoon dried thyme
2 tablespoons butter, melted
¼ cup coarse fresh bread crumbs

1. Preheat the oven to 350°F.

2. Heat the oil over medium-high heat in a large skillet. Add the scallions, garlic, zucchini, and pepper; sauté, stirring frequently, for 5 minutes. Stir in the grated carrot and cook 1 minute more. Season the vegetables to taste with salt and pepper.

3. Stir together the yogurt, ½ cup of the Parmesan, the parsley or basil, and the thyme. Combine with the vegetable mixture, stirring well. Turn all into a shallow 1-quart casserole dish. Toss the melted butter and bread crumbs together and sprinkle over the top. Sprinkle the remaining 2 tablespoons Parmesan over the top as well.

4. Bake the casserole until browned and bubbling, 25 to 30 minutes. Serve hot.

Makes 6 servings

We love to pack the bounty of the land and sea for escapist summer picnics on the water or along the shores of secluded islands.

Baked Summer Corn

This wonderful recipe can be made with either freshly cooked or raw corn off the cob, which makes it perfectly suited for using up ears of corn left from a shore dinner or for doing something a little different with just-picked corn from the garden. While bacon always makes a tasty combination with corn, we find the dish even more delicious when made with one of the salami-type sausages from Smith's Log Smokehouse or Kohn's.

2 tablespoons butter or bacon fat
4 scallions, trimmed and minced
3 cups cooked or raw corn kernels
8 strips crisp, cooked bacon, crumbled, or 3 ounces smokehouse semihard salami, diced small
1/2 cups sour cream
Salt and freshly ground pepper,
   to taste
Pinch of cayenne pepper

1. Preheat oven to 350°F. Lightly butter a 1½-quart shallow casserole dish. Set aside.

2. Melt the butter or bacon fat over medium heat in a small skillet. Add the scallions and sauté until softened, 2 to 3 minutes.

3. In a mixing bowl, combine the scallions, corn, and bacon or salami. Mix in the sour cream and season with salt, pepper, and cayenne. Spread the corn mixture evenly in the prepared casserole dish.

4. Bake the corn until set and lightly browned on top, 30 to 35 minutes. Serve hot.

Makes 6 servings

Nasturtium Salad

We have never seen nasturtiums grow anywhere else as vibrantly and prolifically as they do in Maine. We love the peppery flavor and color that their edible leaves and blossoms add to mixed green salads and often plant them to neighbor lettuce rows in the garden. Using a fruit vinegar, such as raspberry or strawberry, in the dressing will further accent the floral appeal of the salad.

Dressing:
2 tablespoons fruit or wine vinegar
1/2 tablespoon fresh lemon juice
1 teaspoon Dijon-style mustard
1/2 cup olive oil
Salt and freshly ground pepper, to taste

Salad:
10 cups mixed fresh salad greens, washed and dried
1 cup nasturtium leaves, stems removed
1 cup nasturtium blossoms

1. To make the dressing, in a small bowl whisk together the vinegar, lemon juice, and mustard until smooth. Slowly whisk in the olive oil and then season to taste with salt and pepper.

2. Combine the salad greens with the nasturtium leaves and blossoms in a large salad bowl. Drizzle with enough of the dressing to coat all lightly. Serve at once.

Makes 6 servings

Peppery-colored and -flavored nasturtium blossoms and leaves are a favorite addition to summer green salads.

Tomato, Basil, and Chèvre Salad

"Maine has two seasons — winter and Fourth of July." We don't know who coined this often-heard phrase, but it isn't true. Most saltwater farmers don't begin their long and bountiful harvest of the quintessential summer vegetable, the tomato, until late August. Since there are no words that do justice to the sensation of sinking one's teeth into a vegetable that exudes the sunshine-filled heat of the day, this recipe is not worth the effort if perfectly sun-ripened tomatoes are not used.

Fresh greens, such as Romaine lettuce or arugula,
for garnish
2 pounds fresh, unrefrigerated ripe tomatoes, sliced
18 to 24 whole fresh basil leaves
³/₄ pound fresh chèvre, preferably from York Hill Farm or
Seal Cove Farm, sliced into small disks
¹/₄ cup extra virgin olive oil
Freshly ground black pepper, to taste

1. Lay the greens on a large platter. Place a slice of tomato, overlapped by a basil leaf, overlapped by a disk of chèvre on the bed of greens. Continue this process in a decorative manner until all the tomatoes, basil, and chèvre are used.

2. Liberally drizzle the olive oil over the salad. Grind fresh black pepper over the top and serve.

Makes 6 servings

95

A lush summer tart laden with just-picked blueberries and raspberries.(Photo credit: Raymond Chase)

Chapter Nine

Summer Berries

Blueberries properly cooked are delicious. Certainly uncooked berries are just as delicious. A Maine man likes to eat the berries on his breakfast cereal. He likes to eat blueberries on lettuce for his dinner salad. He likes to eat blueberries and cream for his supper dessert. But best of all, he likes to eat a bowlful of berries and milk at bedtime. He takes his snack to his back steps and eats in the dark. He gazes at the stars; he looks at the lightning bugs in the meadow; he listens to the loons on the shore. He is apt to say to himself, "There is nothing as good as blueberries in August."

ESTHER E. WOOD
Saltwater Seasons

IT IS ironic that the vast fields that yield Maine's most prolific berry crop are known as "barrens," for all berries are picked, consumed, and celebrated with revelled abandon throughout the state during the half-warm summer months. I'm convinced that the half-pint unit of measure, so common as a berry container in markets across the nation, simply does not exist in Maine. At the very least, berries — be they strawberries, blueberries, raspberries, or black-berries — are plucked and slurped by the pint, with quarts and bushel buckets being all the more preferable. Any lingering elements of Puritanism and parsimony seem to fall completely by the wayside when you put a Mainer in a berry patch. Then, again, perhaps Down East berry bacchanalia isn't as inconsistent with reserve of character as it first appears. As Louise Dickinson Rich writes in *State O'Maine:*

They [Mainers] avail themselves, as a duty, of foodstuffs that can be had for the taking — fish, shellfish, wild game, dock, fiddlehead and goose-grass greens, and all kinds of pie timber, as it is called, meaning a variety of wild berries. Living off the country does more than save money and satisfy some atavistic urge. It salves the Conscience. To walk about the countryside simply for pleasure on a lovely day would be self-indulgence, and visions of tasks undone at home would rise up to haunt the walker. Staying outdoors in the sun and fresh air all afternoon to pick berries is something else again. It is a useful chore justified by tangible results and some discomfort in the form of scratched hands and a lame back. The discomfort is important to Conscience, which is to the Down-easter as real and painful as an inflamed sciatic nerve and requires equally delicate treatment.

The business of blueberries in Maine began on the barrens of Washington and Hancock counties, an area often referred to today as the blueberry belt. The barrens themselves are defined as wild, desolate, treeless tracts of land with gravelly and strongly acid soil inhospitable to most vegetation, the one remarkable exception being the low-bush blueberry, which tends to grow everywhere over the barrens. These barrens are the product of a glacier that retreated about 12,700 years ago leaving a terrain of gravel, sand, and large boulders, which are thought to have rolled directly off the edges of melting ice. Geological studies have revealed that this sort of glacio-marine delta, which tends to resemble a sci-fi moonscape, is comparatively rare and almost entirely unique to the state of Maine.

Expansive blueberry barrens provide peaceful and plentiful picking for both home consumption and commercial processing.

Somehow, wild blueberry plants managed to take root in the harsh soil surrounding the deposited rocks and boulders, and there is further speculation that the barrens were first burned over by Indians living in Washington County partly for protection from surprise attacks and partly to encourage the continued growth of various wild berries. Blueberries, after all, were an important dietary staple to the Indians, and it is known that they dried blueberries in the sun on brush mats and sold them to the first English explorers. Once seacoast towns were established by white settlers, gathering blueberries on the barrens became a public privilege extending over a hundred years. Whole families traveled from far and wide to pick wild Maine berries, and a local news item from 1860 noted, "The pickers are doing a smashing business on Epping Plains just now. They gather about forty bushels a day and sell them for seven cents a

quart. Purchasers carry them to Rockland and to Bangor to market."

Blueberrying in Maine went through its first major change as a result of the Civil War, which created a great demand for canned goods to keep the Union Army marching. Hence, initial experiments in canning blueberries began in Cherryfield in 1866 with the berries being cooked in an open pan over an old brick-oven fire. The cooked berries were then scooped into cans and capped entirely by hand.

At present, Maine is the nation's only commercial producer of wild blueberries, and more than 95 percent of the crop is processed by high-tech freezing rather than old-fashioned canning. Once picked or commercially raked, the blueberries are rushed from the barrens to plants, where they are winnowed, washed, and then put on a conveyor belt to have both underripe and overripe berries sorted out by a combination of human hands and sensitive electronic equipment. The berries then enter a wind tunnel in which frigid air velocities packing temperatures of 70 degrees below zero quick-freeze each berry individually. Maine blueberries are judged to be more intense and piquant in flavor than plumper, cultivated counterparts and thereby ideally suited for use in commercial baking mixes, since the small and compact size allows for baking without bursting. The year 1990 saw a record harvest of 75 million pounds of berries statewide. High crop yields combined with the dismantling of the Berlin Wall have brought a surge of optimism to Maine blueberry growers, the Germans being the highest per capita consumers of wild blueberries in the world.

While the commercial blueberry industry must be recognized as vital to Maine's economy, raking in respectable yearly revenues of over $70 million, we prefer to forage for our own berries for the making of our own favorite home-baked pie and muffin recipes. We begin to hanker to go berrying in May, when the barrens are transformed into a lush carpet of pink and white bell-shaped blossoms. At this time the smell of smoke often cuts through the sweet spring air, as some barrens are burned in two-year cycles to help remove competing plants and hostile insect pests and thereby increase blueberry yields in years to come. Patience must prevail for a while longer, as it will take until the beginning of July for the low-lying blueberry shrubs to stop growing and sport all of their hard green berries and then until the end of July or beginning of August for the berries to become, at long last, ripe for the frenzy of picking.

Fortunately, Maine has a lovely strawberry season in the interim to sate our appetites. Avid seekers of the state's uncultivated bounty know that June meadows and woodland fringes harbor the wild berries that our beloved Maine mentor Robert P. Tristram Coffin called "the best berries of Summer. . . . If there is a sweeter combination of sunlight and allspice, honey and nectar, gay color and sparkle, and essence and elixir of the earth than this ripest wild strawberry, eaten warm from the stalk, I wish you would write in and tell me about it."

While the bad news is that wild strawberries do not grow in the hardy proliferation of the state's sweet and tiny wild blueberries, the good news is that Maine has many farmers who persist in the tough and arduous task of growing cultivated strawberries, and most of their picturesque farms are open to the public for leisurely days of picking-your-own-berries until your fingers and palms are stained scarlet. In the long daylight hours of June and early July, growers such as Bob and Earlene Chasse of Silveridge Farm in Bucksport and Herb and Phyllis Schartner of Mountain View Fruit and Berry Farm in Thorndike make that old Beatles' tune "Strawberry Fields Forever" seem like a dream brought to life. The Schartners, in particular, delight in making berry picking into an event by providing shaded picnic tables, lounge chairs, and refreshing pitchers of iced tea to all pickers from sunup to sundown.

The enterprising Phyllis is also known for proffering recipe advice of all sorts. To pickers at the farm, she dispenses a bevy of typed strawberry recipes ranging from turnovers, to pink punches, to sweet and exotic pizzas. Jonathan and I tilt to the side of simplicity when it comes to strawberry cookery and second the Mainers' predilection for a Fourth of July shortcake splurge or a "mile-high" pie.

By the end of strawberry season, we feel primed for the more serious, more back-breaking blueberry picking. Berry picking runs deep in our family. It must have begun before we were born, when our mother first came to Maine as a teenager in the company of all six of her brothers. Her father then and there decided that the best way to keep the rambunctious sons industrious and out of mischief would be to set them up in a blueberry-harvesting business on his newly acquired property, Long Island, in Blue Hill Bay, and the business flourished for some time.

My fondest recollections of youthful blueberry picking come from expeditions undertaken with our grandmother. "Ma," as we grandchildren called her, was a jubilant forager who could pick until Maine's considerable tides came in and went out again, and then some. Just as we would be getting ready to cart an afternoon's wealth of blueberries homeward, Ma would, without fail, sight another patch so incredibly rich with juicy berries that she couldn't resist filling one last basket. At the close of each spell of picking mania, Ma would always stop to top her baskets with a green sprig of blueberry shrub so that the memory of our time on the barrens would follow us into the kitchen afterward. Happily, our mother takes after her mother, still continuing the family love of finding a blueberry barren offering a spectacular coastal vista and several hours' worth of picking. Generational improvements have made our mother into such a tidy picker that we have recently bestowed her with the title "the impeccable picker" — a nickname, I must add, that she covets.

When it comes to cooking our blueberry cache, Jonathan and I share in the conservative philosophy of hometown author Esther Wood. She wrote in her *Saltwater Seasons* book, the title of which incidentally inspired our own:

> We Maine people are sensitive about what we consider the misuse of Maine blueberries. I was once served blueberry ice cream. The color was a dismal gray. I tasted the cream: the berries were frozen nuggets, the custard was of poor quality and strange flavor. No proper Maine cookbook contains a recipe for blueberry ice cream. . . . Nor should blueberries be combined with gelatin. . . . Blueberries belong in pies fashioned from home mixed and home rolled pastry, made with sugar, flour, cinnamon, and baked in an oven of decreasing heat. . . . Blueberries also belong in blueberry cake. . . . Blueberries also belong in muffins. They are at home in wheat muffins or oatmeal muffins. The secret of good muffins is using plenty of well-floured blueberries. The secret of superior muffins is using buttermilk or sour milk for the liquid.

Maine is equally blessed with an abundance of what many consider to be the most elegant berry, the raspberry. Raspberries grow wild all over the place, and we used to enjoy picking them in thick entanglements on our grandfather's island. Cultivated raspberries also grow well and easily in Maine, and Jonathan and my father share a sizable thicket in their coastal garden. Lots of roadside stands sell reasonably priced pints and quarts of raspberries in the heart of summer, encouraging the extravagant use of the berries in fresh pies and tarts. My mother makes a special point of freezing some raspberries from our garden each year so that the family can later savor the flavor of summer sunshine in the midst of wintry Christmas holidays. Blackberries bid farewell to summer in Maine, having stored up the warmth of the fairest two months of the year to burst upon the scene in September with perfumed ripeness. We tend not to do much to blackberries except to pick and eat them on the spot where we find them. Robert P. Tristram Coffin was of similar mind, recommending, "Once you get these black beauties home, eat them at once with sugar. . . . Their taste is all their own and the heartiest among berries."

Both cultivated and wild raspberries thrive in Maine's summer climate.

Strawberry Shortcake with Bakewell Cream Biscuits

Bakewell Cream is a leavening agent unique to Maine that was invented in Bangor during World War II, when shortages of cream of tartar threatened to jeopardize Mainers' passion for home-baked biscuits. To this day the secret formula of Bakewell Cream has never been duplicated, and the extra-light and -high biscuits that the product renders keep its back-of-the-box recipe the preferred one for berry shortcakes throughout the state. This true Down East strawberry shortcake is a favorite cap to Fourth of July celebrations that feature fresh salmon and peas. Here is how we make ours.

Mainers like to make their shortcake biscuits with Bangor-based Bakewell Cream as the leavening agent.

Filling:
2 quarts fresh strawberries, rinsed, hulled, and halved
½ cup sugar

Bakewell Cream Biscuits:
4 cups unbleached all-purpose flour
4 teaspoons Bakewell Cream (available through mail
   order outside Maine)
2 teaspoons baking soda
½ teaspoon salt
5 tablespoons sugar
½ cup shortening
1½ cups plus 2 tablespoons cold buttermilk

Finishing:
1½ cups heavy cream
1 teaspoon vanilla extract

1. Combine the strawberries and sugar in a mixing bowl and let sit in the refrigerator for 1 hour.

2. Preheat the oven to 475°F. Sift together the flour, Bakewell Cream, baking soda, salt, and 3 tablespoons of the sugar. Cut the shortening into the dry ingredients with a pastry cutter until the mixture resembles coarse meal. Add the 1½ cups buttermilk and stir quickly with a fork to blend into a sticky dough. Turn out on a floured board and knead 5 or 6 times until smooth.

3. Roll out or pat the biscuit dough to a thickness of ½ to ¾ of an inch. Cut into rounds with a 3-inch biscuit cutter and arrange the biscuits 1 inch apart on a lightly greased baking sheet. Brush the tops of the biscuits lightly with the remaining 2 tablespoons buttermilk and sprinkle with the remaining 2 tablespoons sugar. Bake the biscuits until puffed high and colored light golden brown, a scant 5 to 7 minutes. Let cool.

4. To assemble the shortcakes, whip the cream with the vanilla until it forms soft peaks. Split each biscuit in half horizontally and lavish some strawberries over the bottom of the biscuit. Top with a generous dollop of whipped cream and then the other half of the biscuit. Serve and consume at once.

Makes 12 servings

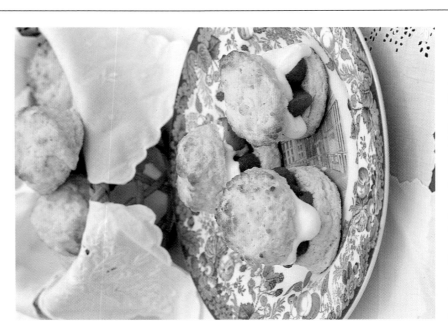

Strawberry Shortcake is a quintessential Down East summer dessert.

Doris Henderson's Strawberry Pie

Doris Henderson is the nearly nonagenarian aunt of food writer Nancy Harmon Jenkins. When Nancy learned that I was researching Maine cooking, she encouraged me to pay a visit to her aunt in Camden, whom she described as a terrific old-fashioned cook with file boxes of recipes and anecdotes to accompany them. I was not disappointed when I stopped in on Doris Henderson one unusually hot August afternoon as she and her eighty-two-year-old husband were busy packing for a two-week stay at their Canadian border summer camp, a wooded place with neither electricity nor plumbing.

As we sat in her kitchen eating freshly baked molasses cookies, Doris vividly recalled her childhood in Machias. Just as I had hoped, she had an ample collection of pie recipes dolloped with strong opinions. This strawberry pie is one of her personal favorites and is similar to the famous strawberry pie served at Helen's Restaurant in Machias. Don't be put off by the strawberry gelatin in the recipe, as Doris assured me that it is the secret to maintaining the bright red color in the filling. She is both wise and right.

Crust:

1 cup unbleached all-purpose flour
3/4 cup Crisco shortening
1/2 teaspoon salt
3 tablespoons sugar
2 tablespoons cornstarch, dissolved in 1/4 cup cold water
1/2 teaspoon salt
2 to 3 tablespoons ice water

Filling:

1 cup sugar
1/2 cup boiling water
1/2 teaspoon salt
1 1/2 quarts fresh strawberries, rinsed, hulled, and halved
1/2 teaspoon white or cider vinegar
2 cups lightly sweetened whipped cream, to garnish

1. To make the crust, combine flour, Crisco, sugar, and salt in a mixing bowl. Blend together with a pastry cutter until the mixture resembles coarse crumbs. Add the vinegar and enough ice water to hold the dough together. Shape into a disk, wrap in plastic wrap, and refrigerate for at least 1 hour.

2. Preheat the oven to 375°F.

3. On a lightly floured surface, roll out the dough into an 11-inch circle. Line a 9-inch pie dish with the dough; trim and crimp the edges decoratively. Line the pie shell with foil and fill with pie weights or dried beans. Bake the shell until light golden brown, 20 to 25 minutes. Remove the foil and weights and cool the shell completely.

4. Meanwhile, make the filling. Combine the sugar, boiling water, salt, and dissolved cornstarch in a saucepan. Bring to a boil over medium heat, stirring constantly, and cook until the mixture is thickened and clear, 5 to 6 minutes. Remove from heat, add the gelatin, stirring until dissolved. Combine the strawberries with the thickened mixture and then pour all into the baked pie shell. Refrigerate the pie until cold and set, at least 3 hours.

5. When ready to serve, cut the pie into wedges and top each serving liberally with whipped cream.

Serves 8

Prudence Sylvester's Blueberry Muffins

This recipe is among the most coveted of all our Maine recipes, for when we were children spending summers in Maine, Prudence Sylvester and her husband, Leon, symbolized the essence of all that was kind and good about the Vacation State. The Sylvesters ran a rural Gulf gas station, small general store, and message center situated next to their own house and between our parents' and grandparents' Blue Hill and Brooklin homes, and we found some reason or another to stop into Sylvester's every single morning. If we were lucky, a batch of these delicious muffins might have just emerged from the oven.

Muffins:

1 cup unbleached all-purpose flour

Wild Blueberry Pie

After a warm July or August day of plentiful wild blueberry picking, this pie is sure to be the unanimous choice for dessert. Mainers tend to be very particular about the simplicity of their wild blueberry pies and allow no more than a pinch of cinnamon and nutmeg to interfere with the fresh blueberry flavor. We personally like a smidgen of fresh lemon juice added to our filling, but such heresy is debatable among the natives. There is no disagreement, however, about topping this quintessential Maine pie with a scoop of pure vanilla ice cream.

Crust:

2 cups unbleached all-purpose flour
8 tablespoons (1 stick) unsalted butter, chilled and
    cut into small pieces
1/2 cup Crisco shortening
1/4 teaspoon salt
1/3 cup ice water

Filling:

4 1/2 cups fresh wild blueberries
2/3 cup granulated sugar
2 tablespoons unbleached all-purpose flour
1 tablespoon fresh lemon juice (optional)
1/2 to 1 teaspoon ground cinnamon
Pinch of grated nutmeg
1 tablespoon unsalted butter

---

1 cup regular oats
3/4 cup granulated sugar
1/2 teaspoon salt
3 teaspoons baking powder
1/2 teaspoon ground cinnamon
1 cup whole milk
3 tablespoons vegetable oil
1 egg
2 cups fresh Maine blueberries

Topping:

2 tablespoons granulated sugar
1/2 teaspoon ground cinnamon

1. Preheat oven to 425°F. Line 12 muffin cups with paper liners.

2. Combine flour, oats, sugar, salt, baking powder, and cinnamon in a mixing bowl. Make a well in the center and add the milk, vegetable oil, and egg. Mix together with a wooden spoon to make a smooth, thick batter, but do not overbeat. Gently fold in the blueberries.

3. Divide the muffin batter among the cups, filling each about three-fourths full. Combine the topping sugar and cinnamon and sprinkle over the top of each muffin. Bake until puffed and light golden brown, about 20 minutes. Serve hot, warm, or at room temperature.

Makes 12 muffins

HERRICK'S BLUEBERRIES

SIZE OF CAN . . . . . NO. 300
CONTENTS . . . . 14 OZ.

BLUEBERRY PIE

Drain juice from one No. 300 can blueberries. Sweeten berries to taste, add one tablespoon flour, 1/4 teaspoon salt and 1/2 cup juice. Line a 9 inch pie plate and put one tablespoon butter on crust. Turn in berries, sprinkle with cinnamon or nutmeg if desired, cover with top crust and bake in hot oven until crust is nicely browned.

BLUEBERRY MUFFINS

2 cups Cake Flour   3 teaspoons Baking Powder
2 Eggs   3/4 teaspoon Salt
3/4 cup Milk   1/3 cup Sugar
4 tablespoons Melted Butter

Fold into the batter 1 cup Blueberries, well drained and slightly floured. 1 Teaspoon grated orange or lemon rind optional. ALSO DELICIOUS FOR SHORTCAKES AND AS SAUCE FOR ICE-CREAM.

Herrick's Blueberries

PACKED IN LIGHT SYRUP

14 OZ. AVOIR.

CONTENTS

DISTRIBUTED BY

E. S. HERRICK, BROOKSVILLE, MAINE.

Evelyn's Blueberry Crumb Pie

Jonathan's wife, Evelyn, frequently tends to the dessert department at the restaurant. Her blueberry pie is a year-round favorite with customers since it may be successfully made with either fresh or frozen Maine blueberries.

Crust:

1 cup all-purpose unbleached flour
2 tablespoons sugar
1/3 cup margarine
2 to 3 tablespoons ice water

Filling:

4 1/2 cups fresh or frozen Maine blueberries
1/2 cup sugar
3 tablespoons tapioca
1 teaspoon ground cinnamon
1 tablespoon lemon juice

1. To make the crust, combine flour, butter, Crisco, and salt in a mixing bowl. Using a pastry cutter, blend the shortening into the flour until the mixture is the consistency of coarse meal. Add all the ice water and continue to work into a soft dough. Shape the dough into a flat disk, wrap in plastic wrap, and refrigerate at least 1 hour. (Alternatively, make the dough in a food processor by the usual machine method.)

2. Preheat the oven to 425°F.

3. Divide the pastry dough in half and roll one half out on a floured surface to fit into a 9-inch pie pan. Line the pan with dough, trimming the edges to fit.

4. In a mixing bowl, toss the blueberries with the sugar and flour to coat evenly. Stir in the lemon juice (if using), cinnamon, and nutmeg. Pile the filling into the pie shell. Dot the top with the tablespoon of butter cut into small pieces.

5. Roll out remaining half of the crust into an 11-inch circle. Place over the top of the pie and crimp the edges to seal the pie and make a decorative crust. Cut several slashes in the top of the pie with a sharp knife to serve as steam vents.

6. Bake the pie until the crust is golden brown and the filling is bubbling, 40 to 45 minutes. Note that this pie bakes at a relatively high temperature for a relatively short period of time. Serve the pie either warm or at room temperature. Be sure to top with a scoop of vanilla ice cream.

Makes 8 servings

This sign says it all when it comes to the Maine passion for pies.

Summer Blueberry and Raspberry Tart

Most of the recipes in this book stem from Maine cooks and time-honored traditions. This one is an exception in that I invented it one summer day to take advantage of blueberries that my mother had just picked and a superb crop of ripe raspberries in Jonathan's garden. The tart is a simple one and too good not to include. Make it only in the summer, when berries are in their prime, as the filling consists of an extravagant amount of both cooked and uncooked berries.

Hot-Water Crust:
3/4 cup unsalted margarine, cut into small pieces
1/4 cup boiling water
1 tablespoon milk
1 teaspoon salt
2 cups unbleached all-purpose flour

Filling:
1 1/2 pints fresh raspberries
2 pints fresh blueberries
1/2 cup sugar
3 tablespoons cornstarch
1/4 cup cold water
1/4 cup Cassis liqueur
1 tablespoon unsalted butter
Vanilla ice cream or whipped cream, to garnish

1. To make the crust, place the margarine in a small bowl and pour the boiling water over it. Stir until the margarine is melted and then blend in the milk and salt. Place the flour in a food processor fitted with the steel blade; with the machine running, pour the margarine mixture in a steady stream through the feed tube to make a ball of soft dough. Wrap the dough in plastic wrap and refrigerate for at least 1 hour.

2. Preheat the oven to 425°F. Roll out the dough on a lightly floured surface into a 12-inch circle. Fit the pastry into a 10- to 11-inch tart pan with a removable bottom. Trim and crimp the edges in a decorative fashion. Pierce the crust in several places with the tines of a fork and then line it with foil. Cover the foil with pie weights or dried beans and bake the crust until lightly browned all over, 15 to 17 minutes.

Evelyn's Blueberry Crumb Pie as served at Jonathan's Restaurant.

Topping:
1 cup unbleached all-purpose flour
1/2 cup oats
1/2 cup brown sugar, packed
1/2 cup margarine

1. To make the crust, mix the flour and sugar together. Cut in the margarine with a pastry cutter, blending until the mixture resembles fine crumbs. Add water until mixture just holds together. Form into a ball, cover with plastic wrap, and chill for at least 1/2 hour.

2. Preheat the oven to 350°F. On a floured surface, roll the dough out to 1/8 to 1/4 inch thick and place it in a 9-inch pie tin. Trim the edges.

3. Make the filling by blending together the blueberries, sugar, tapioca, cinnamon, and lemon juice. Pour the filling into the pie shell.

4. For the topping, mix together with your fingers the flour, oats, brown sugar, and margarine until well blended. Put this on top of the pie. You may have a little extra.

5. Bake the pie until the top is golden, 45 to 50 minutes. Remove from oven and cool slightly or serve at room temperature.

Makes one 9-inch pie

This industrious young boy has turned almost as blue as a blueberry after a hard and rewarding day of picking.

Remove the weights and foil; let cool.

3. In a small saucepan, mash together 1 cup each of the raspberries and blueberries. Sprinkle with the sugar. Stir together the cornstarch, water, and Cassis until smooth; pour over the berry blend. Bring the mixture to a boil, stirring constantly. Continue cooking for a few minutes more until the mixture is thickened and clear. Remove from the heat and swirl in the tablespoon of butter until melted.

4. Arrange half of the remaining uncooked berries over the bottom of the tart shell, using equal amounts of raspberries and blueberries. Cover evenly with the cooked mixture. Arrange the remaining uncooked berries over the top. Serve slightly warm or at room temperature with vanilla ice cream or whipped cream, if desired.

Serves 8

Fresh Raspberry Pie

Phyllis Schartner shared this simple yet elegant prize-winning pie recipe with us. The pie crust recipe from Doris Henderson's Strawberry Pie (see page 102) may be used for the prebaked pie shell or use your own favorite recipe. If the raspberries are nearing the end of the season and are especially juicy or mushy, add an extra tablespoon of cornstarch to compensate. This is one of summer's most opulent pies.

4 cups fresh raspberries
2 tablespoons cornstarch
1/4 cup cold water
1 cup sugar
1 prebaked 9-inch pie-pastry shell
Vanilla ice cream or whipped cream to garnish

1. Place 1 cup of the raspberries in a small saucepan and mash to a pulp. Dissolve the cornstarch in the water until smooth and add to the saucepan along with the sugar. Bring the mixture to a boil and then simmer, stirring constantly, until the mixture is thickened and clear, 4 to 5 minutes. Gently toss the fresh raspberries with the cooked mixture. Pile all into the prebaked pie shell and refrigerate until serving time.

2. Cut the pie into wedges and serve with a topping of ice cream or whipped cream.

Serves 6 to 8

Chapter Ten

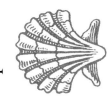

Country Fairs and Farmers' Markets

Anything can happen at a county agricultural fair. It is the perfect human occasion, the harvest of the fields and of the emotions. To the fair come the man and his cow, the boy and his girl, the wife and her green tomato pickle, each anticipating victory and the excitement of being separated from his money by familiar devices.

E. B. WHITE
"Fall"

IN DAYS when America existed as an agrarian society, an annual country fair marked the joyous culmination of the travails of the agricultural year. As with so many other rural traditions in Maine, country fairs still thrive Down East. Indeed, the Maine Department of Agriculture, Food and Rural Resources lists no fewer than twenty-four agricultural fairs on its seasonal schedule. The October Fryeburg Fair is the state's largest, and the August Skowhegan Fair is the oldest, having begun in 1818. Crowded attendance and rich history, however, stand as no guarantee to the power of these events to transport immediately and nostalgically the fairgoer back in time to a century or so ago.

The Blue Hill Fair, having just celebrated its hundredth anniversary, reports difficulty in surviving as an agricultural fair during an era in which so few farms are left. To beef up time-honored livestock exhibits and events, this fair must now merge entrants from as far away as Skowhegan and Fryeburg in the western part of the state with local,

coastal participants. The Bangor Fair, once one of the best and grandest of old-fashioned fairs, is at present more an outrage of fried-dough stands, insipid game concessions, suspicious-looking characters, and noisy neon rides.

Ironically, the most authentic, old-time country fair in Maine — the Common Ground Fair — is also the most progressive. Sponsored by the Maine Organic Farmers and Gardeners Association (MOFGA) and held on the Windsor fairgrounds during the third week in September, the fair was created well over a decade ago to provide counterculture back-to-the-landers with a special event in which to rejoice in alternative life-styles. Neither carnival rides nor cotton candy nor caffeine is allowed at the Common Ground Fair. In their stead are sheepshearing and fiddling contests, nitrate-free lamb sausages on whole-wheat buns, just-pressed gallons of cider, and natural beer- and wine-making supplies. When it comes to feasting, the Common Ground Fair law and goal has been to ensure that by 1992 all permissible foods come from produce, grain products, and oils that are certified organic and that meat and dairy products be free of artificial flavoring, color additives, chemical preservatives, and raised without medication or hormones. The caffeine issue has been a controversial one. MOFGA's position, nonetheless, remains firm with food coordinator Mario Pascarelli stating: "We don't permit caffeine. There's no chocolate and no decaf — even decaf has minute amounts of caffeine. We've been around and around on this and have had a lot of requests to relax our standards. Forget it. We're not going backward. Once you relax one standard, you relax more, and we want to upgrade and evolve our standards." We have noticed that many at the Common Ground Fair adjust amia-

Crowds revel in the truly old-fashioned flavor of the Common Ground Fair.

bly to this restriction by substituting another vice — cigarette smoking. While the mild hypocrisy of this has not been lost on those of us who can't function without our caffeine rushes, Pascarelli is the first to confess: "The Fair isn't perfect, and I'm not perfect either. But I like to think we're taking steps in the right direction."

One would think that such fervent fair guidelines might tend to confine general attendance to those committed to MOFGA's principles. However, simplicity seems to seduce those with more complex ways of life. A recent article in *Down East* magazine reported Common Ground Fairgoers to be 57,000 in 1990, and further noted sighting more "shiny" Mercedes and BMW's than battered VW buses in the parking lots." Since so many of the wonderful people and foods that are profiled in this book are to be found uniquely consolidated at the Common Ground Fair, we can't say that we are confounded by this widespread acceptance.

We can't imagine anyone not wanting to pay a visit to this event if only to savor a 'Stache Pulled Pork Sandwich, or a bushel of Herb and Phyllis Schartner's heirloom apples, or a tub of creamy Mystique goat cheese, or some of Smith's Log Smokehouse's beef jerky, or the spicy crunch of Spruce Bush Farm's dilly beans. Furthermore, entries by individual organic farmers in Exhibition Hall competitions for fruits and vegetables, flowers and herbs, and home-canned and home-baked goods are a visual treat. Homespun crafts — pottery, Abenaki Indian baskets, hand-loomed textiles — at the Common Ground Fair are similarly top-notch with over sev-

A copious and creative Grange exhibit at the Blue Hill Fair.
(Photo credit: Mark Lyon)

Country Fairs and Farmers' Markets

enty exhibitors, preselected by a jury on the basis of skill, quality, and ingenuity of product, housed in three tents.

If the Common Ground Fair sounds a bit too utopian, most other agricultural fairs in Maine offer a more middle ground. We are most familiar with our hometown Blue Hill Fair, held every Labor Day weekend. Although it has had to accept the blight of skyscraping rides and junk-food stands in order to sustain its agricultural heritage, the fair reveals the compromise to be a pretty good one. In 1891, a group of shareholders paying $10 apiece founded the first Blue Hill Fair Association. They set out to create a fair geared toward livestock and produce exhibitions, horse and harness racing, and the then current sports rage of baseball games. Maine Granges contributed a significant agricultural impetus from the

The baked beans at the Common Ground Fair are not to be missed.

start by encouraging their members to enter and display the pride of their home harvests in friendly competition. Early fairs also provided a social setting for members from many different area Granges to meet and exchange helpful tips and information.

Certainly a lot has changed since the turn of the century, yet we are delighted to report that, to this day, the Grange Harvest food display at the Blue Hill Fair is a breathtaking attraction. Fair management deserves some of the credit as it offers special premiums to farm organizations or individuals who enter mixed produce arrangements. Other food contests that carry on a bygone flavor include judgings for the best peck of potatoes or pint of berries, largest squash or pumpkin, most perfect plum or pear, and tastiest two-crusted blueberry pie and/or muffins. Since 1945, 4-H clubs have enthusiastically participated in vegetable, livestock, and craft exhibitions.

Many who look forward to the Blue Hill Fair these days do so for the harness races. Organizers have deliberately sought to keep the annual track event as folksy as possible by not allowing mechanical starting gates and by keeping prize purses to a minimal, two to five hundred dollars per race. A true Down East twist is imparted with the gift of a lobster to each owner who enters a horse in the races. Additional animal-related competitions at the fair include pulling events, which test how far either an ox or a workhorse can pull a set weight; pig scrambles, in which children are let loose in pens with the hope of beating opponents in the successful capture of wiggly, fleet-footed piglets; and sheep dog trials, which try a dog's ability to gather and control a flock of sheep.

Now, if only the Chevy Thunder Show with its pickup truck pyrotechnics, the latest draw at the hundredth anniversary of the Blue Hill Fair, could go the way of those disappearing farms. . . . Yet, as we have learned from our experiences at the Common Ground Fair, no fair is perfect.

Farmers' markets carry a small-scale experience of a country fair to many a township during Maine's fertile months, usually mid-May to mid-October. The extraordinary displays of vegetables and flowers by individual farmers are not created for competitive

The fresh produce at farmers' markets is not only unembellished but also irresistible.

meet the personality behind the produce or product.

Both country fairs and farmers' markets appeal foremost to the senses. We can't bring you the smell of chicken barbecuing at the Common Ground Fair, or the farmers' market feel of soft Angora wool from a rabbit, or the sound of sheep baaing during a shearing competition. We can nonetheless readily share photos from our overflowing albums along with the odd recipe re-creation.

Newly dug potatoes and fresh-cut flowers share table space at this farmers' market concession.

glamour viewing but for actual prodding, purchasing, and eating — and very good eating they are. Bath, Belfast, Blue Hill, and Brewer all play host to farmers' markets as do Camden and Caribou, Southwest Harbor and Waldoboro. All have varying dates, locations, times, and products. Such rain-or-shine improvisation is part of their charm.

A May trip to the Brewer Farmers' Market is likely to yield seedlings or pansy flats from Shoestring Farm or fiddleheads from a local forager, while a trip to the Damariscotta Market may bring a fresh-dressed spring chicken from Maine-ly Poultry or home-baked bread from Joanie's Cakes and Confections. Markets in July and August often convene more frequently, and the array of fresh vegetables, fruits, baked goods, cottage-industry foodstuffs, and handicrafts can be spectacular. This is the time to

Fresh Lemonade

We don't know of a country fair or outdoor summertime lobster festival or chicken barbecue that doesn't sport at least one fresh-lemonade stand. Here is how to bring that old-fashioned flavor home.

6 large lemons
1 large orange
½ cup superfine sugar (instant dissolving)
6 cups cold water
Ice cubes and fresh mint sprigs to garnish

1. Grate the zest from one of the lemons and set aside. Squeeze the juice from this lemon and four others. Squeeze the juice from the orange and combine with the lemon juice. Strain all through a sieve to remove the seeds and put the strained juice into a pitcher.

2. Combine the superfine sugar and grated lemon zest. Place in a food processor or blender and whiz together for 1 minute. Stir into the juice in the pitcher. Slice the remaining lemon and add with the water and stir well. Pour the lemonade into glasses filled with ice cubes and garnish each serving with a mint sprig.

Makes 4 to 6 servings

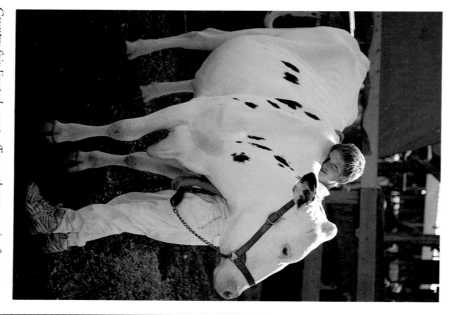

Country fair livestock events offer ample opportunity for young farmers to show pride in their animals. (Photo credit: Mark Lyon)

Wool dyeing, spinning, and knitting are popular pastimes for Maine homemakers. Blue Hill even boasts a Wednesday Spinners Club.

Doris Curtis's Squash Donuts

One aspect of country fairs that most visitors do not encounter is the bustling breakfast business that many of the food stands do for their fellow concession workers. Men who work the rides, livestock exhibitors, and just about anyone else involved with running a Maine country fair either pitch tents or live in campers for the duration of their stay. At 6 A.M., long before the gates open to the public, many of the food concessions equipped to handle breakfast will open for business. These squash donuts, served for years at Doris Curtis's food stand, keep weary fair workers coming back for more. Doris herself exemplifies typical Maine modesty by describing her delicious recipe as merely "a regular donut with a cup of squash mixed in."

1¼ cups granulated sugar
2 large eggs
2 tablespoons melted margarine
1 cup canned squash, preferably One-Pie brand
½ cup buttermilk
1½ teaspoons baking soda
1 teaspoon cream of tartar
1 teaspoon baking powder
½ teaspoon ground ginger
1 teaspoon nutmeg
⅛ teaspoon salt
4 cups unbleached all-purpose flour
2 tablespoons confectioners' sugar (optional)
Crisco, for frying

1. Mix the sugar, eggs, margarine, squash, and buttermilk together in a large bowl. Add the baking soda, cream of tartar, baking powder, ginger, nutmeg, salt, and flour. Mix well.

2. On a well-floured board, roll the dough out to a thickness of ½ inch, working in a little of the flour. With a 3- to 4-inch donut cutter, cut the donuts; you should be able to get about 2 dozen.

3. Using the manufacturer's instructions, fill a deep-fat fryer with the Crisco and heat to 360°F. Place the donuts in batches (4 to 6 at a time, making sure not to crowd them) in the fryer. Cook for 2 minutes. With a slotted spoon or spatula, turn the donuts and cook for 2 minutes longer. Remove the donuts from the fat and drain on paper bags or newspaper. Repeat the process until all the donuts are cooked. Dust with sifted confectioners' sugar, if desired.

Makes about 24 donuts

Wild Blueberry Tea Bread

Homemade tea breads in assorted flavors are frequently hawked at farmers' markets by entrepreneurs with small home-based businesses. Blueberry bread is always a popular choice, and our version is made extra moist by giving Maine's small wild berries a fortifying maceration in a bit of port or Bartlett Sweet Blueberry dessert wine. The combination of blueberries, wine, and walnuts in the bread begs for an accompanying side of fresh local goat cheese.

⅓ cup port or Bartlett Sweet Blueberry wine
1 pint fresh wild blueberries
¼ cup unsalted margarine
¾ cup sugar
1 egg
⅓ cup milk
1¾ cups unbleached all-purpose flour
½ teaspoon salt
2½ teaspoons baking powder
1 teaspoon ground cinnamon
¾ cup coarsely chopped walnuts

1. Combine the port with the blueberries in a small mixing bowl and toss well. Let stand for 15 minutes.

2. Preheat the oven to 350°F. Lightly grease and flour a 9 × 5-inch loaf pan and set aside.

3. With an electric mixer, cream together the margarine and sugar until smooth and fluffy. Beat in the egg and then the milk. Sift together the flour, salt, baking powder, and cinnamon; stir into the creamed mixture to make a thick and smooth batter. Gently fold in the blueberries, port, and walnuts. Turn the batter into the prepared loaf pan.

4. Bake the bread until a toothpick inserted in the center comes out clean, about 1 hour. Cool the bread in the pan for 10 minutes, invert onto a rack, and cool completely. Refrigerate the bread before serving for easier slicing.

Makes 1 loaf

Pulled Pork Sandwich with Maple Barbecue Sauce

Every year Stewart Blackburn entraps hungry fairgoers at the Common Ground Country Fair in Windsor with the intoxicating aromas of sliced pork butt simmering in large kettles with his own "intrepid" Maple Barbecue Sauce over a pit of fiery coals. Three bucks will get you a delicious sandwich and probably send you back again to the end of a long line of people waiting to indulge in this unique rendition of Maine barbecue. Grab plenty of napkins and avoid wearing your favorite tie. We recommend spiking the sauce with a bottle of Geary's Ale for a little extra flavor.

1 5-pound pork butt
2 cups 'Stache's Maple Barbecue Sauce (available in stores and markets that feature Maine products and many specialty food stores nationwide)
1 12-ounce bottle Geary's Ale (optional)
12 large, fresh bakery hard rolls, split

1. In a domed cooker, make a fire for cooking with indirect heat according to the manufacturer's instructions. Roast the pork butt in the cooker with the vents halfway open to achieve an internal temperature of 170°F, about 2 hours. Remove the pork from the cooker and allow to cool for 30 minutes.

2. Cut the pork into 2-inch-thick chunks. Place the pork in a large pot or kettle and cover with the barbecue sauce. Simmer over low heat until the pork shreds easily, 30 to 35 minutes. If the sauce becomes too thick, add a cup or two of water or a bottle Geary's Ale, if using.

3. Spoon the pork generously onto the bottom halves of the rolls, sandwich together with the top halves, and serve at once.

Makes 12 overflowing sandwiches

Barbecued Chicken

Mainers have a uniquely straightforward way of barbecuing chicken so that it, as they like to say, "tastes like itself." Heavy and sweet tomato-based sauces are taboo Down East, where a simple baste of one part cider vinegar, one part water, to one-half part vegetable oil reigns supreme and aromatic. Maine chicken is honestly delicious, and during summer months outdoor chicken barbecues are second in popularity only to lobster bakes. This is the time-honored formula that satisfies at country fairs and public food events across the state.

1 cup cider vinegar
1 cup water
½ cup vegetable oil
Salt and freshly ground black pepper, to taste
2 broiler-fryers (2½ pounds each), quartered

Country fairs and juicy barbecued chickens are synonymous.

115

Country Fairs and Farmers' Markets

1. Whisk together the vinegar, water, and oil. Season with salt and pepper. Arrange chicken in a single layer in a shallow, nonmetallic dish and cover with the marinade. Let stand 1 hour.

2. Meanwhile, prepare a barbecue for grilling. When the charcoal has turned gray, drain the chicken from the marinade and place skin side up several inches above the heat. Turn the chicken pieces every 6 to 8 minutes, basting the side that is up with the reserved marinade at each turning. The chicken should take 50 minutes to 1 hour to cook completely. It may be served hot off the grill, at room temperature, or cold for picnics.

Serves 4 to 6

Pineland Farm Blue Ribbon Pottsfield Relish

This variation of a family recipe handed down through several generations was a blue ribbon winner at the 1991 Common Ground Country Fair. Since their move to midcoast Maine in 1987, Rebecca and David Waddell have been growing and canning their own vegetables at Pineland Farm in Waldoboro. In 1990 they started entering their creations in local country fairs. After you taste Pottsfield Relish it's easy to understand why Rebecca and David are having trouble keeping track of the number of blue ribbons they have snagged in these friendly competitions.

Base:
6 cups finely chopped green tomatoes
6 cups finely chopped firm red tomatoes
6 cups shredded and then finely chopped green cabbage
6 medium onions, finely chopped
3 large red bell peppers, finely chopped
1 orange bell pepper, finely chopped

10 celery stalks, finely chopped
1/2 cup mustard seeds
1/2 cup salt

Syrup:
6 cups vinegar
6 cups sugar
1/2 teaspoon ground cloves
1/2 teaspoon cinnamon

1. On the day before you plan to make the relish, place the green and red tomatoes, cabbage, onions, red and orange peppers, celery, mustard seeds, and salt in a large stockpot and cover with ice water. Keep the vegetables submersed by weighting them down with a plate. Cover the pot and store in a cool place for 18 to 24 hours.

2. The next day, drain the vegetables thoroughly. Press out the excess liquid.

3. In a stockpot combine all the syrup ingredients and bring to a boil over high heat. Add the drained vegetables, reduce the heat, and simmer for 40 minutes.

4. Pack 6 1-quart canning jars, leaving 1/4 inch head room. Seal and process for 10 minutes in a boiling water bath.

Makes 6 quarts

Chapter Eleven

Autumn Fruits and Vegetables

You couldn't start with a better season in Maine. For practically everything is coming to ripeness and readiness then. This is the time the law goes off deer and duck, off smelts and wild geese, and Summer tourists. . . . Of course, cranberries and crab apples are growing red in the marsh and along the woods, to add their spicy jellies and color to the meat. . . . Potatoes are bursting up through the hills. Apples thunder from trees. . . . The smokehouse is full. And the year runneth over.

ROBERT P. TRISTRAM COFFIN
Mainstays of Maine

AUTUMN in New England has been romanticized for centuries. But, of all the New England states, we think autumn is best in Maine. To the bonfire colors of the rest of New England, Maine adds the backdrop bonus of a spectacular coastline whose waters turn a shade of blue intense enough to compete with the deepest crimson of a neighboring blueberry barren, richest golden birch tree, or most incendiary maple. Think of those male birds of most vibrant plume, such as cardinals and peacocks, and you'll begin to have a metaphor for the colors of Maine in September and October. Autumn, there can be no doubt, is dress season Down East.

Out of this ripeness of landscape comes a truly outstanding bounty of autumn fruits and vegetables. We are reminded of lines from a Robert Frost poem — "And who's to say where / The harvest shall stop?" — as we find ourselves surprisingly eager to

Phyllis Schartner on her tractor during a rare moment of repose.

trade the sunny softness of a vine-ripened tomato for the juicy crackle of the first orchard apple of the season. Our appetites and anticipation become all the more stirred as we venture out on a roller-coaster drive through farm-laden countryside to pay a sea-

117

An exquisite harvest of autumn fruits from Schartners' Mountain View Farm in rural Thorndike.

sonal visit to the lush orchards of Herb and Phyllis Schartner in Thorndike.

The Schartners married in Massachusetts a dozen or so years ago and five years later bought their Maine farm and moved to Thorndike so Phyllis could be closer to her native Canada. As we pulled into their hilltop driveway one idyllic September day, we caught a glimpse of Phyllis on her tractor barreling up between orchard rows at at least 30 miles an hour to greet us. We could immediately understand (a) how Phyllis could have been a beauty queen and

model during her teenage years and (b) how deserving she and Herb were of having been named the Maine State Grange Family of the Year in 1990. Herb stuck steadily to his work while Phyllis led us on an exuberant tour through fruit-filled orchards as tempting to us as imagined visions of the Garden of Eden.

We were soon to discover that Phyllis's passion for what she grows is equaled by her love of heirloom varieties of fruits. As we roamed, more common apples such as McIntoshes, Cortlands, and Macouns were busily being picked by friends of the Schartners

118
Saltwater Seasonings

for shipment to England. Crab apple orchards had been planted to border these, Phyllis explained, to allow for the cross-pollination of breeds so vital to sustaining healthy apple development. But it was as we crossed the street that divides the farm that Phyllis's knowledge of apple varieties really shone. Apples were originally native to Europe and Asia, and the first apple seeds were brought to America by the Pilgrims in 1620. Apples were a favorite food of the Colonists because they were tasty, versatile, and lasted through long, cold winters. By 1800, there were over a hundred American-bred varieties, and it is these early breeds that captured the attention of Phyllis Schartner. A source of pride and joy is her Tolman Sweet tree, well over a hundred years old and still bearing its large, acid-free golden apples originally developed for people with special dietary needs. One test bite from a dropped Tolman Sweet encouraged Phyllis to sing the praises of many another forgotten apple: "Spitzenburgs, Thomas Jefferson's favorite apple; Chenango Strawberries, from the seventeen hundreds; Wolf Rivers, the best baking apples; Northern Spys, the apples highest in vitamin C; Dutchess of Oldenburgs, Pippins, and Rhode Island Greenings," and so on down the staggering list.

Apples, however, are not the only fruit in the Schartners' orchards. There are also trees bearing pears and plums aplenty, and the juiciest white peaches we have ever tasted. When not hawking her crops at the Common Ground Fair or the Brewer Farmers' Market, or working the acres of land on their farm, Phyllis is most likely to be found concocting batches of homemade jams, jellies, and pickles. Everything from apples to elderberries to mint leaves and zucchini seems to be fair game for Phyllis's creative efforts.

All farmers we encounter at this time of year seem to be similarly industrious in finding ways to savor the autumn windfall. Much of their activity is spurred on by the race against the first killing frost. Will it come as early as the harvest moon toward the end of September, or will it be kind enough to hold off until Columbus Day? Summer berry picking mania is easily transferable to apples as many orchards across the state open in mid-September for weekends of family picking. There are apple pies to

be baked and country fair contests to be entered. An October visit down Cape Rosier way is likely to find organic gardener Stanley Joseph either fashioning a wacky, Tibetan-style small boat known as a coracle from homegrown willow shoots or making sauerkraut from the year's cabbage harvest. Wife Lynn Karlin is apt to be engaged in making dried wreaths from assorted pods, herbs, and flowers or baking pies from pumpkin pulp scooped out in the process of making jack-o'-lanterns. Up the road, in South Brooksville, Stan and Lynn's friend and neighbor Tom Hoey will probably be gearing up to press hard cider now that he's taken the leap of making his Sow's Ear Winery into a small, commercial enterprise.

Jonathan and I like to join in the frenzied fun by shifting our culinary gears toward fall's new crops and root vegetables. Jonathan can't wait to combine a gift of some of Phyllis Schartner's apple butter with coppery sliced rutabagas, and I am eager to cook with parsnips, Brussels sprouts, and winter squashes. We also both crave the comfort we know is lurking within the new crop of Maine potatoes. Potatoes, however, have presented a dilemma for us in the context of this book because we have tried to limit our food coverage to within a thirty-mile radius of the Maine coast in a state that never ceases to amaze us with its distances. Yet we know that we cannot possibly ignore that 95 percent of Maine's potatoes are grown inland in faraway and humongous Aroostook County. This is not to say that there are not lots of gentlemen farmers who grow coastal potatoes on their saltwater farms, but their crops are literally "small potatoes" compared to what goes on up in Aroostook. Curiosity convinced me to make the four-hour trek from home base in Blue Hill to Presque Isle in the heart of Aroostook County.

As I departed at dawn, my mother staggered from her bed to bid me farewell with the sort of kiss one would plant on a loved one embarking on a grueling adventure to the North Pole or an Amazonian rain forest. I drove and drove and drove through the mists of this gray day until I at long last arrived at my destination. "The County," as Mainers like to call this 6,400-square-mile area, is utterly beautiful with cultivated fields stretching as far as the eye can see. Were it not for the architecture of the farmhouses

Mainers always grow plenty of pumpkins for pies and jack-o'-lanterns.

and the omnipresent potato chip trucks on the road, I would have thought that I had been transplanted deep into the remotest parts of rural France. Even in the rain, the colors of the fall foliage were stunning, and it was easy to imagine the pinks of potato blossom time in July to be just as gorgeous.

I headed directly for the Maine Potato Board on Main Street in Presque Isle, as their secretary had promised to hook me up with some local potato growers. What I had heard about The County became immediately evident — life and conversation in Aroostook does indeed center around one thing: the past, present, and future of potatoes. At the Potato Board, however, I soon learned that this had not always been the case. The first potato had been planted in The County in June of 1807, a good fifty years after Scotch-Irish settlers had brought potatoes

with them to Maine. For several years potatoes were grown only for home consumption, livestock feed, and bartering purposes. In 1862, the seeds of change were sown when a potato prophecy by "S" appeared in the *Maine Farmer* stating: "Of all the places in Maine where potatoes will pay best, Aroostook will excel as soon as it shall have railroads." The railroads arrived during the decade of 1870–1880 and the potato industry flourished as predicted thereafter. Today, Maine ranks third, after Idaho and Washington, in total potato production in the United States. Come autumn, Aroostook remains the only county in the nation where children can be excused from school to help with the potato harvest.

In another life or another cookbook, we could devote a whole fat chapter to the riches of potato farming in Aroostook. But we must content our-

Butternut Squash and Cider Soup

Root cellars were important to surviving long winters in New England before the days of mass transportation and twenty-four-hour supermarkets. Rural Mainers still retain a great fondness for these sustaining crops, and this autumn soup is a simple yet alluring marriage of two harvest favorites — vine-matured, golden butternut squash and fresh, locally pressed cider.

The accompanying Walnut and Cheddar Crisps tap into the Colonial practice of pairing soups with bite-size savories and, of course, celebrate that great Yankee flavor combination of apples with sharp Cheddar cheese.

5 tablespoons unsalted butter
1 large onion, minced
1 tablespoon caraway seeds
1 large butternut squash (3½ to 4 pounds), peeled, seeded, and cut into 1-inch chunks
6 cups sweet cider
Salt and freshly ground pepper, to taste

1. Melt butter over medium heat in a large stockpot. Add the onion and caraway seeds and sauté until the onion is quite soft, about 10 minutes. Add the squash, cider, and water to the pot. Bring to a boil and simmer uncovered until the squash is very tender, about 45 minutes.

2. Purée the soup in batches in a blender until smooth. Return to a clean pot and season to taste with salt and pepper. Serve hot, ladled into bowls and surrounded by several Walnut and Cheddar Crisps. The soup can also be made ahead and reheated.

Serves 6 to 8

Label alone is likely to sell Tom Hoey's Normandy-style hard cider.

selves here with this brief overview, because just as "the year runneth over" in autumn, so, too, do the recipes in this chapter. We know when it is time to trade the pen for the pot and switch from prose on the page to productivity in the kitchen.

Walnut and Cheddar Crisps

1/2 cup (1 stick) unsalted butter at room temperature
2 cups grated sharp Cheddar cheese
1 tablespoon cream sherry
1 1/2 teaspoons baking powder
1/4 teaspoon pumpkin pie spice
1/4 teaspoon salt
1 1/4 cups unbleached all-purpose flour
1 egg, beaten with 1 tablespoon water
1 cup finely chopped walnuts

1. Using an electric mixer, beat the butter and Cheddar together until well combined. Beat in the sherry. Add the baking powder, pumpkin pie spice, salt, and flour and stir to form a moderately stiff dough. Shape dough into a disk, wrap in plastic wrap, and refrigerate for at least 2 hours.

2. Preheat oven to 375°F.

3. Cut the dough into quarters and roll each quarter out into an 8-inch circle on a lightly floured surface. Brush each circle generously all over with the beaten egg and water. Sprinkle the walnuts evenly over the top of each pastry circle. Press into the surface of the dough by rolling over lightly with a rolling pin. Cut each circle with a sharp knife or pastry wheel into 12 triangular wedges.

4. Place the wedges slightly apart on lightly greased cookie sheets. Bake until light golden and crisp, 8 to 10 minutes. Transfer to a rack to cool and serve at room temperature.

Makes 4 dozen crisps

Parsnip Stew

Having spent the past decade breathlessly striving to keep abreast of the New York-to-California food world's fickle fads, I never cease to be amazed by how fantastic old-fashioned, straightforward Yankee food can be. Parsnip Stew was originally invented as a poor man's chowder, but I think it tastes like a sophisticated lady's private passion.

In New England, parsnips are usually dug just after the first frost, but Mainers take special pride in letting a portion of their crop hibernate snug in the ground throughout the long, cold winters. Those that survive are called "spring-dug," and they are super-sweet and flavorful. No matter what the season, this simple stew or soup is a winner.

1/4-pound piece salt pork
2 tablespoons unsalted butter
1 medium onion, minced
1 pound parsnips, peeled and cut into 1/2-inch chunks
1 pound Maine potatoes, peeled and cut into 1/2-inch chunks
5 cups water
2 cups milk or half-and-half
Freshly ground pepper, to taste
Paprika to garnish

1. Place the salt pork in a small saucepan, cover with water, bring to a boil, and simmer for 5 minutes. Drain. Cut the salt pork into a 1/4-inch dice.

2. In a medium-size stockpot, melt butter over medium heat. Add the diced salt pork and cook until lightly brown but not quite crisp, 5 to 6 minutes. Add the onion and sauté for 5 minutes more.

3. Add parsnips, potatoes, and water to the pot. Bring to a boil and then simmer uncovered until the vegetables are tender, 25 to 30 minutes. Blend in the milk and season to taste with pepper. Let the stew mellow or age off the heat for at least 1/2 hour. Return to low heat to reheat. Serve hot, ladled into soup bowls and topped with a sprinkling of paprika.

Serves 6

1. Bring a large pot of water to a boil and blanch the Brussels sprouts just until crisp-tender, about 6 minutes. Drain in a colander.

2. Meanwhile, brown the bacon in a large skillet over medium-high heat. When the bacon is crisp, remove from the skillet with a slotted spatula and drain on paper towels. Add the vinegar and maple syrup to the hot fat in the skillet, taking care to stand back, as the mixture may sputter. Add the Brussels sprouts to the skillet and stir to coat with the sauce. Season with freshly ground black pepper. Return the crisped bacon bits to the skillet, stirring to distribute evenly. Serve at once.

Serves 6 to 8

Waldorf Salad

A good, freshly made Waldorf salad is too often a forgotten taste. This is how chef Alan Dodge makes his at the popular and scenic Le Garage Restaurant in Wiscasset. To keep the salad crunchy, it is prepared half an hour before the lunch rush to accompany all omelets on Le Garage's menu.

6 Macoun or Granny Smith apples, cored and cut into ½-inch chunks
2 tablespoons fresh lemon juice
4 stalks celery, diced
¾ cup dark raisins
¾ cup coarsely chopped walnuts
¾ to 1 cup mayonnaise, preferably Hellmann's

Toss the apple chunks with the lemon juice in a large mixing bowl. Mix in the celery, raisins, and walnuts. Add enough mayonnaise to moistly bind the salad together. Serve at once or store in the refrigerator for no more than 3 hours for best flavor results.

Makes 6 servings

Baked Rutabaga with Onion and Apple Butter

We sweeten a satisfying autumn combination of golden rutabaga slices and caramelized onions with our friend Phyllis Schartner's fruity apple butter. We recommend it as an accompaniment to a sputtering pork roast or the Thanksgiving turkey.

5 tablespoons unsalted butter
1 large onion, peeled, halved, and thinly sliced
1 rutabaga (2 to 2½ pounds), peeled, quartered, and thinly sliced
4 tablespoons apple butter (see Phyllis Schartner's recipe on page 147)
3 tablespoons cider vinegar
1 cup Bartlett Coastal White wine, or substitute sweet apple cider
Salt and freshly ground pepper, to taste

1. Preheat oven to 350°F. Butter a 1½-quart casserole dish.

Sweet and Sour Brussels Sprouts

It is no secret that Mainers take a strong fancy to both pies and pickles. This recipe for autumn Brussels sprouts attests to Mainers' love for sweet-and-sour flavors.

1½ pounds Brussels sprouts, trimmed and cut with an X on the bottom
4 strips bacon, cut into a small dice
2 tablespoons cider vinegar
2 tablespoons maple syrup
Freshly ground black pepper, to taste

Recently unearthed rutabagas look foreboding before being tamed by peeling, slicing, and baking with a baste of sweet apple butter.

2. In a large skillet, heat 3 tablespoons of the butter over medium-low heat. Add the onion and sauté, stirring frequently, until the onion begins to turn a pale golden color, about 20 minutes.

3. Meanwhile, bring a large pot of lightly salted water to a boil and blanch the rutabaga slices until they are almost crisp-tender, 8 to 10 minutes. Drain and set aside.

4. Add the apple butter, vinegar, and wine (or cider) to the onions in the skillet, stirring until blended. Increase heat to medium-high and let the mixture reduce by a third, 5 to 7 minutes.

5. To assemble the dish, use a slotted spoon to place a thin layer of the onion mixture over the bottom of the casserole dish. Follow with a thin layer of rutabaga slices, seasoning lightly with salt and pepper. Repeat the process several times, ending with a layer of rutabagas on top. Pour any liquid remaining in the skillet over the top of the casserole and dot with the remaining 2 tablespoons of butter. Cover the dish with aluminum foil and bake until the rutabagas are quite tender, about 40 minutes. Serve hot.

Serves 8 to 10

Golden Potatoes

Basic mashed potatoes take on a lovely autumn hue when combined with boiled carrots. Sometimes turnip or rutabaga is used in place of carrots.

6 large Maine potatoes, peeled and cut into coarse chunks
1 pound carrots, peeled and cut into 1-inch pieces
6 tablespoons unsalted butter, at room temperature
3/4 cup milk or half-and-half
Salt and freshly ground pepper, to taste
Pinch of ground nutmeg

1. Place the potatoes and carrots in separate pots, cover with water, and boil each until very tender. Drain thoroughly.

2. Combine the hot potatoes and carrots in a large mixing bowl. Using a potato masher or a hand-held electric mixer, beat the vegetables until smooth and well combined. Work in the butter and milk. Season to taste with salt, pepper, and nutmeg. Serve at once.

Makes 8 to 10 hearty servings

Potatoes and white enamel pots are Maine staples. These potatoes take on a harvest hue by being mashed with boiled carrots.

Maine Potato Stovies

Many think that the name for this popular dish came from its stovetop preparation, but it actually is the name of a peasant dish brought to America by Scottish and English settlers. Helen Nearing, Maine's first lady of vegetarianism, included a recipe for stovies in her cookbook, *Simple Food for the Good Life*, which eliminated the customary salt pork base. We, however, continue to side with those who view salt pork and bacon fat as the backbone of traditional Maine cooking.

¼ pound salt pork, cut into a ¼-inch dice
2 medium onions, peeled and thinly sliced
4 large Maine potatoes, peeled and thinly sliced
1 cup water
Salt and freshly ground pepper, to taste

1. Place the diced salt pork in a large skillet and cook over medium heat until lightly browned but not quite crisp. Add the onions and sauté until limp, 5 to 6 minutes.

2. Add the potatoes to the skillet and toss to coat with the onions and fat. Pour in the water, season with salt and pepper, and cover the skillet. Simmer over medium-low heat until the potatoes are tender and most of the water has evaporated, 35 to 40 minutes. Check the potatoes from time to time to see if more water is needed to prevent sticking to the bottom of the pan. Serve the stovies hot as a side dish to roasted meats.

Serves 6

The Best Two-Crusted Apple Pie in the State of Maine

Yes, Maine does sponsor a Two-Crusted Apple Pie Competition, which has been held at the Annual Agricultural Trade Show in Augusta for the past five years. The rules are simple yet serious: the pie must have two crusts made from scratch, the filling must be made with Maine apples, and the recipe must be accurately written and displayed in front of the pie during the judging. The recipe that follows won the competition in 1990 and belongs to Laurie Jones of Livermore Falls, who has been baking pies for over twenty years. Laurie learned her apple pie recipe from her mother who, in turn, learned it from her mother.

We tested the recipe (at Jonathan's Restaurant) on an audience who unanimously agreed with the judges from Augusta. I made one slight alteration by sprinkling a few tablespoons of sugar over the top of the pie crust for the sake of final appearance and crunchy taste and was immediately admonished for the affectation by an old-time Mainer.

Hints from winner Laurie Jones include working the shortening evenly into the flour with a minimum of strokes and mixing the ice water as quickly as possible into the flour-shortening mixture. For apples, Laurie likes to use McIntosh drops, which she gathers from a local orchard.

Crust:

2 cups unbleached all-purpose flour
⅔ cup plus 2 tablespoons Crisco shortening
Pinch of salt
6 to 8 tablespoons ice water

Filling:

6 cups peeled and thinly sliced apples, preferably
    Maine McIntosh
1 cup granulated sugar
1 tablespoon unbleached all-purpose flour
½ teaspoon cinnamon
½ teaspoon nutmeg
1 tablespoon unsalted butter

Topping:

2 tablespoons milk
2 tablespoons granulated sugar (optional)

1. Preheat oven to 425°F.
2. To make the crust, in a mixing bowl blend the

A quintet of Laurie Jones's award-winning apple pies.

flour, Crisco, and salt together with a pastry cutter until the mixture resembles coarse meal. Add water and toss with a fork until the flour is moistened and forms small peas. Gather half the pastry into a ball and roll out into an 11-inch circle on a floured surface. Transfer to a 9-inch pie pan and trim overhanging edges of pastry ½ inch from rim of pan.

3. For the filling, combine apples, sugar, flour, cinnamon, and nutmeg in a large mixing bowl. Toss until the apples are well coated and then mound into the pie shell. Dot the top of the pie with the tablespoon of butter cut into small bits.

4. Roll out the other half of the pastry into a thin circle. Place over the apple filling and trim edges to 1 inch from the rim. Fold and roll the top edge of pastry under the lower edge of the rim to seal. Pinch edges to crimp decoratively. Lightly sprinkle the milk and sugar (if using) on the top crust and cut several

slits with a sharp paring knife in the crust to let steam escape.

5. Bake the pie until the crust is golden brown, 35 to 40 minutes. Serve warm or at room temperature.

Makes 8 servings

Bean Pot Poached Pears.

Bean Pot Poached Pears

A bean pot is a staple of most Maine kitchens, and this recipe for poached pears is a good one to keep handy when a simple yet elegant dessert is in order. Depending on menu and mood, we use either fruity Bartlett Coastal White or Coastal Red for the poaching liquid. A few pungent slices of York Hill's Capriano goat cheese will offer a lovely contrast and accompaniment.

2 cups Bartlett Coastal White or Coastal Red wine
1/2 cup granulated sugar
2 tablespoons fresh lemon juice
2 teaspoons minced fresh ginger
8 whole cloves
1 cinnamon stick
8 firm but beginning to ripen Bartlett, Anjou, or
    Bosc pears, peeled and left whole
1 1/2 tablespoons cornstarch dissolved in 1 1/2 tablespoons
    cold water

1. Preheat oven to 350°F.

2. Pour white or red wine into a 2-quart bean pot or casserole dish. Stir in the sugar, lemon juice, ginger, cloves, and cinnamon stick. Immerse the pears in the liquid and cover the pot.

3. Bake the pears, turning in the liquid from time to time, until tender but not mushy, about 45 minutes. Using a slotted spoon, remove pears to a serving platter and arrange upright.

4. Strain the poaching liquid into a clean saucepan. Stir in the dissolved cornstarch and bring to a boil over medium-high heat, stirring constantly. Continue cooking until the liquid is clear and thickened, 4 to 5 minutes. Spoon the thickened sauce over the pears. Serve warm or at room temperature.

Makes 8 servings

Hale-and-hardy Black Angus cows sniff the salt air at pictur-esque Wolfe's Neck Farm in Freeport.

Chapter Twelve

Maine Meat

Over the years a great many of our Maine recipes have commenced, "Try out a piece of salt pork." It's an old-fashioned expression and we don't use it as much now. We are more apt to say, "Melt margarine. . . ." For one thing, we use less animal fat but, fondly, we recall that salt pork was the backbone of Maine cooking. You just couldn't get along without salt pork. You needed it for frying purposes but especially you needed it for flavor.

MARJORIE STANDISH
Cooking Down East

BY NOW it should come as no surprise that recipe after recipe in cookbook after cookbook on Maine food calls for the use of salt pork in one way or another. The rural isolation, the climate, and the thriftiness inherent in the character of a typical Down Easter made raising a pig almost obligatory in earlier times, for the pig was the main source of meat for families facing a long and unrelenting winter. Salt pork was, and still is, one of the benefits enjoyed by those who continue with this yearly practice. Before modern transportation, good roads, electricity, and refrigeration made their way to these parts, salt curing, brining, smoking, and canning were the options available to preserving the precious protein of the pig for the long cold months. To this day, raising a pig is still commonplace among Mainers. Jonathan did it a few years back with the help of a friendly neighbor (a native, of course), lots of plate scraps from his restaurant, and surplus vegetables from his garden.

The meat of a homegrown pig, that being several notches

above store-bought pork; the flavor is more concentrated, the fat more aromatic and intense when melted, and the bacon free of the artificial taste infused by nitrates and other preservatives. Natives continue to use salt pork in many a recipe, from fish chowders to the larding of lean roasts of wild venison.

For those not inclined to raise their own animals for meat, a little searching can uncover many sources of locally raised meat products. It is not uncommon for roadside vegetable stands to have a freezer tucked away in a barn holding an array of homegrown meat cuts. A perusal of the classifieds of local newspapers or *Uncle Henry's* (a folksy "swap and sell" weekly) can lead one to just about any kind of homegrown meat produced in the area. Organically raised lamb or mutton will have a wild or attractively "gamey" taste to it. We find it sublime eating when slowly roasted on the bone in a dome cooker with native green alder branches, an addition that our grandfather often used to enhance the flavor of meat cooked outdoors. Maple-cured bacon, smoked using the proprietor's own secret formula, can elevate a BLT to new heights.

Fresh rabbit meat, though nowhere to be found in the grocery stores, is readily available from independent farms. There is even an Eastern Maine Rabbit Breeders Association. Although most of the rabbits raised Down East are either for show or wool, an increasing number are being raised for dining pleasure. The meat itself is all white, very lean, and of very high nutritional value; it lends itself to braising or grilling and can be substituted for chicken in many recipes.

We have found that the best and most alluring products are those raised in an organic fashion.

A woolly, wintertime scene at Horsepower Farm.

Indeed, organically raised, range-fed chickens and turkeys have a taste and intensity of flavor to which mass-produced brand-name products cannot hold a candle. So superior is the taste that growers of these birds begin to take orders for Thanksgiving turkeys from exhibit booths at country fairs come late summer. Others will sell their stock directly to friends and perennial customers without any advertising at all.

Other feathered friends are also to be found along the coast. Jim and Laurie Olmstead, proprietors of Foggy Ridge Gamebird Farm in Warren, have for several years raised a variety of game birds — partridge, pheasant, quail, chukar, and duck, to name a few. From the incubation to the butchering and in some cases freezing stage, the Olmsteads run a tight operation, which when all is said and done does not appear to yield a particularly lucrative living. Nevertheless, that personal dedication exhibited so often

by so many of the other enterprising people we encounter is at once evident at Foggy Ridge. Jim moved to Maine from Virginia as a teenager and began raising his first birds for sentimental reasons — he missed the southern sounds of bobwhite quail singing. While we're not sure if this was the sole inspiration for the birth of Foggy Ridge Gamebird Farm, Jim maintains that it played a major part. The Olmsteads' brochure emphatically states that birds at Foggy Ridge are grown "with the dignity they deserve." This means that they do not live in little stalls or coops, nor are they force-fed grain laden with antibiotics and growth hormones; rather, these lucky birds spend their time in vast flight pens that cover incredibly scenic acres surrounding a modest poultry barn. This existence allows the birds to exercise and forage freely and with a minimum of stress. The result is tastier cooked poultry with an "unmanufactured" flavor. The majority of the Olm-

Foggy Ridge's bird pen offers lots of room for the birds to spread their wings and an incomparable view.

Jim Olmstead holds a young pheasant at his Foggy Ridge Gamebird Farm.

steads' birds are sold to restaurants and gourmet shops; they can also be ordered directly from the farm, and a good portion find their way to preservation at nearby Kohn's Smokehouse.

More than passing mention is due Wolfe's Neck Farm in Freeport. Wolfe's Neck Farm was the original brainchild of a couple who came to Maine in the late 1950s in search of a way to produce organically raised quality beef using ecologically responsible methods. Our first visit to Wolfe's Neck was in mid-March of 1991, and Jonathan and I were immediately taken with everything that went on at this exquisite coastal promontory. The farm superintendent was Dave Degrandpre, a gentle man devoted to the mission he had inherited. We arrived mid-morning and

131

had to wait for Dave to meet us for our interview, for he was busily assisting in the birthing of several calves. Upon seeing these newborns — mere minutes after their arrival into the serene surroundings of Wolfe's Neck — we both were astounded by the adept coordination exhibited by calves that had been still in the womb when we began our journey from Blue Hill that morning. We were touched by the genuine affection that Dave and other farm employees show their bovine charges.

Wolfe's Neck Farm stretches over six hundred acres and has an average herd of three hundred head of Black Angus beef cattle, one hundred of which are brood cows. It has been a forerunner in the implementation of technological improvements, including being the first beef farm in the state of Maine to use large rolled hay bales and "cafeteria" feeding. Wolfe's Neck Farm also pioneered the use of newspaper bedding in animal stalls, which has proved to be an ecologically sound way to recycle paper fiber. The farm, having been given to the University of Southern Maine in 1985, now recycles all the newspaper from the university campus. The animals themselves, in compliance with the guidelines and requirements of organic farming, eat no hay that has been grown with chemical fertilizers, receive no artificial growth hormones or antibiotics, and exist in an environment that is deemed to be less stressful than nonorganic alternatives. The expansive grazing fields overlooking Casco Bay provide the animals with what Dave has described as "the best view on the farm." Cattle health and happiness can best be gauged by noting that the only veterinarian bills on the farm are for pregnancy and birth-related problems.

The approach at Wolfe's Neck is void of "barnyard blindness," a term Dave used to describe traditional beef farming where it is the norm to accept old practices rather than to try new ways. It is the willingness to experiment and innovate using organic and ecologically safe practices that will keep Wolfe's Neck Farm true to the mission set forth by its founders for years to come.

The organic beef from the farm is a bit leaner than typical choice or prime USDA beef, and it has a slightly darker color than that in the meat case of a local supermarket. It also has a tendency to cook a bit faster than nonorganic beef. All Wolfe's Neck

beef is flash-frozen and wrapped in white freezer paper — an ecologically responsible alternative to the use of plastic Cryovac packaging. The products are sold from freezers on premise and available for purchase by restaurants and home cooks alike.

On a return visit to Wolfe's Neck in early May, we were deeply saddened to learn of the untimely, accidental death of Dave Degrandpre. We shall not forget his generosity to us or his enthusiastic devotion to a praiseworthy mission.

Although we have thus far focused on domesticated animals that are either commercially bred or homegrown, we cannot ignore that which is wild and hunted, namely, the white-tailed deer. In days gone by it was the barren winters that would coax hunters into the woods in pursuit of deer because, as with the pig, this was a source of meat that could sustain a family for many months. These days, hunting is more sport, and, as controversial as it has become in recent years, it is a tradition firmly entrenched in the lives of Mainers. "Get your deer yet?" is one of the most frequently posed questions during the three-week hunting season that commences in early November and ends on or around Thanksgiving.

The usually lean deer meat needs the extra-special culinary care required of all game. The aversion that many game neophytes have to venison stems from the improper handling, aging, and cooking of the meat.

Any large animal, such as the pig, lamb, or steer, will offer several cuts of meat that will demand different types of preparation. When the animal is wild, as is the case with the white-tailed deer, the texture of the meat will vary depending on the size and age of the animal and the environs from which it has been snatched. Recipes for canned venison mincemeat are more common in older Maine cookbooks primarily because freezers were not considered a necessity in the early days of this century; now, however, the tough shoulder cuts that would have been spiced for mincemeat are more commonly ground into "venisonburger" and customarily frozen in small packages to be consumed as convenient. Roasts tend to be quite lean and require larding with, as one might guess, salt pork. We have included two of our own venison recipes, one for a long-simmering chili made from chunky stew meat and another for a slowly braised sauerbraten whose marinating process begins at least two days before it is a finished dish.

Meat is undoubtedly important in the diets of Mainers. While it is true that health concerns have resulted in lower consumption of red meat, and there are certainly more and more vegetarians Down East than years ago, one pass through Moody's Diner in Waldoboro at "supper" time will show that "meat and potatoes" is still king among the natives. Every seat, be it counter or booth space, is apt to be taken by locals enjoying such standbys as pot roast and gravy, meatloaf and mashed potatoes, liver and onions, or, naturally, a big and hearty New England boiled dinner. Coffin, to be sure, knew whereof he spoke when he stated: "Maine men are built on the square, and ride rolling decks well, because they and their ancestors have eaten square meals for three hundred years. A Maine man expects to rise five pounds heavier and handsomer, five pounds more independent and self-possessed, when he gets up from the table."

Roasted Loin of Pork

Pea contest winner and pig farmer Lawris Closson roasts ovensful of pork loins for frequent dinners held at local Oddfellows Halls. Lawris says that the key to keeping the meat moist is to roast it at a low temperature for a relatively long time. Buttery mashed potatoes are Lawris's favorite accompaniment to this succulent roast.

1 pork loin, butt end, 4 to 5 pounds, boned, rolled, and tied
1 stick margarine, melted
Salt and freshly ground black pepper, to taste
1 large onion, sliced

1. Preheat the oven to 275°F. Place the pork loin on a large sheet of heavy-duty aluminum foil. Brush the loin with half of the margarine. Season the roast with salt and cracked pepper. Place the onions around and on top of the pork.

2. Loosely wrap the meat, making sure, however, that it is sealed. Place the meat on a baking sheet and roast for 2 hours.

3. Increase the oven heat to 375°. Remove the meat from the oven and loosen the foil so the top of the meat is exposed, being careful not to spill the juices that have accumulated around the pork. Baste the pork with the remaining margarine. Return the meat to the oven and roast for an additional 15 minutes or until the top of the roast begins to brown.

4. Remove the meat from the oven and transfer it to a platter. Pour the juices and onion slices over the meat. Allow the meat to sit for 10 minutes before carving into slices ½ inch thick. Serve at once.

Makes 6 to 8 servings

Smothered Pheasant

When we asked Foggy Ridge's Jim Olmstead his favorite way of enjoying the fruits of his labor, he raved over his wife's recipe for pheasant smothered with sour cream, onions, and paprika. Taking his cue, we revamped our family recipe for paprika-rich Hungarian chicken to accommodate the long cooking time required for Jim's feisty free-range pheasants. We bake our Smothered Pheasant until the meat is literally falling off the bone.

3 pheasants (2 to 2½ pounds each), quartered
½ cup flour
4 tablespoons best-quality paprika

This paprika-colored enamel pot is perfect for slow simmering paprika-laced Smothered Pheasant to falling-off-the-bone tenderness.

Salt and freshly ground pepper, to taste
3 tablespoons unsalted butter or margarine
3 tablespoons vegetable oil
2 cloves garlic, minced
2 medium onions, thinly sliced
1 pound mushrooms, wiped clean and sliced
2 teaspoons dried marjoram
2 to 3 cups Bartlett Coastal White or other dry white wine
1 cup sour cream
1/2 cup minced fresh parsley

1. Dredge the pheasant quarters in the flour mixed with 2 tablespoons of the paprika and some salt and pepper. Heat the butter and oil together over medium-high heat in a large Dutch oven or other large ovenproof casserole. Brown the pheasant pieces in batches until all are seared on all sides. Remove to a platter.

2. Preheat the oven to 325°F.

3. Add the garlic and onion to the fat and crispy bits remaining in the Dutch oven and sauté for 5 minutes. Add the mushrooms and continue to cook, stirring frequently, for another 10 minutes. Stir in the remaining 2 tablespoons paprika and the marjoram. Pour in 2 cups of the wine and return the pheasant to the pot. Cover the pot tightly and transfer to the oven.

4. Bake for 3 hours, adding more wine if the casserole seems too dry at any point. Remove the pheasant from the pot and keep warm on a covered platter. Gently mix the sour cream into the liquid and vegetables in the Dutch oven. Taste for seasoning, adjusting if necessary, and then return the pheasant to the pot to coat with the sauce. Serve at once with buttered egg noodles and sprinkle each portion generously with parsley.

Serves 6 to 8

Drunken Rabbit with Maple Barbecue Sauce

Maine has an active Rabbit Breeders' Association, and the number of small rabbitries in the state seems to be — well — multiplying like rabbits! Farm-raised rabbit is tender and delicate, unlike tough and stringy wild rabbit. Rabbit is nutritious, low in cholesterol, and we think irresistible when soused with Geary's Ale and 'Stache's Maple Barbecue Sauce.

Rub and Marinade:
2 rabbits (2 to 2½ pounds each), cleaned and cut into serving pieces
4 cloves garlic, coarsely chopped
2 tablespoons dried thyme
2 tablespoons dried rosemary
2 teaspoons dry mustard
2 teaspoons salt
1/2 cup olive oil
1/2 cup cider vinegar
2 bottles (12 ounces each) ale, preferably Geary's

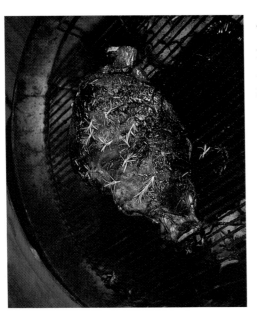

Jonathan infuses a hefty local leg of mutton with the rich and dark smoke of green alder twigs.

Sauce and Finishing:
3 cups bottled barbecue sauce, preferably 'Stache's Maple Barbecue Sauce
1 large onion, peeled, halved, and thinly sliced
Salt and pepper, to taste

1. On the day before you plan to serve the rabbit, place rabbit in a large stainless-steel or glass bowl and toss with the garlic, thyme, rosemary, salt, and mustard. Let stand 2 to 3 hours in the refrigerator.

2. Combine the olive oil, vinegar, and ale; pour over the rabbit, and let marinate in the refrigerator overnight. Turn the rabbit pieces occasionally.

3. The next day, preheat the oven to 350°F. Drain the rabbit pieces from the marinade, and arrange them in a single layer in a large roasting pan.

4. Place the reserved marinade in a saucepan, bring to a boil over high heat, and cook until reduced by a third, 12 to 15 minutes. Add the barbecue sauce and onion and bring back to a low boil. Pour the sauce evenly over the rabbit in the roasting pan.

5. Cover the roasting pan tightly with aluminum foil and bake until the rabbit is tender, about 1 to 1¼ hours. Serve at once.

Makes 6 servings

Alder-Smoked Leg of Mutton

For years our family has frequently smoked whole turkeys over coals in an outdoor dome cooker with outstanding results. Jonathan has adapted the same method to cooking large legs of lamb and mutton. The addition of green alder twigs, a technique our grandfather used when cooking steaks over an open fire, imparts a subtle flavoring that is most complementary to the strong flavor of the mutton.

1 bottle (750 ml) Bartlett Nouveau Blueberry or other light, fruity red wine
½ cup cider vinegar
3 tablespoons lightly chopped fresh rosemary
1 tablespoon coarsely chopped fresh parsley, stems included
1 large onion, halved and thinly sliced
½ cup lightly chopped celery leaves
1 medium head of garlic, peeled and coarsely chopped
1 teaspoon salt
½ teaspoon freshly ground pepper
2 tablespoons Dijon-style mustard
1 cup olive oil
1 leg of mutton, 8 to 10 pounds, bone in
Sprigs of fresh rosemary for garnish

1. Place all the ingredients except the olive oil and mutton in a large bowl and mix thoroughly. Stirring with a wire whisk, slowly pour in the olive oil. Place the mutton in a large nonreactive dish. Pour the marinade over the mutton. Marinate for 8 hours or more, turning the mutton several times.

2. Prepare an outdoor dome cooker for smoking according to the manufacturer's instructions. When cooker is ready, remove mutton from marinade and place it on the center of the grilling grate inside the cooker. Reserve marinade. Insert 8 or 10 small alder twigs through the grate handles on each side directly onto the coals. Cover the cooker and smoke the mutton for 1 hour.

135

Maine Meat

3. After 1 hour repeat the process of adding alder twigs. Pour 1 cup of reserved marinade over the mutton, cover the cooker, and smoke for 1 more hour. Repeat this process one last time and smoke for ½ hour longer, or until a meat thermometer registers between 130° and 140°F when inserted into the center of the meat close to the bone. Discard remaining marinade.

4. Remove mutton from grill and place it on a carving board or platter. Cover loosely with a foil tent and let it rest for 10 minutes. Slice the meat rather thinly on an angle and spoon the juices that have collected on the bottom of the platter over the meat. Serve at once, garnished with rosemary sprigs.

Makes 10 to 12 servings

Yankee Pot Roast

In 1972, the Lady Editors of *Yankee* magazine compiled the cookbook *Favorite New England Recipes* and included a lengthy story about the pot roast served at a Maine rest-and-refreshment stop called Half-Way House. The generous use of seasonings in Half-Way House's recipe intrigued us enough to use it as the inspiration for our own version of this most satisfying of Yankee meat dishes.

1 4-pound pot roast, preferably chuck or bottom round
1 teaspoon salt
Flour to coat the meat evenly
4 tablespoons unsalted butter
2 cloves garlic, crushed
1 large onion, sliced
12 whole black peppercorns
2 teaspoons ground allspice
1 teaspoon whole fennel seeds
1 bay leaf, crumbled
1 tablespoon prepared horseradish

¾ cup dry red wine
1 cup water
1 rutabaga, peeled and cut into chunks
1 pound carrots, peeled and cut diagonally into 1-inch chunks
2 tablespoons chopped fresh dill

1. Rub the meat with salt and flour to coat evenly. Melt the butter in a large skillet over medium heat. Add the garlic and sauté for 2 minutes, lowering the heat if necessary so the butter does not brown. Add the meat to the skillet and gently brown on all sides. This will take about 10 minutes.

2. Lay the onions on the bottom of a Dutch oven or any large pot with a tight-fitting lid. Place the browned meat on top of the onions. Add the butter, garlic, and juices that have accumulated in the skillet. Add the peppercorns, allspice, fennel seeds, bay leaf, horseradish, wine, and water. Bring the liquid to a simmer and then reduce the heat to very low. Cover tightly and cook for 2 hours or, alternatively, braise the pot roast in a 275°F oven for the same amount of time.

3. Remove the lid from the pot and add the rutabaga and carrots. Add a little more water to the pot if necessary. Return to heat, cover, and cook for 45 minutes longer. Remove from heat and transfer the roast to a large platter. Slice the meat diagonally across the grain. Surround the meat with the vegetables from the pot and pour the liquid over the meat. Garnish generously with chopped fresh dill and serve.

Makes 6 to 8 servings

Venison Sauerbraten

A lean rump roast marinated for days in Bartlett Nouveau Blueberry and select spices gives a unique Maine twist to a recipe for classic German sauerbraten — a type of pot roast in a sweet-and-sour sauce thickened with crushed gingersnaps. Serve our rendition on a bone-chilling night with more blueberry wine and boiled Aroostook County potatoes.

Marinade and Meat:

1 bottle (750 ml) Bartlett Nouveau Blueberry wine, or substitute French Beaujolais or California Gamay
2 cups water
2 cups cider vinegar
1 large onion, peeled, halved, and thinly sliced
24 juniper berries, lightly crushed
24 black peppercorns
6 bay leaves
1 tablespoon salt
1 teaspoon dried thyme
3 cloves garlic, peeled and halved
1 venison rump or top round roast, 4 to 5 pounds

Cooking Ingredients:

½ cup plus 3 tablespoons unbleached all-purpose flour
6 slices bacon, cut into ¼-inch dice
2 tablespoons vegetable oil
2 cups diced onions
2 cups peeled and diced carrots
1 cup diced celery
2 cups water
¾ cup crushed gingersnap crumbs
Salt and freshly ground black pepper, to taste

1. At least 2 days in advance, prepare the marinade. Place all the marinade ingredients in a nonreactive pot and bring to a boil. Remove from heat and cool to room temperature.

2. Place venison in a deep ceramic crock or stainless-steel pot just large enough to hold it comfortably. Pour the marinade over the meat and turn to moisten all sides. Cover, place in the refrigerator, and marinate 2 to 4 days; turn the meat at least once a day.

3. When ready to cook the sauerbraten, preheat oven to 350°F. Remove the venison from the marinade, reserving the marinade, and pat the meat dry. Dust the meat with ½ cup of the flour, shaking off any excess.

4. Heat a large skillet over medium heat and sauté the bacon just until the fat has been rendered. Add the vegetable oil and brown the venison evenly on all sides, taking care not to let the fat burn. The browning should take about 20 minutes. Then transfer the meat to a Dutch oven. Pour off and reserve the fat from the skillet. Deglaze the skillet with ½ cup of the marinade, being sure to scrape up any brown bits clinging to the bottom of the pan, and pour over the roast in the Dutch oven.

5. Return 3 tablespoons of the reserved fat to the skillet and heat over medium-high heat. Add the onion, carrot, and celery; sauté until softened, about 5 minutes. Sprinkle in the remaining 3 tablespoons of flour and continue cooking and stirring until the flour begins to brown, 3 to 4 minutes. Add all the reserved marinade to the skillet and bring to a boil. Pour contents over the venison, cover, and roast in the oven for 2½ hours.

6. Remove the roast from the Dutch oven and keep warm. Strain the cooking liquid through a sieve, pressing down hard on the vegetables to extract as much flavor as possible. Discard the pulp and skim the fat off the remaining liquid.

7. Place strained liquid in a saucepan with 2 cups of water. Bring to a boil and slowly stir in the gingersnap crumbs. Reduce heat to low and cook, stirring constantly, until the sauce is quite thick, 10 to 15 minutes. Season to taste with salt and pepper.

8. To serve the sauerbraten, carve the meat into ½-inch-thick slices, arrange on a platter, and nap with half of the sauce. Put the remaining sauce in a gravy boat and pass at the table. Serve at once.

Serves 8 to 10

Practical pig farmer and colorful character Lanris Closson.

Venison Chili

Maine's big-game hunting season takes place in the fall with well demarcated seasons for deer, black bear, and moose. Deer are most plentiful, and it is not unusual for successful hunters to share part of their bounty with relatives and neighbors. Jonathan was the happy recipient of a care package of tender venison, which inspired this Maine-style chili. We think it tastes best after a vigorous day of cross-country skiing in Acadia National Park. Ice-cold cider or extra Geary's Ale afoam in a frosty mug are welcome thirst quenchers.

In our opinion, chili should always be made in a big pot and in quantity. This recipe is no exception with a hefty yield of 24 servings. Why not plan a party!

6 cups dried red kidney or soldier beans
4 strips bacon, cut into a ¼-inch dice
2 tablespoons vegetable oil
2 large onions, coarsely chopped
6 cloves garlic, minced
2 cups coarsely chopped celery stalks
2 green or red (or a combination) bell peppers, seeded and diced
1 tablespoon dried thyme
2 tablespoons fennel seeds
1 tablespoon cumin seeds
2 teaspoons hot red-pepper flakes
2 tablespoons chili powder
2 tablespoons ground cumin
1 teaspoon dry mustard
3 pounds venison top round, cut into ¼-inch cubes
4 bottles (12 ounces each) ale, preferably Geary's
2 cups bottled barbecue sauce, preferably 'Stache's Maple Barbecue Sauce
16 cups water
2 cinnamon sticks
2 cans (28 ounces each) whole tomatoes, undrained
Salt to taste
Sour cream to garnish

1. The day before, place the beans in a large bowl and cover amply with cold water. Let soak overnight. Drain the next day and set aside.

2. In a large pot, sauté the bacon over low heat until the fat has been rendered. Add the vegetable oil and then the onion, garlic, celery, peppers, thyme, fennel, and cumin seeds. Sauté until the vegetables begin to soften, about 5 minutes.

We can't think of a better way to fortify body and soul after an invigorating day of cross-country skiing than with a hearty bowl of Venison Chili and a frosty bottle of Geary's Ale.

3. Add the red-pepper flakes, chili powder, cumin, and mustard to the pot and increase the heat to medium high. Cook, stirring constantly, until the spices become very aromatic and begin sticking to the bottom of the pot, about 5 minutes. Add all the venison and toss continuously with the vegetables and spices until the meat loses its deep red color, about another 5 minutes.

4. Add the ale, barbecue sauce, and water to the pot. Stir in the reserved beans and the cinnamon sticks. Bring the chili to a boil and then reduce to a simmer. Cook, uncovered, stirring occasionally, for 2½ hours. Add the canned tomatoes and continue simmering until the beans are very tender and the venison meat begins to shred, another hour or so. Season the chili to taste with salt.

5. Serve the chili piping hot in shallow soup bowls or crocks. Garnish each serving with a generous dollop of sour cream.

Makes 24 servings

139

Maine Meat

Goats graze in an idyllic setting at the Seal Cove Farm.

Chapter Thirteen

Cottage Industries

IN THE dictionary, cottage industry is defined as the production, for sale, of goods at home, as the making of handicrafts and foodstuffs by rural families. When that *home* is the exquisite coast of Maine, it becomes a cinch to understand why there are so many cottage industries burgeoning Down East. Indeed, it is the beauty of place that first strikes a customer at Morse's Sauerkraut or Seal Cove Goat Cheese Farm, followed by the enticement of discovering a unique, quality food product. These days Maine boasts rural, home-based industries ranging from apiaries and breweries to seaweed harvesters, Shaker herb farms, and water-powered organic grain mills.

One of the oldest cottage industries in all of New England is the R. B. Swan & Son honey company in Brewer, Maine. Reginald Swan and his son, Harold, began packing honey in 1942, and Harold's handsome son, Richard, is at the helm of the family business today. Honey is actually the by-product of a more important role performed by the bees — crop pollination. Since the widespread use of insecticides over the last thirty years has eliminated many of the state's native pollinating insects, growers must now import thousands of migratory bees, with the bulk of the hives coming to Maine from Florida. R. B. Swan & Son is one of the largest beekeepers in the state, tending to approximately 1700 hives. Beekeeping season begins in May in both blueberry barrens and apple orchards. As the season progresses, the bees will be moved to pollinate wild raspberry bushes that take hold in clearings left by loggers, buckwheat

crops in the northerly potato-growing county of Aroostook, and late summer's wildflowers statewide. The significance of such transience has not been lost on those of us researching this book, as many are the times that we personally felt as if we were traveling on the same circuit as the honeybees. Such fertile country is Maine!

Richard Swan drives the bees from their hives in order to collect their warm, wild-raspberry honey.

141

We caught up with Richard Swan one bright and sunny July day when he was out gathering raspberry honey from hives close to home in Brewer. In this particular instance the hives had not been hired out for crop cultivation purposes, but placed in an open field in exchange for supplying the owner of the land with a share of the resulting honey. We watched with guarded fascination as Richard drove the bees from their pastel hives with a combination of pine-needle smoke and a stinky ointment, appropriately named "Bee-go," smeared on wooden palettes. Once the bees had cleared out and the honey emerged, we couldn't resist throwing caution to the wind by succumbing to the tempting offer of sticking our fingers right into the comb to taste the oozing, warm honey within.

Beekeeping operations require a vast number of wooden boxes and frames to serve as bee housekeeping units, along with trucks and forklifts to transport the hives and buildings to house equipment and processing paraphernalia. In a company as large as that of R. B. Swan, the initial capital investment can run as high as $100,000. Then there is that ever-ominous bane of unpredictable weather to take into consideration. Maine's chilly climate does not normally allow bees to gather enough nectar for the excess honey they need to survive a harsh winter. Most Maine beekeepers therefore supply their hives with extra honey. Additionally, the image of a big black bear frolicking next to a beehive is much more than just a quaint illustration Down East; it is a frightful reality. The Swans once lost eight hundred pounds of honey and twenty hives to bears in a scant two-week period. It is little wonder that black bear hunting is still a popular sport in Maine.

Swan's honey is invitingly packaged in hexagonal jars with hand-painted labels designed by a local artist. Wild Blueberry and Wild Raspberry are the most sought-after flavors in the line, although the Summer Wildflower Nectar and dark, heavy-bodied Buckwheat Honey also have their loyal followings. Back-to-the-landers with their strict adherence to using natural foods make honey cookery popular in Maine. As back-to-the-kitchen authors, we have included two favorite honey recipes in this chapter.

A cottage industry that is much more recent in its Down East origins than beekeeping is making goat cheese. Over the last fifteen years, we have witnessed near herds of goat cheese producers appearing on the scene. Marjie Lupien, owner of Mystique Goat Farm in Waldoboro, started making goat cheese with eight goats and a Home Food Manufacturing License fifteen years ago, "before it was chic." She learned the craft from nuns in Canada and translated their instructions from French to English. The name of the operation stems from the owner's belief that goats are mysterious creatures. The goats at Mystique are Nubian, the only dual-purpose (milk and meat) breed of dairy goat, and they produce milk for ten months of the year. From the beginning, Marjie has displayed a gifted hand for the often grueling and temperamental task of transforming raw milk into creamy goat cheese. Mystique's goat feta has amassed raves at the American Cheese Awards, and the goat cheese disks bottled in peppered olive oil once won the prestigious California Goat Cheese Association Award. Despite such national acclaim, Marjie Lupien remains a firm disciple of the "small is beautiful" school of thought. Mystique goat cheese is sold only through local farmers' markets, the Common Ground Fair, and in five retail stores between Rockport and Wiscasset. Marjie, in fact, believes that "it is bad luck to stray too far from the coast." No problem, as Jonathan and I don't mind a couple of hours of coastal driving for the reward of getting our hands on the most exceptionally smooth feta we've

A few of the many varieties of Swan's Honey.

We are convinced that the most picturesque goat cheese farm in all of Maine is that of Seal Cove on Mount Desert Island. Owner Barbara Brooks moved from Boston to Maine in 1973 to be with her true love. She and her husband bought their farm on Seal Cove and started pastoral life first with a chicken and pig. They next purchased a goat, and it was that goat that really stirred something in Barbara. To this day she claims that it is her love for goats rather than their cheese that keeps her in the business. Finding that "goats are nice and friendly, and they don't eat as much as a cow" has inspired Barbara to develop a scientific and genetic fascination with her herd. Today Seal Cove Farm resembles a scene from a Swiss fairy tale as all of the goats there are healthy Swiss breeds — a combination of Alpine, Toggenburg, and Saanen.

If Barbara had her choice, she would rather sell goat's milk than goat's cheese, but she has resigned herself to the fact that the market is currently in cheese. She learned how to make goat cheese by taking courses in Canada and by apprenticing with Camilla Stege in Dixmont, a woman who was a true pioneer in Maine goat cheese making. Seal Cove sells both fresh chèvre and goat feta at local farmers' markets. Barbara admits that she finds the feta trickier to master than the chèvre but that she persists "because

Baby diapers are used to drain whey from curds in the goat-cheese-making process at Seal Cove. Here, freshly laundered ones bob along with delphiniums in the ocean breeze.

Seal Cove goat cheese maker Barbara Brooks proudly displays a tray of soft and fresh chèvre destined for discriminating palates at the country French restaurant Le Domaine.

ever tasted or a tub of Mystique's unique Orange Goat Cheese Spread, which we enjoy as a topping on Deer Isle Gingerbread or Wild Blueberry Tea Bread.

We are equally fond of the goat cheeses made inland at York Hill Farm in New Sharon. Owners Penny and John Duncan were lured into the field by a desire to work at an economically viable rural enterprise. Furthermore, the couple has found that "the meshing of the science and art of cheesemaking offers an endlessly fascinating and rewarding pursuit." York Hill makes the usual array of fresh goat cheeses with flavor options of pepper and herbs, but it is the unusual aged Capriano — a sort of texture and taste cross between pungent Cheddar and good imported Parmesan — that really excites our palates.

143

Cottage Industries

A handsome red barn dominates the lovely landscape surrounding Morse's Sauerkraut business in Waldoboro.

Julia Child happened to stop by the farm last summer and she encouraged me to keep making it."

Another cottage industry with a pungent product and picturesque setting is Morse's Sauerkraut on rural Route 220 in North Waldoboro. Waldoboro was originally settled by German immigrants, and the first sauerkraut business was begun there in 1918 by Virgil Morse. The business stayed in the family until 1988, when retired U. S. Navy Commander Thomas (Tom) D. Cockroft purchased it. Morse's farm is dominated by a splendid red barn surrounded by forty acres of cabbage fields. Pumpkins are often planted as an alternate crop to the cabbages as they are known to restore nitrogen to the soil. We visited Morse's on a perfect October day when both pumpkin harvesting and sauerkraut making were in full swing. One thing that makes Morse's Sauerkraut so good is that all the cabbage is still cored by hand before being shredded, brined, and packed into barrels in which it is aged by being weighted down by large rocks beachcombed from Maine's jagged coastline. Tom says that he can make three to five barrels of sauerkraut a day. Since taking over the business, he and his wife, Rebecca, have expanded the product line to include tangy Aunt Lydia's Beet Relish and spicy Cabbage Fever Reliever.

In addition to cabbage-based creations, the shop at Morse's Sauerkraut Farm sells a wealth of Maine-

made food products, local produce, and prepared German-style sandwiches and baked beans. In fact, Tom reports that 80 percent of the people that travel to Morse's on any given Saturday come to eat sauerkraut and baked beans.

Not too far from Waldoboro, down Damariscotta way, in a little seaside alcove known as Hockomock Hollow, resides William Stewart Blackburn, a colorful and erudite character who runs Maine's most worldly and academically informed cottage industry, 'Stache Foods. Blackburn's concoctions run the gamut from locally inspired Loud's Island Tomato Conserve and Valhalla Maple Barbecue Sauce to incendiary Jamaican Jerk Slather, Nirvana Pistachio Green Goddess Dressing, Krakatoa Satay Sauce, and Xanadu Cashew Ginger Sauce. 'Stache Foods was started in 1985 and named for the owner's trademark, flamboyant auburn-colored handlebar mustache. After graduating from Bowdoin College, Blackburn found that an interest in food was literally

Tom Cockroft packs freshly shredded cabbage into barrels for curing into pungent sauerkraut.

Phyllis Schartner's colorful assortment of the preserved fruits of her labor.

kindled when he began to cook the wild mushrooms he was supposed to be studying on a fellowship in New Zealand over a campfire for fellow biology field-mates. Once back stateside, Blackburn pursued cooking, gleaning French polish from courses at the California Culinary Academy and honing grilling skills during a stint working in Alaska at a salmon-bake restaurant renowned for its nightly feasts of pit-grilled foods to feed a thousand.

It is not surprising, then, that the catering of grilled events has developed into a compatible component to Blackburn's bottled sauce sorcery. When I ran my food shop on Nantucket, I couldn't keep 'Stache's Maple Barbecue Sauce on the shelves, and recipes within these pages for Crab Louis, Drunken Rabbit, Pulled Pork Sandwiches, and Venison Chili are all improved by the addition of 'Stache's ingenious sauce.

We can't end a discussion of Maine cottage industry before giving brief mention to the many who put up dilly beans and fruit preserves. Dilly beans are a Down East favorite, and we think the best ones are bottled in North Whitefield at Spruce Bush Farm in owner Ellis Percy's sugar shack. Percy also raises Registered Red Wattle hogs, makes sausages, and jars dark amber maple syrup. But it is the special balance of seasonings in the pickled beans — garlic, fennel seeds, hot red-pepper flakes, and dill, of course — that makes a trip deep into the backroads of Lincoln County to Spruce Bush truly worth the time and effort. Ellis Percy is no fool, and he wasn't about to share the secret and successful dilly bean recipe with us, so we are humbly offering our approximation as inspired by Percy's product. To obtain the real McCoy, look for Spruce Bush Farm's Dilly Beans at the annual Common Ground Fair and in selected midcoast food stores.

Maine's native bounty of summer berries and autumn fruits induces a fury of preserving in the making of jams, jellies, and chutneys. Whistling Wings Farm in Biddeford, Downeast Delicacies in Kennebunkport, and Nervous Nellie's on Deer Isle are but a few of these sweet and savory cottage industries. Lots of individual growers put up their own fruits on a small and sporadic scale to be sold at farmers' markets and roadside stands. Phyllis Schartner was kind enough to share with us her

apple butter recipe, which she simmers from McIntoshes or Macouns from her Thorndike orchards. This apple butter is the key to Jonathan's rutabaga recipe in the "Autumn Fruits and Vegetables" chapter and always nice on a piece of morning toast.

The individuals we have met behind Maine's thriving cottage industries all seem to be intent on going to extra lengths to make their foodstuffs out of the ordinary; such dedication readily inspires us to drive the extra Maine mile to seek them out.

Toast o' Maine

We read about this treat in Allene White's (E. B. White's daughter-in-law) food column, "Mutual Benefit," which appears weekly in the *Ellsworth American.* She had sampled it at the Full Circle Fair in Blue Hill, where it was the talk of the fair. While delighted customers weren't quite sure what combination of ingredients made Toast o' Maine so irresistible, Allene's sleuthing revealed it to be a French toast type of sandwich of heavy-textured whole-wheat bread, soft cream cheese, and Maine honey. Here is our recipe taken from the mouth-watering description in Allene's column.

If you are at all like us, you may prefer to confine the honey to the sandwich's interior, though the original Toast o' Maine was served with a honey syrup over the top to further saturate the bread.

4 slices homemade-quality, hearty whole-wheat or oatmeal bread
⅔ cup whipped cream cheese, softened
2 tablespoons honey, preferably from Maine
1 egg
½ cup whole milk
½ teaspoon vanilla
1 tablespoon each butter and margarine
Additional honey and whipped butter for serving, if desired

1. Spread ⅓ cup cream cheese evenly over each of 2 slices of bread. Drizzle a tablespoon of honey over each and top with the remaining 2 slices of bread.

2. In a shallow dish, such as a pie plate, whisk together the eggs, milk, and vanilla until well blended. Dip the sandwiches in the egg mixture, turning once, to saturate both sides.

3. Melt the butter and margarine together in a large skillet or griddle over medium heat. Brown the sandwiches well on both sides, taking care not to burn. Slice the sandwiches in half on the diagonal and serve at once, gilding the lily further with a topping of more honey and butter, if desired.

Makes 2 servings

Honey-Roasted Onions

Bees are kept busy in Maine beginning with the pollination of the blueberry barrens in May. Come summer there are plenty of raspberry bushes and fields of wildflowers to visit. The by-product is a thriving cottage industry of apiaries and honey bottlers. A favorite use for Maine honey is to drizzle it over these onions, which literally melt in your mouth. The onions may be either foil roasted in the oven or over hot coals on an outdoor grill. We like the sweet contrast they offer to the saltiness of many a Maine main dish.

1 large onion
2 teaspoons honey, preferably from Maine
Salt and freshly ground pepper, to taste

1. Place the onion on a large square of heavy aluminum foil. Cut the onion into 8 equal wedges, leaving just the bottom root end of the onion uncut in order to keep the onion whole. Spread the wedges open so the onion looks like a blossoming flower. Drizzle the honey, salt, and pepper over the center. Put the onion back together and wrap tightly with the foil to make a sealed ball. Prepare as many onions as needed in the same manner, allowing a half to a whole onion per person.

2. To cook the onions, either roast in a 450°F oven or place on top of hot coals on an outdoor grill. The onions will be soft and tender in 45 minutes to 1 hour. Open the foil packets, savor, and serve.

Makes 1 serving

Phyllis Schartner's Apple Butter

We've always been fans of the nutty brown color and smooth flavor of apple butter. This jamlike spread is not terribly difficult to make at home, thanks to Phyllis's perfected and straightforward recipe.

10 to 12 McIntosh or Macoun apples
½ teaspoon ground allspice
1 teaspoon ground cinnamon
7½ cups sugar
3 ounces (½ bottle) liquid pectin

1. Coarsely chop the apples — peel, core, and all — and place in a large pot with ¾ cup water. Bring the apples to a simmer and cook uncovered, stirring occasionally, until the pulp becomes very soft, 30 to 40 minutes.

2. Put the fruit pulp through a sieve to remove the skin and seeds. Measure 5 cups of the pulp and place in a large, clean saucepan. Add the allspice, cinnamon, and sugar, mixing well. Bring the mixture to a full rolling boil, stirring occasionally. Boil hard for 1 minute, stirring constantly. Remove from the heat and immediately stir in the pectin.

3. Skim any foam from the surface of the butter and continue to stir the mixture for 5 minutes. Allow the mixture to cool for 10 to 15 minutes.

4. Meanwhile, sterilize 6 pint jelly jars according to manufacturer's instructions. Ladle the apple butter into the jars and seal following manufacturer's instructions. Store in a cool place.

Makes 5 to 6 pints

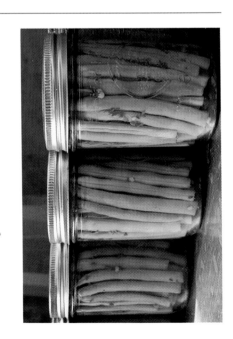

Dilly Beans

When we run short of Spruce Bush Farm's Dilly Beans, we are forced to make our own, and this is the recipe we use to sate our craving. Keep an eye out for 1½-pint wide-mouth canning jars as they are the perfect size for pickling and storing dilly beans.

2 pounds fresh green string beans, trimmed
4 cups cider vinegar
2 cups water
1 teaspoon hot red-pepper flakes
1½ teaspoons fennel seeds
3 tablespoons coarse (kosher) salt
4 medium cloves garlic, cut into coarse slivers
Several sprigs of fresh dill

1. Bring a large pot of water to a boil and blanch the beans for exactly 1½ minutes; drain and refresh under cold running water. Pack the beans upright and compactly into 4 or 5 1½-pint wide-mouth canning jars that have been sterilized according to manufacturer's instructions.

2. Place the vinegar, water, red-pepper flakes, fennel seeds, and salt together in a nonreactive saucepan. Bring to a boil and let boil for 1 minute. Pour the vinegar mixture directly over the beans in the jars to come within ⅓ inch of the top of the jar. Tuck several slivers of garlic and dill sprigs into each jar.

3. Seal the jars according to manufacturer's instructions and store the beans in a cool place until ready to use. We like to refrigerate dilly beans for a few hours before serving.

Makes 4 or 5 1½-pint jars

The best dilly beans we've ever tasted are made in this sugar shack at Spruce Bush Farm in North Whitefield.

Green Bean and Goat Feta Salad

While pickled dilly beans are the first choice of most Down Easters, we are equally fond of the just-picked flavor fresh string beans offer during the summer. To celebrate the cool crispness of this prolific pod vegetable, we often combine a fresh harvest with Mystique's peerless goat feta, slivered red onions, and toasted walnuts.

Dressing:

1 tablespoon Dijon-style mustard
1/4 cup red wine vinegar
1 clove garlic, minced
1/2 cup olive oil
Salt, to taste

Salad:

1 pound fresh green string beans, trimmed
1 small red onion, halved and cut into thin crescent slivers
1/4 pound goat feta, crumbled
1/2 cup lightly toasted and coarsely chopped walnuts
Freshly ground black pepper, to taste

1. To make the dressing, whisk together the mustard, vinegar, and garlic. Slowly whisk in the olive oil and then season to taste with salt; set aside.

2. Bring a large pot of salted water to a boil, add the beans, and cook until they are just crisp-tender, 3 to 4 minutes. Drain and at once immerse in a bowl of ice water to stop the cooking and set the bright green color. Drain again and pat dry with a towel.

3. In a mixing bowl, combine the beans, onion, and 1/2 cup of the dressing, tossing well. Refrigerate until ready to serve. Just before serving, mix in the feta, walnuts, and any remaining dressing. Season generously with black pepper and serve.

Makes 6 servings

Seal Cove goat cheese is presented for tasting at a local farmers' market.

Crab or Lobster Louis

This recipe comes straight from sauce maker Stewart Blackburn's suggestion sheet on uses for his versatile Maple Barbecue Sauce. We have taken the liberty of garnishing this light and luxurious summer salad with a few color enhancements from the garden.

2 cups mixed leaf lettuces
1 pound fresh crabmeat or picked lobster meat
1 cup mayonnaise, preferably Hellmann's
1/3 cup 'Stache's Maple Barbecue Sauce
1/3 cup whipped cream
2 tablespoons grated onion
Lemon slices to garnish
Cherry tomatoes or nasturtium blossoms to garnish
Fresh parsley, tarragon, or dill sprigs to garnish

1. Line 4 salad plates with the mixed lettuces. Mound one-fourth of the crab or lobster meat in the center of each plate.

2. Mix together the mayonnaise, Maple Barbecue Sauce, whipped cream, and grated onion. Spoon the sauce equally over the crab or lobster. Garnish each plate with lemon slices, cherry tomatoes, or nasturtium blossoms and the herb of choice. Serve at once.

Makes 4 servings

Sauerkraut Supper

Morse's fresh sauerkraut baked slowly with apples, potatoes, caraway seeds, sausage, and beer or apple cider makes a satisfying one-dish supper. We find the combination tastes particularly good when made with the extraordinary fresh bratwurst sausage from Kohn's Smokehouse in nearby Saint George, though another fresh sausage or kielbasa may be substituted in the recipe. For a less filling side dish, omit the sausage altogether and serve as an accompaniment to a pot of autumn baked beans.

3 tablespoons bacon fat
1 large onion, minced
1 tablespoon caraway seeds
3 large tart apples, peeled, cored, and cut into
    coarse chunks
2 pounds Morse's fresh sauerkraut, briefly rinsed and
    then drained
6 medium red-skinned potatoes, washed and sliced into
    1/3-inch-thick slices
2 1/2 cups lager beer or orchard cider
2 bay leaves
12 black peppercorns
6 whole cloves
2 to 2 1/2 pounds fresh bratwurst, poached in water just
    until cooked through or the same amount smoked
    kielbasa cut into 3-inch lengths

1. Heat the bacon fat in a heavy skillet over moderate heat. Add the onion and sauté until quite soft, about 10 minutes. Stir in the caraway seeds and cook a minute more. Add the apples and stir to coat with the onion mixture for a couple of minutes. Remove from heat.

2. Preheat the oven to 350°F.

3. Combine the apple-onion mixture with the sauerkraut in a large bowl. Have ready a 2 1/2- to 3-quart casserole dish. Layer half of the sliced potatoes over the bottom of the dish. Top with half of the sauerkraut mixture. Layer the rest of the potatoes on top and then finish with the remaining half of the sauerkraut. Pour the beer or cider over all.

4. Cut a small square of cheesecloth and place the bay leaves, peppercorns, and cloves in the center. Tie the square together at the top to make a little bag or pouch. Bury the seasonings in the middle of the sauerkraut casserole.

5. Cover the casserole tightly with foil and bake undisturbed for 1 hour. Uncover the casserole and insert the sausages evenly throughout the sauerkraut. Return to the oven and bake uncovered for another 1/2 hour. Remove from oven and let sit a few minutes before serving. Serve hot with dark bread and frosty mugs of more lager beer or cider.

Makes 6 servings

The best Christmases are indeed saltwater ones!

Chapter Fourteen

Christmas Down East

Christmas goes with Maine as naturally as drawn butter goes with lobster.

CASKIE STINNETT
"Christmas in Maine"

AT NO time does Maine's nickname, the Pine Tree State, seem more appropriate than at Christmas. Even if Mainers weren't such sentimentalists about honoring the yuletide celebration, the landscape would seem already festively decorated. Closed-for-the-season lobster pound signs linger as red as Santa's suit, as crisp winter air heightens favorite scents of the season by mingling balsam, pine, and spruce with woodsmoke from every home's warming stove or fireplace. Meanwhile, Mother Nature tends deftly to natural ornamentation by richly icing twinkling garlands of snow over each and every evergreen in Maine's vast larder. The Pine Tree State becomes one great fairyland of Christmas trees.

One senses as much, if not more, Christmas spirit standing silently alone in the middle of the Maine woods as strolling through the holiday bustle of a humanly festooned village port such as Camden or Kennebunk. When it comes to Christmas, Mainers love to take up where nature leaves off and deck home and hall with all the symbols of the season.

A December drive along coastal Route 1 reveals roadside trucks hawking balsam wreaths of every size in the very same spots where summer's itinerant fish peddlers previously held sway. Most seaside nurseries will also celebrate a last seasonal hurrah by overflowing with native Christmas greens before battening

down for the required long spell of hibernation in a northern clime. In a final splurge, the entire state takes on the intoxicating fragrance of those ubiquitous balsam keepsake pillows sold in every tourist trading post from Kittery to Calais. For wreathmaking is big business in Maine, with nearly two million balsam fir wreaths produced yearly to decorate not only Down East doorways and mantels but also those of homes all across the United States. Mail-order evergreen advertisements start appearing in local publications as early as September, offering long-lasting wreaths garnished with such native flora and fauna as reindeer moss, pine cones, rose hips, acorns, chestnuts, dried berries, sea lavender, and seashells. *Long-lasting* is a most important, operative word as Mainers are known to practice a unique tradition of leaving their Christmas wreaths hanging

Christmas Down East is both a time of dressing up and battening down for the long winter ahead.

Many isolated Christmas tree farms rely on the honor system.

until the snows begin to melt in March. This custom brings a small but bright spot of color and cheer to the bleakness of the winter landscape throughout the barren months of January and February.

Mainers are equally proud of the quality of their Christmas trees, as more than three hundred farms grow over three hundred thousand trees, supplying both the state and many parts of the nation. The Maine Christmas Tree Association promotes high standards among growers by grading trees for market by characteristics such as density, color, taper, and freshness. The next best thing to having your own Maine woods in which to cut down a tree is buying a fresh and fragrant, top-quality Maine-grown tree. Balsam firs, the Christmas trees of choice for most Mainers, are the state's biggest sellers, though species such as Scotch pine, white pine, fraser fir, and white, blue, and Colorado spruces also enjoy popularity.

Ask any number of people what else is special about Christmas in Maine besides the bounty of evergreen boughs, and they are likely to speak of a deeply embedded sense of tradition. David Robichaud and Henry Fecker, who run the most irresistible Christmas decor shop on the coast of Maine, 51 BayView Street in Camden, say they must have the store in full holiday regalia by the beginning of October to satisfy the anticipation of their clientele. As 51 BayView is a tony home-furnishing mecca during Camden's touristy summer season, I sus-

pected that it might have been summer-home owners returning for a final holiday recess who supported this fabulous collection of nostalgic Christmas ornamentation, both festive and frivolous. But the owners faithfully assure me that it is mostly the natives who succumb to the delight of decorating their year-round homes with the season's choicest finery.

I can neither doubt nor dispute this as I have witnessed how many Maine villages traditionally dress for the holidays, holding old-time tree-lighting ceremonies, craft fairs and festivals, open houses, and caroling parties. Christmas-by-the-Sea celebrations abound, with Santa being just as likely to arrive by lobster boat as by sleigh. Ogunquit, for example, sponsors a traditional tree lighting, inn tour, and series of Christmas concerts, while the Bath Garden Club plays host to the Festival of Trees, for which several town trees are decorated by area merchants and organizations. Kennebunkport's two-week-long Christmas Prelude and Post-Prelude grows in popularity each year, and Portland's Old Port makes a quaint cobblestoned shopping stop away from the craziness and conformity of shopping malls. Camden bonds with its neighbors on either side, Rockport and Lincolnville, for more tree lighting, caroling, and a special holiday house tour. Just a couple of coastal nooks away, Boothbay Harbor concentrates on a nautical theme by decking the masts of its schooners.

Moving still farther down east, Searsport — with its old sea captains' mansions proudly ablaze with sparkling lights — is always a favorite town to pass through as I journey toward Blue Hill. The Penobscot Marine Museum in Searsport presents a Victorian Christmas each year with a delightful Saturday-afternoon stroll through six decorated sea captains' homes turned into bed-and-breakfast inns. The afternoon tour is followed by Victorian Christmas refreshments in one of the inns. Special holiday exhibits in the museum itself feature scenes of antique toys and dolls and staged holiday baking activities. Festivities in Bar Harbor are equally toothsome, with the entire commercial center of town being re-created in the form of a miniature gingerbread village. If a piece of summer property in elite Bar Harbor has always been out of your price range, then perhaps an edible edifice will content as all Christmastime gingerbread properties are offered for

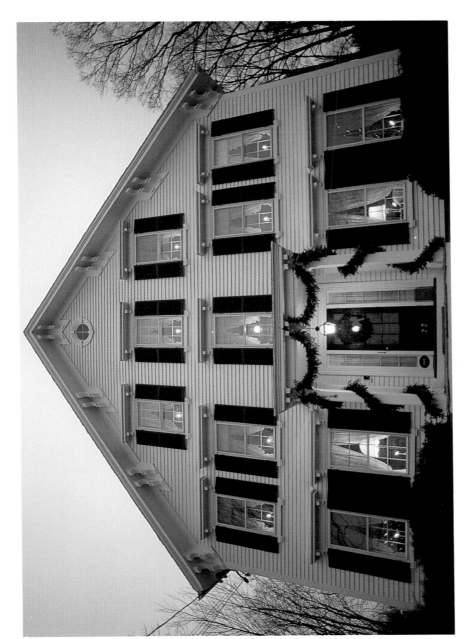

Old sea captains' mansions lend themselves to impressive holiday decoration.

sale at prices far more modest than the real McCoy, with some of the proceeds going to charity.

Christmas to most, whether Mainers or not, means going home to be with family. We are fortunate that home these days means our parents' waterfront place on Blue Hill Bay. Robert P. Tristram Coffin certainly would have approved, as he insisted in his lively essay "Recipe for Christmas" that the best Christmases were saltwater ones. Like other coastal villages, Blue Hill has its share of yuletide events. The historic Holt House, walls charmingly restored with stencils found in old Blue Hill homes, dresses for the season and warms guests with tea served in front of a roaring fireplace. The people of the village like to dress as well, and gay apparel is the rule at Jonathan's Restaurant's Candlelight December dinner or at the Bagaduce Chorale's hymnal Christmas Eve concert at the Congregational Church. But

the best and most old-fashioned Christmas experience of all in Blue Hill is being on a sleigh ride at the Birdsalls' Horsepower Farm. Now, sleigh bells may ring across the country, but Horsepower Farm is one of the few places I know of in the nation to carry on the dying art of a picture-perfect Currier and Ives–style open sleigh ride, for children and adults alike, through fields of fluffy, new-fallen snow.

Sleighs played an important part in the early life of agrarian New England. Spring, summer, and fall were seasons of rigorous farm work, while winter signaled the only leisure spell for travel and socializing. Century-old accounts from Maine reveal that most people with the means to keep a horse also owned a sleigh. Paul and Mollie Birdsall not only believe that the ways of a hundred years ago still hold plenty of merit today, they practice them daily at Horsepower Farm. When not taking customers on

153

Christmas Down East

Paul Birdsall readies his horses for an old-fashioned winter sleigh ride.

for Scalloped Scallops. But, perhaps, the delicate flavor of these cold-water oysters is best savored in a thin stew of nothing more than fresh, quivering oysters, butter, milk, cream, and a smattering of seasonings. Such simple yet elegant stews were all the rage in nineteenth-century New England and still bring a perfect beginning to a sit-down Christmas dinner.

Baking cookies is another popular Christmas pastime in Maine, though you won't find the international array of slick city Christmas sweets Down East. The sugarplums that dance in Mainers' heads are born of old-fashioned ingredients like molasses, brown sugar, cinnamon, nutmeg, raisins, and nuts. Candy is a frugal miracle made from sweetened mashed potatoes, while homey and practical hermits and soft molasses cookies are accepted over buttery shortbreads and daintily decorated Spritz cookies. That puritanical Yankee attitude toward food clings to Maine like seaweed to the rocks of its rugged coastline, making typical Down East fare, even at Christmastime, substantial and good but by no means fancy. This type of food, after all, is what is needed to survive in a climate where Christmas carols are experienced first as a breathy shape in the frosty air in the seconds before they ring with musical warmth on the frostbitten ear.

Logger's Joy

This potent brew is an old Maine recipe from the long and grueling days of lumberjacking in the dense woods of northern Maine. We have revived it as a uniquely Down East toddy for toasting the Christmas season. The warm libation is also a particularly rewarding treat after a frosty day's work readying the home woodpile for the long winter ahead.

sleigh rides, the Birdsalls have been known to relax long enough to enjoy a sleigh-ride party of their own. Because riding in an open sleigh through a snow-becalmed Maine landscape is often a chilling though thrilling adventure, Mollie likes to warm guests afterward with mugs of simply mulled local cider and hearty bowls of lamb stew made from the farm's own mutton.

It is such satisfying, soul-nourishing food, rather than ostentatious banquets, that tends to be the rule at Christmas celebrations throughout Maine. A roast goose or turkey surrounded by root vegetables makes a likely Christmas dinner, followed by a steamed pudding or squash or mincemeat pie for dessert. There are many Mainers who still make their own mincemeat from scratch in the fall, utilizing scraps of meat and suet left from hunting expeditions or green tomatoes left on garden vines as a base. It is this type of homemaking that gives weight to the traditional flavor of Christmas in Maine. As Coffin suggests, the best formula for making a first-class Christmas requires one to "go out and run it down in the barnyard, shoot it out of the pasture pines, dig it out of the bay at ebb tide. But get it right out of the old home acres."

While my family still practices many Polish Christmas traditions from my father's heritage as we always had before Maine became home, we also now pay homage to the saltwater splendor before us in Blue Hill Bay. When bald eagles, and not Santa's reindeer, grace yard and shorefront on Christmas morning, it becomes mandatory to halt all peeking into stockings and gift exchanging in order to stop and reflect on the incredibly unspoiled wild bounty of the setting before us. From the churning bay bottom, no more than a hundred yards beyond the Christmas tree whose top tickles the ceiling of our dining room, will come lobsters — already the color of Christmas when the scarlet steamed shells mingle with the crustaceans' green tomalley. More often than not, the sweet meat ends up scrambled into our eggs on Christmas morning. We are also likely to honor the colonial custom of indulging in yuletide oysters. Cultured Maine Pemaquid or Spinney Creek oysters are a treat steamed just until opened over a fireplace fire or scalloped richly in a baked casserole with butter and crumbs in a manner similar to our earlier recipe

1 tablespoon fresh lemon juice
2 teaspoons sugar
1/3 cup applejack
2/3 cup boiling water
1 lemon slice to garnish

Makes 1 drink

Put lemon juice, sugar, and applejack in a mug. Pour in the boiling water and stir. Garnish the drink with a lemon slice and begin sipping at once.

Mulled Cider

The cider that warms sleigh riders at Horsepower Farm is based on Fannie Farmer's original recipe but mulled with a tad less sugar.

1 quart orchard cider
1/2 teaspoon whole allspice
1/2 teaspoon whole cloves
1 3-inch stick cinnamon
1/4 cup brown sugar, lightly packed

1. Simmer the cider and spices together in a pot over medium heat for 15 minutes. Stir in the brown sugar and continue to simmer for 10 minutes more.
2. Ladle the hot cider into mugs, straining out the whole spices if desired.

Makes 4 servings

Holiday Oyster Stew

A seafood stew cooked in the simple Maine manner is made particularly elegant by the lavish use of freshly shucked oysters from icy Down East waters.

4 tablespoons unsalted butter
1 1/2 cups finely minced celery
1 pint freshly shucked oysters and liquor
1/2 cup medium or cream sherry
3 cups half-and-half
1 cup heavy cream
1/2 teaspoon ground nutmeg
Freshly ground white pepper, to taste
Paprika to garnish
Minced fresh parsley or snipped fresh chives to garnish

1. Melt the butter in a soup pot over medium heat. Add the celery and sauté until quite soft, about 10 minutes. Stir in the oysters, their liquor, and the sherry. Continue to cook just until the edges of the oysters curl and the centers are barely cooked through, 3 to 4 minutes.
2. Meanwhile, in a separate saucepan, heat together the half-and-half and heavy cream just until hot to the touch. Be careful not to let the mixture boil or it may curdle. Slowly stir the hot cream blend into the oyster mixture. Season the stew with the nutmeg and white pepper. (Salt is unnecessary because of the briny flavor of the oysters.)
3. Ladle the stew at once into shallow soup bowls and garnish the top of each serving with a generous sprinkling of paprika and a scattering of parsley or chives.

Makes 4 to 6 rich servings

Ingredients are laid out in preparation for Mollie's Sleigh-Ride Stew.

Mollie's Sleigh-Ride Stew

Mollie Birdsall recommends this homey lamb stew as a warm and fortifying finish to an old-fashioned Horsepower Farm yuletide sleigh ride. Mollie uses the farm's own organically raised lamb in her version to impart the distinctively gamey lamb flavor that she and the sleigh-ride master, husband Paul, prefer.

3½ to 4 pounds lamb shoulder cut into 1½- to
    2-inch cubes
½ cup unbleached all-purpose flour
Salt and freshly ground pepper, to taste
2 tablespoons butter
2 tablespoons olive oil
2 medium onions, peeled and sliced
3 cloves garlic, minced
1 cup dry red wine
4 cups boiling water
2 beef bouillon cubes
3 tablespoons coarsely chopped fresh rosemary or
    1 tablespoon dried rosemary
2 russet-type potatoes, peeled and cut into ½-inch cubes
¾ pound carrots, peeled and cut into 2- by ½-inch strips
¾ pound green beans, trimmed and cut diagonally into
    thirds
24 small white boiling onions, trimmed and then
    blanched in boiling water for 5 minutes to remove the
    skins

1. Toss the lamb cubes with the flour seasoned with some salt and pepper in a shallow dish to coat lightly and evenly all over.

2. Melt the butter and olive oil together over medium-high heat in a Dutch oven or large stew pot. Sear the lamb cubes in batches until nicely browned all over, about 10 minutes per batch.

157

Christmas Down East

The lamb chunks for the stew are seared atop an old Home Clarion stove.

Remove cooked batches with a slotted spoon to a bowl and keep to the side.

3. Once all the lamb has been seared, add the sliced onions and garlic to the pot. Sauté, stirring for 5 minutes. Pour in the wine and stir to loosen any brown bits sticking to the bottom of the pot. Pour in the boiling water and add the bouillon cubes, stirring constantly until they are dissolved. Return the lamb to the stew pot, add the rosemary, and check the seasoning for salt and pepper. Cover the pot and simmer slowly over low heat, stirring occasionally for 2 hours.

4. Add the potatoes, carrots, green beans, and peeled boiling onions to the stew. Cover and continue simmering until vegetables are tender, 45 minutes to 1 hour longer. Serve the stew hot, ladled generously into shallow soup bowls.

Note: This stew may also be made a day or so in advance and then reheated, as many people believe a stew becomes more flavorful if allowed to mellow in the refrigerator for a day or two before serving.

Makes 10 to 12 servings

Cranberry Irish Soda Bread

Since the Scotch-Irish were responsible for bringing potatoes to Maine around 1750, it should come as no surprise that Irish soda bread recipes crop up now and again in Down East cooks' files. This spectacular one, dotted generously with ruby red cranberries, looks especially festive at Christmastime. We think it is the perfect bread to accompany Mollie's Sleigh-Ride Stew.

2½ cups unbleached all-purpose flour
½ cup whole-wheat flour
¾ cup light brown sugar, packed
1 tablespoon baking powder
1 teaspoon baking soda
½ teaspoon salt
1¾ cup buttermilk
2 large eggs, lightly beaten
3 tablespoons unsalted butter, melted and cooled
1½ cups coarsely chopped cranberries
Grated zest of 1 orange
1 tablespoon caraway seeds

1. Preheat oven to 350°F. Butter a 9-inch springform pan and set aside.

2. Sift flours, sugar, baking powder, soda, and salt together into a large mixing bowl. Make a well in the center. Place buttermilk, eggs, and butter in the center of the well. Using a wooden spoon, mix all together until just combined. Blend in the cranberries, orange zest, and caraway seeds just until evenly distributed.

3. Spread the batter evenly in the prepared springform pan. Bake until golden brown, 55 minutes to 1 hour. Serve the soda bread slightly warm or at room temperature.

Makes one 9-inch round loaf

Molasses Cookies

Maine cookbooks and card files overflow with recipes for molasses cookies. Some people like them thin and crisp while others prefer them plump and chewy. In the old days, lard was often used for the shortening. After much research and testing, we have decided we fall into the camp of soft and chewy cookie connoisseurs, and at Christmastime we like to dress up this perfected recipe by adding a little orange zest to the batter. These cookies are especially good with a cup of rum-spiked eggnog or mulled cider.

1 cup vegetable shortening
1 cup light brown sugar, packed
1 cup dark molasses
2 eggs
4 cups unbleached all-purpose flour
2 teaspoons baking soda
½ teaspoon salt
1 tablespoon ground cinnamon
1 tablespoon ground ginger
½ teaspoon ground cloves
Finely grated zest of 1 orange
½ cup granulated sugar

1. Preheat oven to 350°F. Grease baking sheets.

2. In a large mixing bowl, cream together the shortening and sugar until light and fluffy. Beat in molasses and eggs until smooth.

3. Sift together flour, baking soda, salt, cinnamon, ginger, and cloves. Using a wooden spoon, gradually work in the dry ingredients to make a moderately stiff dough. Work in the orange zest until evenly distributed.

4. Roll dough between the palms of your hands to form large walnut-size balls. Roll each ball in a small bowl of the granulated sugar to coat lightly. Arrange the balls 1 inch apart on the baking sheets. Flatten each ball into a cookie by crisscrossing with the tines of a fork.

5. Bake the cookies until lightly browned but still a little soft in the center, 12 to 15 minutes. Transfer with a spatula to a wire rack to cool. Store in a covered cookie jar or tin.

Makes 4 dozen large cookies

Christmas cookies and Mulled Cider are hard to resist.

Hermits

To my knowledge, the long-standing debate over whether authentic hermits should be made as drop cookies or bars has never been resolved. I do know that both versions are equally popular with Maine bakers, as covered family recipes have been pridefully handed down through generations. I am told by some that the cookies are most fondly remembered as a summer treat packed for dessert on island picnics and served with a wedge of sharp Cheddar cheese. I think hermits also make a welcome addition to an old-fashioned Christmas cookie tray.

Personally, I cast my vote with the hermit *bar* bakers and like to use a combination of dark and golden raisins in my batter, though many older recipes call for larger muscat raisins. The coffee icing lends a festive frost to the bars, but if you're planning to serve the hermits with Cheddar cheese, omit it.

3/4 cup unsalted margarine
1 1/2 cups dark brown sugar, packed
2 tablespoons molasses
2 eggs
1 teaspoon vanilla
3 cups unbleached all-purpose flour
2 teaspoons cinnamon
1 teaspoon ground nutmeg
1/2 teaspoon ground cloves
1/2 teaspoon salt
1/2 teaspoon baking soda

1/2 cup buttermilk or thin sour cream
3/4 cup coarsely chopped golden raisins
3/4 cup coarsely chopped dark raisins
1 1/4 cup coarsely chopped walnuts

Coffee Icing:
1 1/2 tablespoons unsalted margarine
1 cup sifted confectioners' sugar
1/2 teaspoon vanilla
1 to 2 tablespoons strong black coffee

1. Preheat the oven to 350°F. Grease a 9 × 13-inch baking pan.

2. In a large mixing bowl, cream together the margarine and brown sugar until smooth. Beat in the molasses, eggs, and vanilla until well combined.

3. Sift together the flour, cinnamon, nutmeg, cloves, salt, and baking soda. Add to the batter alternately with the buttermilk or sour cream to make a smooth, thick batter. Spread the batter evenly in the prepared baking pan.

4. Bake the hermits until just set in the center, 20 to 25 minutes. Be careful not to overbake as the bars are meant to be moist. Let cool completely. If frosting the hermits, beat the margarine and confectioners' sugar together in a small bowl until smooth. Beat in the vanilla and enough coffee to thin the icing to spreading consistency. Drizzle the icing over the hermits and cut into 1 × 2-inch rectangular bars.

Makes about 36 hermits

Needhams

Needhams are a fudgelike confection made from mashed native potatoes, and they epitomize old-time Maine ingenuity and resourcefulness. For the uninitiated they are an acquired taste or, more often, a taste never acquired. Needhams are most often made for Christmas giving, and I am fond of the magical, snow-white look they lend to Maine Christmas cookie platters.

Some recipes for needhams call for a waxy chocolate topping, which I personally dislike. If needhams must be made with chocolate, try mixing a cup of miniature chocolate chips into the potato batter. Vanilla is the traditional flavor, but I prefer almond extract in my needhams, which gives this unique candy the aura of a Maine marzipan.

1 cup unseasoned mashed potatoes
1/2 teaspoon salt
8 tablespoons (1 stick) unsalted margarine
2 pounds confectioners' sugar
1/2 pound flaked coconut
2 teaspoons almond extract
1 cup miniature chocolate chips (optional)

1. Combine the mashed potatoes and salt. Melt the margarine in the top of a double boiler over simmering water. Mix in the mashed potatoes, confectioners' sugar, coconut, and almond extract. Cook, stirring continually, until well combined, 4 to 5 minutes. Remove from heat and let cool to room temperature. Fold in the chocolate chips, if using.

2. Grease a 10 × 15-inch jelly-roll pan and then spread evenly with the potato batter. Place the needhams evenly with the potato batter. Place the needhams in the refrigerator or other cool place to harden for at least 24 hours. When hard, cut the needhams into small squares or diamonds. Store needhams in an airtight tin in a cool place.

Makes about 5 dozen

Christmas Jam Sticks

This delightful and exquisite cookie is inspired by a recipe from the collection cleverly packaged in a brown paper sack by the fun-loving trio of women known as the Maine Bag Ladies. While the original recipe by Hancock dweller Terry Flettrich Rohe calls for apricot jam as a filling, I prefer to use a native and homemade blueberry, raspberry, or strawberry jam to bring the taste of distant outdoor summer pleasures into the snow-drifted December landscape.

1/2 cup unsalted butter
1 1/4 cups sugar
1 tablespoon grated lemon zest
2 eggs, separated
1 cup unbleached all-purpose flour
1/2 teaspoon salt
1/4 teaspoon baking powder
1 cup berry jam
3/4 cup chopped walnuts
Confectioners' sugar

1. Preheat the oven to 350°F. Butter a 9 × 13-inch baking pan.

2. In a mixing bowl, beat together the butter, 1 cup of the sugar, and the lemon zest until smooth and creamy. Beat in the egg yolks, one at a time, beating well after each addition.

3. Sift together the flour, salt, and baking powder. Add to the creamed mixture to make a moderately stiff dough. Pat the dough evenly over the bottom of the prepared baking dish. Spread the jam in a thin layer over the top of the dough. Sprinkle the walnuts over the jam.

4. In a small bowl and with clean beaters, beat the egg whites until foamy. Gradually beat in the remaining 1/4 cup sugar and continue beating until shiny and stiff. Spread the meringue over the jam and walnuts.

5. Bake the jam sticks until set and lightly browned, about 30 minutes. Cool and then dust the top with sifted confectioners' sugar. Cut into small sticks and serve or store in an airtight container.

Makes about 4 dozen

Chapter Fifteen

Trending

Our Captaine discovered up a great river, trending alongst into the Maine about forty miles, . . . the beauty and goodnesse whereof I cannot by relation sufficiently demonstrate. . . . As we passed with a gentle wind up with our ship in this River, any man may conceive with what admiration we all consented in joy. . . . The farther we went, the more pleasing it was to every man, alluring us still with expectation of better.

JAMES ROSIER
A True Relation — of Capt. George Waymouth's discovery of the St. George's River, 1605
As quoted in Kenneth Roberts's *Trending into Maine*

THE book by Maine author Kenneth Roberts, whose title we have abbreviated for this, our final chapter, opens with an unforgettable line: "I don't pretend to know much about the State of Maine. . . ." Many are the times that we, in our quest to pursue knowledge that we hoped would make us experts of sorts, have felt as ignorant and overwhelmed as the esteemed Mr. Roberts. Indeed, travels through the state's vast woodland resources have often called to mind that apt axiom of not being able to tell the forest from the trees.

However, with our publisher's deadline pending, when it boiled down to sorting between the blueberries and baked beans, the pine trees and lobster pots, and the sardines and salt pork, we decided to make a conscious effort to devote most of our energies to bringing our readers time-honored Maine

The Belmont sign is understated yet inviting.

foods and flavors. Frequently, throughout *Salt-water Seasonings*, we have allowed ourselves a wonderful indulgence in childhood memories of the way Maine was (and often still is), but at the same time we have tried not to let our nostalgia blind us to the fact that nearly a quarter of a million new people have moved into the state in the last decade. This influx has inevitably encroached on old Maine ways and brought change, both for better and worse. The good news is that most of those who have moved, or *trended* if you will, into Maine have been motivated more by respect for the pristine beauty of the state than by the drive to make mighty bucks in virgin territory. How reassuring it is to realize that newcomers experience a sensation of discovery and aesthetic fulfillment little changed from that of James Rosier's *Relation* of 1605.

As the theme of this book is food, and good food at that, our focus in this chapter is the gastronomic dividends that have come Down East to the delight of many during the past decade or so. Because we have in our travels become both friends and avid followers of a few inspirational, epicurean trenders, we wouldn't want to leave readers with the impression that Maine is still all baked bean suppers and simple yet satisfying Bagaduce Lunch crab rolls. While we believe you should absolutely seek out these native pleasures, we also feel strongly about introducing you to a bottle of Bartlett Blueberry wine or a literal "pig-out" at Uncle Billy's SouthSide Barbecue in Portland.

No one better illustrates this new spirit of culinary excitement and adventure in Maine than Samuel F. Hayward. I first sampled Sam's magic at a moment when my weary mind and jaded palate were uncharacteristically void of a yen for extraordinary food.

Chef Sam Hayward and gardener extraordinaire Frank Gross inspect mammoth cabbages to strains of classical music.

This was because I had just finished catering myself to the point of near exhaustion on Nantucket before heading off-island to Maine for book research at our base in Blue Hill. Finding myself too tired to drive farther, I stopped in Brunswick to spend the night. Having recently read about local chef Sam Hayward's food genius in some trade publication or another, I felt unenthusiastically obliged to check out his restaurant, 22 Lincoln. It was a Sunday evening and only the café section of the restaurant, the Side Door, was open for business. What I savored at the Side Door that evening bolted me out of my culinary malaise.

Most of the dishes on this menu started from a base of ingredients indigenous to Maine, but it was right there that all Yankee practicality and attitude ended. Where a Mainer might make a "wiggle" from local shrimp, Sam fashioned a stylized "ceviche" with the succulent pink shellfish bathed in an intensely

infused citrus oil and further contrasted by the surprise of cracked whole coriander seeds rather than the more customary Mexican fresh cilantro. The good ol' Maine crab roll was elevated from its humble toasted bun base to a homemade herbed brioche roll while still managing to maintain an essential simplicity. Foggy Ridge pheasants found their way through the Side Door into dense and aromatic pâtés sauced with wild Maine mushrooms.

Since getting to know Sam personally, it has become difficult to decide which we enjoy more—his cooking or our conversations with him. Both pulsate with energy. Sam grew up in Louisiana, where, he says, his mother was a good Southern cook. The love for Maine developed appropriately enough during a Down East honeymoon. The lure of cooking began in 1974 at Cornell University when he took a summer job preparing meals for researchers at a marine laboratory on the Isles of Shoals off the coast of Portsmouth, New Hampshire. In a manner reminiscent of sauce maker Stewart Blackburn on wild mushroom expeditions in New Zealand, Sam began his culinary career by cooking biological specimens dragged off the ocean floor by scientists. He enjoyed this venture into "maritime cooking" so much that he continued to do it for another two summers. Somewhere along the way a passion for music diverted Sam from the kitchen to the guitar, but after several frustrating years of travel and vacillation between rock and classical music, he returned to a culinary career, purchasing the 22 Lincoln Restaurant in 1981. Sam has referred to this change in careers as "the process of transferring my artistic pretensions from one medium to another."

Although Sam is the first to admit that he held no clear objective when he became proprietor of the restaurant, he soon found that his arts training and background would serve him well by continuing "to instill the sense of urgency to do something with excellence" despite realistic considerations such as profit, locale, and audience. Sam ran 22 Lincoln for ten years and says it was during that decade that he achieved artistic maturity. More than any other single influence, it was the arrival of organic gardener Frank Gross at the restaurant's back door one day early on in the game that was to conspire to give definition to Hayward's emerging cooking style. Gross, a musician turned gardener, established an immediate bond with the idealistic chef. And once Sam tasted Frank's produce, he knew that from there on in his stylistic approach would be rooted in the maxim of "good cooking beginning with perfect ingredients." Sam soon entered into a total "symbiotic relationship" with Gross, which seems to flourish as well as the extraordinary produce harvested from Gross's three-acre organic garden in nearby Lisbon. We went with Sam one day to visit the garden and must confess to never in our lives having seen such spectacular and unusual vegetables growing in such luxurious and fluffy soil. We wondered if the classical music being piped over the gardens from the greenhouse had anything to do with our experiencing the mere uprooting of a leek as a transcendental experience.

These days Sam is in the kitchen in Freeport's Harraseeket Inn working as the "artistic director" as opposed to "cook-chef." He closed 22 Lincoln and

made this switch because he felt the need to give up "the burden of ownership." He continues his rich and rewarding restaurant rapport with Frank Gross, though he has never been one to broadcast his organic preferences for fear of being labeled as the proprietor of a "hippie, weed-and-seed-eater establishment." Sam states emphatically: "I use organic vegetables simply because they taste better; they are raised by craftsmen who care." With artistic maturity securely established, Sam's goal is to become known as "a practitioner of refined New England cooking using superb ingredients and impeccable technique." There is no doubt in our minds that Sam Hayward has what it takes to be a culinary maestro in Maine, if not all of America.

Many people have at one point or another in their lives entertained the romantic pipe dream of opening and running a quaint bed-and-breakfast inn in New England. Two who have actually persevered through the grueling insanity of seeing this dream to fruition are Jerry Clare and John Mancarella, good friends of mine on Nantucket for several years before they trended into Maine. Both had strong backgrounds in running all aspects of a restaurant business, and both were eager to create something of their own together in New England. As real estate prices became increasingly outrageous on Nantucket, they decided to head north and ended up in Camden, mostly because it reminded them of a Nantucket they had known and loved twenty years earlier. After a summer passed Down East confirming their instincts, they purchased a place that had earned the reputation of being one of Maine's finest and most up-to-date restaurants, Aubergine, at 6 Belmont Avenue on the fringes of Camden proper. An inn also came along with the restaurant.

Jerry says he was drawn to the demanding challenge of transforming Aubergine into a very special bed and breakfast for two major reasons: "The place was a total wreck and I loved looking at it from the angle of potential — shining the building up — putting a new dress on it — and I've always loved coastal towns. They have a laid-back quality but with some umph!" After months of hard labor combined with shopping sprees at local auctions and antique shops, Aubergine was at long last remade in 1989

A typical wake-up breakfast tray features blueberry pancakes at The Belmont in Camden.

into The Belmont, a six-bedroom bed and breakfast plus dinner restaurant.

Waking up to a bountiful breakfast in bed at the inn, one would never suspect that Jerry Clare believes he isn't "a morning person." Somehow, though, a bed and lunch didn't quite have the right ring, so he and John now alternate turns behind the stove in the morning. Dinners at The Belmont are a true team effort, and the dining room has rapidly turned into a mecca for seekers of good food with country warmth and innovative flair. Belmont crab cakes are served with a spicy red-pepper mayonnaise rather than the traditional tartar sauce, and local lobster often strays far from its backyard origins to appear as part of a risotto or scrambled into Asian pan-fried noodles. John unleashes his Italian heritage by kneading chewy and rustic breads baked on premise every day. The reward to both Jerry and John for all those long hours of toil is in knowing that they have created a place of beauty for their valued guests to match the external panorama of hills and bays that surround them in Camden.

As cozy and elegant as The Belmont is, Uncle Billy's SouthSide Barbeque Restaurant in Portland is frumpy and funky — and on purpose. The owner and storyteller behind Uncle Billy's is Jonathan St. Laurent, a Yankee of French-Canadian descent. And, it is often hard to determine which is better — Jonny's sense of humor or his sense of seasoning. The seeming contradiction inherent in Down East barbecue is easily brushed aside and justified by St. Laurent: "What is a clam bake if not clam barbecue?"

To say the least, the food at Uncle Billy's is exuberant. The menu is chock-full of traditional and newfangled barbecue treats such as Pork Shoulder Sandwiches, Brisket and Burnt Ends, Voodoo Jerk Chicken, and Teriyaki Bluefish. Accompaniments like Mother's Mountain Cole Slaw, named for a locally made mustard in the dressing, and Barbeque Billy Beans are fabulous. We've heard that vegetarians travel from great distances to sit at the counter of this meat-pit to polish off bowl after bowl of the spicy, molasses-rich beans. Desserts at Uncle Billy's usually center on one concoction or another based on his "world-renowned" Death by Chocolate Sauce.

The finest accompaniment to any barbecue is, as St. Laurent attests, "a cold brewed beverage," and there are two Maine-based beers that are part of the New England resurgence in microbreweries. Geary's Pale Ale is brewed right in Portland and in a manner to emulate classic English pale ales. We love its lobster label, coppery color, and slightly bitter, intense flavor. We cook with Geary's Ale, and we quench our thirst with it. Portland Lager is milder than Geary's yet rich and full-bodied. A lot of this lager's appeal comes from being aged for a full five weeks; most other American lagers are aged for only three weeks. Like so many other Maine products with their emphasis on purity, Portland Lager contains no added chemicals, starches, or sugar. While we like our Geary's Ale served as frosty as possible, Portland Lager is best consumed at a temperature between 40 and 50 degrees — room temperature in many a Down East abode.

Beer is by no means the only libation being made in Maine. Throughout this book we have made countless references in recipes to the fruit wines from the Bartlett Winery in Gouldsboro. These miraculous wines fueled much of the early inspiration for

Saltwater Seasonings. In waiting until now to tell the story of Bob and Kathe Bartlett, we have saved the best for last. The Bartletts originally dreamed of making wine on the coast of Maine in the more traditional manner from grapes. Initial experimentation with more than a dozen French-American hybrid grapes led them to the discouraging conclusion that there were not enough warm days in Maine to ripen grapes adequately for the production of quality wine. Disappointed but not defeated, Bob and Kathe came up with the sound idea of making wine from the resources available to them, namely Maine's abundant berries and autumn fruits.

Bob and Kathe came to Maine in the midseventies with backgrounds in studio arts, and it was during an interlude as head of the glass program in the Fine Arts Department at Ohio State University that Bob started to study oenology, or winemaking,

with passion and a plan. The Bartletts returned to Maine three years later and began building their state-of-the-art environmentally conscious winery in 1981. After overcoming legislative hurdles to allow for the sale and tasting of wines on premise, the pair opened the Bartlett Maine Estate Winery in 1983 with a production of 600 gallons of wine made from blueberries, apples, and pears. These days the Bartletts produce 15,000 gallons of wine per year in a dozen or more different styles. The winery has garnered over thirty-five awards since opening, in both regional and international competitions. While blueberry, apple, and pear wines along with house blends thereof remain Bartlett Estate standbys, newer innovations include strawberry, raspberry, and honey dessert wines as well as a spectacular brut apple and pear sparkling wine made according to the French *méthode champenoise.*

The Bartletts have managed to convince many potential customers to put aside the stigma generally attached to fruit wines by being uncompromising sticklers for quality and by insisting on the use of the most modern winemaking equipment available in conjunction with a deep respect for centuries-old fermenting techniques. Many of their Maine fruit wines emerge surprisingly dry and complex from aging in American and French oak barrels. Bob explains: "Fruit wines have to be serious to overcome people's perceptions, and using French oak indicates that you are serious about winemaking." Interestingly enough, the fruits that go into Bartlett wines often cost more than grapes. The premium blueberries are purchased from the University of Maine's Blueberry Hill Experimental Farm in nearby Jonesboro and cost roughly $1,000 a ton in comparison to $700 a ton for standard California grapes. Raspberries for dessert wine come from a woman in Winterport who commits her entire crop to the winery; all apples are also native; only some pears are purchased from out of state, in Massachusetts. Bob and Kathe believe that it is crucial to support a home agricultural base and thereby cultivate "a symbiotic relationship between the winemaker and grower."

Kathe feels that the bottling of serious wines should be fun, and the Bartletts' Nouveau Blueberry was invented and released as a tongue-in-cheek spoof on French Beaujolais Nouveau. Not to be outdone

At first glance, the Bartlett Winery appears to be totally hightech, but expansive windows make the natural wooded setting felt at all times.

by the French ritualistic fanfare of flying Beaujolais Nouveau to America's chic restaurants and cafés via the Concorde every November 15th, the Bartletts chartered a 1941 WACO biplane in 1986 to fly several cases of their first Nouveau Blueberry wine forty miles down the coast to Blue Hill for uncorking and revelry at Jonathan's Restaurant. When the plane touched down at Blue Hill International Airport (a dusty and paltry landing strip bordering the town dump), the wine was rushed to Jonathan's in a 1917 Ford Model T driven by local Tea and Tobacco shop owner William Petry. Newspaper and television crews had a field day, and all Down East tasters were happier for the event. Nouveau Blueberry wine is created by the same carbonic maceration process

used for French Beaujolais Nouveau, which allows for the fermenting of whole rather than crushed fruit. This light and whimsical wine is perfect for quaffing as an antidote to the encroaching cold of a November night. The Bartletts now incorporate the release of the current year's Nouveau Blueberry into holiday festivities at the winery showroom in Gouldsboro. Meanwhile, Jonathan and I continue to make a family tradition of serving this appealing young berry wine every Thanksgiving.

The Bartletts maintain that their foremost objective has always been to make good wines to accompany good food. Success at this noble task is easily measured by looking at the Maine coast restaurants that have enthusiastically hosted memorable wine-

Blueberry wine is aged in French oak barrels.

*Bob and Kathe Bartlett toast a current blueberry harvest with a sip of their blueberry wine from a previous year.
(Photo credit: Stephen O. Muskie)*

Blueberry Pancakes Belmont

Bountiful breakfasts are but one of the many splendors awaiting lucky guests at Jerry Clare and John Mancarella's Belmont Inn bed and breakfast in Camden. Jerry often makes these pancakes when it's his turn to cook breakfast and prefers to drop the blueberries onto the pancakes once they are on the griddle rather than mixing them into the batter. The pancakes are served with more blueberries on the top, maple syrup, and a savory side of John's special Lavender Morning Sausage.

1 cup unbleached all-purpose flour
3 teaspoons baking powder
½ teaspoon salt
2 tablespoons sugar
1 egg
1 cup milk
¼ cup sour cream
½ teaspoon vanilla
2 tablespoons unsalted butter, melted
½ cup wild or high-bush blueberries
Additional blueberries for garnishing
Sifted confectioners' sugar for garnishing
Maple syrup

1. Sift the flour, baking powder, salt, and sugar together into a mixing bowl. Beat together the egg, milk, sour cream, and vanilla and pour over the dry ingredients. Stir to combine thoroughly. Mix in the melted butter.

2. Heat a lightly greased griddle or skillet over medium-high heat. When hot, drop about ¼ cup batter onto the griddle for each pancake. Drop a few blueberries onto each pancake. Cook the pancakes until lightly browned on both sides. Keep warm in a low oven while cooking the rest of the batter.

3. Serve 4 to 6 pancakes per person. Top each serving with a handful of fresh blueberries and a sprinkling of confectioners' sugar. Accompany with a pitcher of maple syrup.

Makes about twenty 3-inch pancakes

tasting dinners featuring Bartlett wines exclusively. The Nickerson Tavern in Searsport has featured Ducktrap Smoked Trout Sausage in a Cheddar and Apple Beurre Blanc with Bartlett Dry Apple wine. The Osprey in Robinhood favors the French Oak Reserve Pear with a plate of Crab and Four Peppercorn Fettucine. And an all-time favorite combination from the many wine-tasting dinners at Jonathan's Restaurant is the match of Sweet Raspberry wine with Atlantic salmon sauced with a spicy Ginger-Leek Beurre Blanc. At the winery, Bob and Kathe also offer many enticing suggestions for foods to accompany and highlight their wines.

Most European wine connoisseurs insist that fine wine is the embodiment of three factors: soil, climate, and the people involved. We feel wholeheartedly that the same applies to the local fruit wines of Bob and Kathe Bartlett. Dom Pérignon may have tasted stars in Champagne, but when we sip any one of the Bartlett Estate wines, we become at once thoroughly inebriated with the rustic splendor of the entire state of Maine.

Lavender Morning Sausage

Innkeeper John Mancarella makes up this sausage mixture the night before so that it is ready to sizzle on the griddle first thing the following morning, sending irresistibly herbaceous aromas wafting toward the sleeping guests.

1½ tablespoons olive oil
1 small onion, minced
1 pound lean ground pork
½ pound lean ground lamb
Finely grated zest of 1 orange
1 tablespoon chopped fresh lavender or rosemary
1 teaspoon fennel seeds
Salt and freshly ground pepper, to taste

1. Heat the olive oil over medium-high heat in a small skillet. Add the onion and sauté until soft and translucent, 5 to 7 minutes.

2. In a mixing bowl, combine the onion with the pork and lamb, mixing well. Season with orange zest, lavender, fennel, salt, and pepper. The mixture can be used at once or refrigerated overnight.

3. When ready to cook the sausages, heat a griddle or large skillet over medium-high heat. Form the sausage mixture into small patties, about 1¼ inches in diameter. Fry the sausage in batches until well browned and crusted on each side. Serve hot.

Makes about 24 small patties

Cheese Fondue with Fruit Wine

Kathe Bartlett came up with the brilliant idea of using the winery's Dry Pear or Coastal White fruit wine in an otherwise traditional Swiss fondue recipe. This fabulous fondue is just about the best culinary antifreeze we know for the cold of a Maine winter.

2 cups Bartlett Dry Pear or Coastal White wine
2 cloves garlic, cut in half
3 cups grated Swiss-style cheese (Jarlsberg, Gruyère, or Emmentaler)
1 tablespoon cornstarch
2 tablespoons butter
2 to 4 tablespoons heavy cream
Salt and freshly ground pepper, to taste
3 tablespoons pear brandy or Calvados
Chunks of French bread for dipping

1. Combine the wine and garlic in a fondue pot or chafing dish. Bring to a boil and continue to cook until the wine is reduced to 1½ cups. Remove and discard the garlic.

2. Toss the cheese with the cornstarch to coat lightly and evenly. Over low heat, stir the cheese, a handful at a time, into the wine reduction. Wait for each batch to melt before adding the next. Be sure to stir the fondue constantly and to be careful that it doesn't get too hot. Whisk in the butter and enough cream to thin the mixture slightly. Season to taste with salt and pepper and, finally, stir in the pear brandy or Calvados.

3. Keep the fondue warm over a Sterno-type flame and serve with the proper accoutrements of long forks and plenty of bread.

Serves 4

Poached Salmon with Ginger-Leek Beurre Blanc

Jonathan has both a passion and a palate for pairing food with wine. Matching this salmon preparation with a glass of Bartlett Sweet Raspberry wine is a favorite from the many dinners the restaurant has hosted over the years. Serving a sweet wine with fish may strike some as odd, but the spicy bite of the ginger in the salmon sauce has a wonderful affinity with the lush berry flavor and pleasant astringency of the wine.

For the salmon poaching liquid, use either a court bouillon or combination of fish stock and water.

Ginger-Leek Beurre Blanc:
1 shallot, minced
1 medium leek, cleaned, trimmed, and minced
3/4-inch piece fresh ginger, peeled and minced
1/4 cup raspberry or wine vinegar
1/4 cup dry white wine
1 bay leaf
1/2 teaspoon ground ginger
12 tablespoons (1 1/2 sticks) unsalted butter
2 tablespoons heavy cream
Salt and freshly ground pepper, to taste

Salmon and Serving:
2 cups Jonathan's Quick Fish Stock (see page 26)
3 cups water
6 fresh salmon fillets (6 to 8 ounces each)
Julienne of leek stalks to garnish
Bartlett Sweet Raspberry wine

1. To make the Ginger-Leek Beurre Blanc, place shallots, leeks, and fresh ginger in a small saucepan or skillet. Cover with the vinegar and wine and add the bay leaf and the ground ginger. Bring the mixture to a boil and cook until all but a tablespoon of liquid remains in the pan. Reduce the heat to the lowest possible setting. Whisk the butter into the reduction, 1 tablespoon at a time, waiting for each to become incorporated into the sauce before adding the next. The sauce should turn to a thick and silky emulsion. Whisk in the cream and keep the sauce in a warm place while poaching the salmon.

2. To prepare the salmon, fill a large shallow skillet with the fish stock and water (or substitute court bouillon). Immerse and arrange the salmon fillets in

Poached Salmon with Ginger-Leek Beurre Blanc is paired with Bartlett Sweet Raspberry wine for a wine-tasting dinner at Jonathan's Restaurant.

the liquid so that they don't overlap. Bring the liquid to a simmer over medium-high heat and let the salmon poach until just cooked through in the center, 8 to 10 minutes.

3. Remove the salmon fillets from the poaching liquid with a slotted spatula, draining well. Place each fillet on a serving plate. Top each with a generous drizzle of the Ginger-Leek Beurre Blanc. Garnish the fillets by strewing with a few of the julienned leek stalks. Serve at once accompanied by a chilled glass of Bartlett Sweet Raspberry wine.

Makes 6 servings

French-Style Chicken with Nouveau Blueberry Wine

Since the Bartletts employ French techniques and oak aging in the production of many of their wines, it is not surprising that the French inspire much of their cooking as well. Kathe has adapted the classic Burgundian chicken stew, or *coq au vin*, to a recipe using their own Nouveau Blueberry. The chicken will have an extra delicious and potent wine flavor if made ahead and reheated the following day.

Onions:
½ pound salt pork, cut into 1½ × ¼-inch strips
16 small white boiling onions, peeled

Mushrooms:
2 tablespoons unsalted butter
2 tablespoons finely minced shallots
½ pound button mushrooms, wiped clean

Chicken:
2 to 3 tablespoons vegetable oil
2 frying chickens (2½ pounds each), cut into serving pieces
2 large cloves garlic, minced
½ teaspoon dried thyme
2 whole bay leaves
¼ cup brandy or cognac
½ cup chicken broth
2½ cups Bartlett Nouveau Blueberry wine
Salt and pepper, to taste
2 tablespoons unsalted butter
2 tablespoons unbleached all-purpose flour
2 tablespoons minced fresh parsley

1. Preheat oven to 350°F.
2. To prepare the onions, brown the salt pork strips in a heavy skillet over medium heat until crisp, 6 to 8 minutes. Remove strips with a slotted spatula to drain on paper towels and reserve. Brown the onions in the rendered fat, shaking the pan frequently so the onions roll and color evenly all over.

Apple Blush

a blend of 96% apple & 4% wild Maine blueberry wine!

A semi-dry light and refreshing wine. Serve chilled with lighter dishes of pasta, poultry and seafood.
A favorite with Maine lobster.

Located in coastal Maine, an area rich in its natural beauty, Bartlett Maine Estate Winery is dedicated to producing quality wines. Robert & Kathe Bartlett cordially invite you to taste this and other award-winning wines from Bartlett Maine Estate Winery.

For Tour and Tasting Schedules call or write
RR #1 Box 598 Gouldsboro, Me 04607
(207) 546-2408

Gouldsboro
23 miles east of Ellsworth just off route #1

Sam's Maine Cassoulet

This is an adaptation of restaurateur Sam Hayward's Maine Cassoulet. Jonathan's version of this dish sidesteps the impassioned inventor's use of concentrated stocks, infusions, and esoteric vegetables to which many home cooks would not normally have access. We offer this rendition as a tribute to a man who is a pioneer of contemporary Maine cooking.

Beans:
1 pound soldier beans
4 strips lightly smoked bacon
1 cup apple cider
1 tablespoon maple syrup
1 tablespoon duck or bacon fat
Salt and pepper, to taste

Hash:
2 strips bacon, very finely diced
3 parsnips, peeled and finely diced
2 carrots, peeled and finely diced
1 leek (top third of tough green leaves removed), cleaned and finely diced
1 clove elephant garlic, finely diced
1 tablespoon chopped fresh rosemary
½ teaspoon dried thyme
3 leaves fresh sage, chopped
2 slices day-old bread, lightly toasted and crumbled into small chunks
4 links maple breakfast sausage, cut into small pieces, cooked, and drained

Quail:
2 tablespoons unsalted butter
8 quail (4 to 5 ounces each), deboned

Topping:
2 slices day-old bread, lightly toasted and crumbled into small chunks
1 tablespoon olive oil
Fresh rosemary or parsley sprigs to garnish

1. On the day before, place the beans in a large bowl and amply cover with cold water. Soak overnight.

2. The next day, drain the beans, place in a pot with the bacon, cover with water, and bring to a boil. Reduce heat and simmer uncovered until

Remove onions from skillet, place in a bowl, and reserve the onions and fat separately.

3. Prepare the mushrooms by melting the butter over medium heat in another skillet. Add the shallots and sauté for 1 minute. Toss in the mushrooms and sauté for an additional 3 minutes. Add to the bowl with the onions and set aside.

4. Transfer the reserved fat to a Dutch oven and add enough vegetable oil to coat the bottom of the pot in a thin layer. Heat over medium-high heat and brown the chicken pieces, turning frequently to brown all over, about 10 minutes. Remove the chicken from the pot and add the garlic, reserved onion-mushroom mixture, thyme, and bay leaves. Pour in the brandy and, standing back, ignite with a match. When the flames subside, add the stock and the wine. Bring to a boil, scraping up any brown bits clinging to the bottom of the pot. Season the sauce with salt and freshly ground pepper, to taste.

5. Return the chicken to the Dutch oven and stir to coat evenly with the sauce. Cover the Dutch oven and bake until the chicken is tender, 45 minutes to 1 hour.

6. Meanwhile, make a roux by melting the butter in a saucepan over medium heat. Whisk in the flour and cook, stirring constantly, for 3 to 4 minutes. Drain the sauce from the chicken and slowly whisk into the roux, stirring until the sauce is smooth and thickened, about 5 minutes. Pour the sauce back over the chicken. If serving immediately, divide the chicken and vegetables among 4 serving plates and top each portion with a sprinkling of the reserved pork bits and some minced parsley. If making ahead, let the chicken cool to room temperature in the Dutch oven, refrigerate overnight, and bring back to room temperature before reheating in a 350° oven for 30 minutes or so.

Makes 6 servings

The beans for Sam's Maine Cassoulet glisten in their reduction of apple cider and maple syrup.

almost done (beans should retain a little resistance when cut into with a knife or bitten into), about 45 minutes to 1 hour.

3. While the beans are cooking, make the hash. Sauté the diced bacon over low heat to render fat. Add the parsnips, carrots, elephant garlic, and leek. Sauté until vegetables begin to soften, about 8 minutes. Add the rosemary, thyme, and sage and sauté for another 3 to 4 minutes. Add the crumbled bread and sausage and mix thoroughly.

4. When the beans are done, drain, and while still hot toss them with duck fat and salt, to taste. Place the beans in a large skillet and cover with cider and maple syrup. Turn heat to medium and simmer until liquid is reduced by two-thirds, about 12 minutes.

5. While the beans are simmering, preheat the broiler to 450°F. Rinse and dry the quail. Stuff each bird quite tightly with the hash. Cross the legs or tie them to cover the cavity and place the birds breast side up on a lightly greased baking sheet. Brush the birds with melted butter. Place on the middle rack of the oven and broil until the skin begins to brown, 5 to 6 minutes. Turn oven to bake, reduce heat to 375°, and roast until cooked through, 12 to 15 minutes.

6. Make the topping by sautéing the crumbled bread in the olive oil over medium heat until crisp, 3 to 4 minutes.

7. Assemble the cassoulet. Discard the bacon strips from the beans and with a slotted spoon divide them evenly among 4 plates. Reserve the reduced cider mixture. Place 2 roasted birds together, breast side up, on one side of each plate. Sprinkle the bread topping over the beans. Pour the reduced cider mixture over the quail. Garnish each plate with a fresh rosemary or parsley sprig. Serve at once.

Makes 4 main course servings

Grilled Porterhouse Steak with Heifer Pat Down

Our grandparents were beef-eaters, and when they arrived in Maine for their summer stay, the butchers at Merrill and Hinckley, the general store in Blue Hill, were soon to know that Mrs. Florian was in town. Thick steaks and ground-to-order lean beef — our grandmother would stand for nothing less, and our grandfather, the outdoor, open-wood-fire meat master, would certainly let her know if the steaks were anything but top-drawer. We've inherited a small carnivorous streak of our own, and it is in memory of our grandparents that we have married audacious chef Jonathan St. Laurent's Heifer Pat Down with a hefty cut of steak. Adding green alder twigs or apple-wood chips to the grill imparts a subtle but key flavoring to the meat. For authentic new-wave Maine flavor, use organically raised beef from Wolfe's Neck Farm in Freeport and accompany the feast with a bottle of Bartlett Blueberry wine aged in French oak.

Heifer Pat Down from Uncle Billy's SouthSide Barbeque:

3½ ounces cumin
3½ ounces granulated garlic
2½ ounces salt
2 ounces ground black pepper
1½ ounces coriander
1 ounce dry mustard
½ ounce ground anise seeds
½ ounce ground marjoram
½ ounce ground lavender leaves
⅛ ounce ground cloves
¼ ounce ground allspice
¼ ounce ground thyme

Meat:
1 2-inch-thick porterhouse steak, 3 to 4 pounds

1. To make the Heifer Pat Down: Combine all the herbs and spices in a mixing bowl and then store in a plastic bag or airtight container to use as needed.

2. Pat 4 to 5 tablespoons of the Heifer Pat Down evenly over both sides of the steak, pressing lightly to make it adhere. Wrap the beef in plastic wrap and refrigerate for at least 4 hours.

3. Prepare an outdoor charcoal grill (dome cooker), and when the coals are ready and glowing, sprinkle on a few alder twigs or apple-wood chips. Place the steak on the grill, 4 to 5 inches from the heat. Cover the grill with its dome top and close the vents halfway. Let the meat cook/smoke for 15 minutes; flip, re-cover the grill, and cook for another 8 minutes for medium-rare meat. Cook longer if more well done meat is desired.

4. Transfer the meat to a carving platter and let it stand for 10 minutes. Slice the meat thinly on an angle, across the grain. Serve at once, spooning juices that have accumulated on the platter over the sliced beef.

Serves 6 to 8 hungry beef-eaters

The cassoulet, when finished and presented, is sophisticated without being overly arranged or fussy.

Resources

LOBSTERS

Stonington Lobster Co-op
P.O. Box 89
Indian Point Road
Stonington, ME 04681
207-367-2286
lobster, crabmeat

Trenton Bridge Lobster Pound
Route 3
Trenton, ME 04605
207-667-2977
shipped lobsters

Bagaduce Lunch
Brooksville, ME 04617
roadside stand featuring crab rolls and lobster rolls

MAINE MOLLUSKS

Abandoned Farms, Inc.
P.O. Box 551
Damariscotta, ME 04543
207-563-3935
farmed mussels

Cape Split Seafood
RFD 1, Box 468
Addison, ME 04606
207-483-4600
diver-harvested mussels; periwinkles

Dodge Cove Marine Farm, Inc.
P.O. Box 211
Newcastle, ME 04553
207-563-8168
farmed oysters

Great Eastern Mussel Farms, Inc.
P.O. Box 141
Tenants Harbor, ME 04860
207-372-6317
farmed mussels, Mahogany clams

Spinney Creek Oyster Company, Inc.
1 Howell Lane
Eliot, ME 03903
207-439-2719
farmed oysters

FIN FISH

Maine Shellfish Company, Inc.
Water Street
Ellsworth, ME 04605
207-667-3336
fin fish, mollusks, lobsters, crab

Ocean Products, Inc.
Estes Head
Eastport, ME 04631
207-853-6081
farm-raised Atlantic Salmon

Portland Fish Exchange
2 Portland Fish Pier
Portland, ME 04104
207-773-0017
seafood auction

SARDINES

Maine Sardine Council
470 North Main Street
P.O. Box 337
Brewer, ME 04412
207-989-2180

SMOKEHOUSES

Ducktrap River Fish Farm, Inc.
RFD 2, Box 378
Lincolnville, ME 04849
207-763-3960
smoked seafood specialties

Horton's Downeast Foods, Inc.
P.O. Box 430
Waterboro, ME 04087
207-247-6900
smoked seafood specialties

Kohn's Smokehouse
CR 35, Box 160
Thomaston, ME 04861
207-372-8412
smoked meats and seafoods

Smith's Log Smokehouse
Back Brooks Road
Brooks, ME 04921
207-525-4418
smoked Maine meats

GRANGES

Maine State Grange
146 State Street
Augusta, ME 04330
207-623-3421

SALTWATER FARMS

Hay's Farm Stand
P.O. Box 92
Blue Hill, ME 04614
207-374-2822
organic produce

Horsepower Farm
RFD 1, Box 63
Blue Hill, ME 04614
207-374-5038
organic produce, dried beans, lamb, and mutton

Stanley Joseph and Lynn Karlin
Harborside, ME 04642
207-326-4062
organic produce, including high-bush blueberries

SUMMER BERRIES

Bakewell Cream & The Apple Ledge Company
RFD 2, Box 6640
East Holden, ME 04429
207-942-5532
Down East biscuit mix

Blueberry Hill
University of Maine
Experimental Station
RFD Box 805
Addison, ME 04606
207-434-2291
experimental blueberry cultivation

Wild Maine Blueberry Company
Elm Street
Machias, ME 04654
207-225-8364
blueberries

Silveridge Farm
Route 1
Orland, ME 04472
207-469-7836
organic produce; pick-your-own strawberries

COUNTRY FAIRS

The Blue Hill Fair Association
Blue Hill, ME 04614

Maine Organic Farmers and Gardeners Association
P.O. Box 2176
Augusta, ME 04338
207-622-3118

Agricultural Fairs
Maine Department of Agriculture, Food and Rural Resources
State House Station 28
Augusta, ME 04333
207-289-3221

AUTUMN FRUITS AND VEGETABLES

Schartner's Mountain View Fruit and Berry Farm
Route 220
P.O. Box 82
Thorndike, ME 04986
207-568-3668
old and new variety apples, pears, plums; peaches; pick-your-own strawberries

Sow's Ear Winery
Brooksville, ME 04607
207-326-4649
Normandy-style hard ciders

MAINE MEAT

Foggy Ridge Gamebird Farm
P.O. Box 211
Warren, ME 04864
207-273-2357
game birds

Howland Farm Rabbitry
HCR 66, Box 62
Howland, ME 04448
207-732-5100
rabbits

Pinebrook Rabbit Processing
Box 2665
Sam Allen Road
Sanford, ME 04075
207-324-3390
rabbits

Sunset Acre Farm
RR 1, Box 101
Brooksville, ME 04617
207-326-4741
piglets, chickens, turkeys

Wolfe's Neck Farm Foundation
RR 1, Box 71
Freeport, ME 04032
207-865-4469
organic Black Angus beef

COTTAGE INDUSTRIES

Virgil L. Morse and Son, Inc.
Morse's Sauerkraut
RFD 2
Waldoboro, ME 04572
207-832-5569
sauerkraut, Maine products

Mother's Mountain Mustard
Tan-Man
110 Woodville Road
P.O. Box 6044
Falmouth, ME 04105
variety mustards and ketchups

Mystique
Friendship Street
Waldoboro, ME 04572
207-832-5136
goat cheeses

Seal Cove Farm
Route 102
Seal Cove, ME 04674
207-244-3017
goat cheeses

Spruce Bush Farm
RR 1, Box 1715
North Whitefield, ME 04353
207-549-7070
maple syrup, dilly beans,
pickled fiddleheads

'Stache Foods
P.O. Box 705
Damariscotta, ME 04543
207-529-5879
variety sauces

R. B. Swan & Son, Inc.
25 Prospect Street
Brewer, ME 04412
207-989-3622
honey

York Hill Farm
York Hill Road
New Sharon, ME 04955
207-778-9741
goat cheeses, including
Romano-style "Capriano"

CHRISTMAS DOWN EAST
51 BayView
51 Bayview Street
Camden, ME 04843
207-236-4272
designs for home furnishing;
distinctive gifts, original
Christmas ornaments

TRENDING

The Bartlett Maine Estate Winery
P.O. Box 598
Gouldsboro, ME 04607
207-546-2408
outstanding wines made from premium
Maine-grown fruits

The Belmont
Belmont Avenue
Camden, ME 04843
207-236-8053
bed and breakfast inn;
dinner restaurant

D. L. Geary Brewing Company
38 Evergreen Drive
Portland, ME 04103
207-878-2337
distinctive English-style ales

Maine Coast Brewing Company
P.O. Box 1118
Portland, ME 04101
207-773-7970
Portland Lager Beer

Uncle Billy's SouthSide Barbeque
Ocean Street
South Portland, ME 04106
207-767-7119
unique Maine barbecue restaurant;
Uncle Billy's "Death by Chocolate
Sauce"

Index